PANI STEFA AND THE ORPHANS

Dedicated to the legacy of Dr Janusz Korczak, to his children, past, present and future and to all those who are working to keep his legacy alive

Jerry Nussbaum, President, the Janusz Korczak Association of Canada

This publication of PANI STEFA AND THE ORPHANS: OUT OF THE SHADOW OF KORCZAK was made possible through the efforts of Dr Anton Grunfeld and Jerry Nussbaum from the Janusz Korczak Association of Canada.

Pani Stefa and the Orphans

Out of the Shadow of Korczak

Magdalena Kicińska

Translated by Sean Gasper Bye

VALLENTINE MITCHELL
LONDON • CHICAGO

First published in 2021 by Vallentine Mitchell

Catalyst House,
720 Centennial Court,
Centennial Park, Elstree WD6 3SY, UK

814 N. Franklin Street,
Chicago, Illinois
60610 USA

www.vmbooks.com

British Library Cataloguing in Publication Data:
An entry can be found on request

ISBN 978 1 912676 78 1 (Paper)
ISBN 978 1 912676 79 8 (Ebook)

Library of Congress Cataloging in Publication Data:
An entry can be found on request

BOOK INSTITUTE

©POLAND

This publication has been supported by the ©POLAND Translation Program

THE JANUSZ KORCZAK
ASSOCIATION OF CANADA

Contents

Author Acknowledgements

A huge thank you to the translator, Sean Gasper Bye, who transferred this story to the world of a foreign language without losing even a bit of meaning. His patience and reliability inspire my great admiration.

Many thanks to The Janusz Korczak Association of Canada, without whom the publication of this book would not be possible. I am very grateful for your work on popularizing the work of Janusz Korczak. I would like to express my special thanks to Jerry Nussbaum, the good spirit of this book, whose determination and faith that Pani Stefa's story should be told in the world made it possible. I owe him his kindness and conviction about the power of the story of a woman who devoted her life to caring for others.

I dedicate this book to her – and to other women who are still nameless and lost in oblivion.

This book would not have been written without the help, generous advice and support I received from so many people.

Thank you to Monika Sznajderman, not only for the trust you put in a début author.

To Marta Ciesielska from the Korczakianum, the research centre of the Museum of Warsaw, without whom I would have been lost in the world of Korczak archives, for her enormous support and rooting for this idea from the very beginning.

To Agnieszka Witkowska-Krych, not only for her help counting the stairs in the building at 92 Krochmalna Street.

To Itzhak Belfer, boy number 43.

To Ilan Bernstein – Lena from Ein Harod.

To Batia Gilad, President of the International Janusz Korczak Society.

To Anat Bratman-Elhalel, Director of the archives of the Ghetto Fighters Kibbutz.

To the MCKA Bay of Art Foundation, for giving me – through their artistic residency – the ideal conditions for my creative work.

To Grażyna Pawlak, Director of the Mojżesz Schorr Foundation, who has done so much to restore the memory of Stefania Wilczyńska.

To my editors: Łukasz Najder and Tomasz Zając, among other things for their patience and attention to the text and every word within it.

I thank the wonderful women who answered my questions, cheered me up, incessantly inspired me and whom I have so much to learn from: Lidia Ostałowska, Angelika Kuźniak, Sylwia Chutnik, Justyna Pobiedzińska, Magdalena Szkarłat, Anna Czerwińska, Sylwia Szwed, Agnieszka Wójcińska, Małgorzata Rejmer and Urszula Jabłońska.

Thank you to my family.

To my friends: Marta, Joanna, Michał, Justyna, Michał, Ola, Juliusz, Gosia, Basia.

And special thanks to Shlomo Nadel, my guide to the Home and my friend.

Magdalena Kicińska

Acknowledgements from the Janusz Korczak Association of Canada

For the past twenty years the Janusz Korczak Association of Canada has been working towards the dissemination of the legacy and heroism of Dr Janusz Korczak to English-speaking audiences. Our efforts would not be complete without introducing Stefa Wilczyńska, the closest co-worker and partner to Dr Korczak in making his orphanage a home for thousands of children throughout the existence of the Home for Orphans. Stefa Wilczyńska worked and sacrificed her life alongside Dr Korczak and this wonderful book by Magdalena Kicińska has finally offered us an opportunity to present Stefa to the English-speaking world. We are immensely grateful to Ms. Kicińska for bringing from the shadows the story of a woman who dedicated her life to the children and, together with Dr Korczak, became family for so many children.

The translation and publication of this book would not have been possible without the many people and organizations who have contributed to this effort. We would like to thank them all.

On behalf of the Janusz Korczak Association of Canada we would like to thank the Polish Book Institute whose generosity supported the translation costs.

We would like to acknowledge the long-standing support of Rabbi Dr Yosef Wosk and a generous grant from the Yosef Wosk Family Foundation.

We would like to thank the Paul and Edwina Heller Memorial Foundation, Mr. Zygmunt Rolat, the Koret Foundation and many other individual supporters for their generous contributions.

The Janusz Korczak Association of Canada also wishes to express its deep gratitude to Karolina Kołpak, who generously shared her knowledge to bring the reader closer to the reality of life in the pre-war Warsaw. Thank you to Professor Marci Shore for becoming a part of the project.

We thank Toby Harris, of Vallentine Mitchell publishers, for assisting us with all aspects of the publication process. Our thanks go out to Sean Gasper Bye, for the wonderful translation, and to the Museum of Warsaw,

Korczakianum Center for Documentation and Research for the iconography.

We are deeply grateful for the many contributions that made this translation a reality.

Jerry Nussbaum, President, the Janusz Korczak Association of Canada
Dr Anton Grunfeld, Member of the Board, the Janusz Korczak Association of Canada
Project coordinators

Introduction

On 7 October 1912 a group of Jewish children moved into the modern, beautiful building of the Orphans' Home at 92 Krochmalna Street in Warsaw. The splendour of this new institution stood out amidst the immense poverty and filth of the street located in the city centre. Isaac Bashevis Singer, a 1978 Nobel Prize in Literature laureate who grew up on Krochmalna Street, recalled its destitution in many of his works. This is how he described the apartment building in which he lived:

> There was no gas in the building, in the apartment a kerosene lamp was used for light, and the toilet was located in the courtyard, and its key was shared between all tenants of the building. There was no shortage of rats and mice, and little children, instead of relieving themselves in the outhouse, preferred to do it on the staircase. What's even worse, some women treated it as a garbage dump.[1]

On the way to the Orphans' Home, one would pass a huge marketplace, then small shops and slaughterhouses located in various tenement houses. Everyday bustle rang throughout the east side of the street, complemented by smells of fish, meat and vegetables but also waste and the gutter. Closer to the Orphans' Home, factories and industry dominated: brewing of beer and production of chocolates and sweets. Krochmalna was a Jewish street with prayer houses and *mikvehs* for ritual baths, elementary schools called *cheders,* and inhabitants who ran their everyday affairs in Yiddish.

The director of the Orphans' Home was Janusz Korczak, and its Matron and chief educator was Stefania Wilczyńska. Korczak and Wilczyńska met sometime in 1909 through a Jewish association called the Orphans' Aid Society. The chairman of the society was Dr Izaak Eliasberg, a prominent doctor and social activist of Warsaw. The goal of the Orphans' Aid Society was to care for Jewish children who were neglected, abandoned and orphaned. That year, both Korczak and Wilczyńska were hired to work with a group of the society's orphans, the future residents of the Orphans' Home on Krochmalna. Korczak was a doctor, educator, social activist, columnist and writer. His career was on the rise, and he was an increasingly well-known figure in Warsaw and beyond. At the turn of the twentieth century he gained recognition, first from his publications in Warsaw's weeklies *Kolce* (*Thorns*) and *Czytelnia dla Wszystkich* (*Reading Room for All*), and perhaps more notably, for his close cooperation with the leftist, progressive *Głos* (*Voice*) and its continuations. He also published a few positively received novels, in particular *Child of the Drawing Room* (1904), a sharp social criticism of Warsaw's wealthy class. By 1912, the list of his novels, short stories, articles, and scholarly publications was gaining in length and quality, and his reformist aspirations and interest in pedagogy and child-rearing pushed him towards new ideas and projects. In his undertakings Korczak could increasingly count on the support of Jewish and Polish colleagues and friends. The Orphans' Home was to become his most important project, a 'school of life' he conjured in one of his literary fantasies just five years before.

In 1909, when Stefania Wilczyńska met Korczak and began her collaboration with the Orphans' Aid Society, she had just returned to Warsaw from her studies abroad. She spent a summer semester at the University of Geneva in 1906, where she audited a course in botany and organic chemistry. The following two academic years she spent at the University of Liège in Belgium, studying natural and medical sciences. She did not, however, complete her studies there. Sometime before 1909, she took courses in kindergarten training. Now in Warsaw, she began looking for a job, which brought her to the Orphans' Aid Society. Stefania Wilczyńska knew the Eliasberg family through her brother's marriage to Dr Izaak Eliasberg's daughter, Irena. Perhaps due to this personal tie, Wilczyńska, just twenty-three years old, was hired by the Orphans' Aid Society to take care of dozens of orphans despite her lack of experience. Yet her few years of collaboration with Korczak must have convinced him and the board members of the Orphans' Aid Society that she was the right candidate for the position of Matron of the Orphans' Home.

***

Stefania Wilczyńska, born on 26 May 1886, and Janusz Korczak, born on 22 July 1878/1879, were raised in the western periphery of the Russian Empire known as the Kingdom of Poland. It was a peculiar entity. On the one hand, it belonged to the Russian Empire and its inhabitants were imperial subjects. On the other hand, however, most of the elites of the

Kingdom of Poland never accepted imperial authority and considered themselves a separate nation with an opposing system of values, traditions and customs. There was a general sense of distrust between the imperial Russian state and the Kingdom, and the elites of the latter struggled to maintain some national autonomy under conditions which they perceived as oppressive. This state of affairs caused many intellectuals in the Kingdom of Poland to comment on its predicament in the political, economic, social and cultural spheres. The Kingdom seemed to be lagging behind Europe, constricted by a despotic state and unable to run its affairs freely. In this climate, the Kingdom of Poland became full of paradoxes, mismanagement and shortcomings. According to Korczak, for example, everything in the Kingdom of Poland 'took on exceptional, caricatural forms'. In April 1904, as a student of medicine, he wrote a sharp article where the abnormality of the Kingdom described by him would have struck a chord with the contemporary reader.

> The ambulance services [wrote Korczak about Warsaw] are a lively and vivid proof of our squander; our Philharmonic among illiterates; our 14,269 rubles of expenses for publications of the Music Association and 10 rubles as capital for the publication of hygiene brochures (by the Warsaw Hygiene Association); our nine-ruble ambulance trip to provide those who are weakened with a few vouchers for cheap lunches; and [our] 2,130 children not sent to the summer camps because of the lack of funds. But there is much to be said about this…[2]

Much was lacking, and the Kingdom could not afford frivolity and recklessness.

Since the late eighteenth century, the territories of the former Polish-Lithuanian Commonwealth had been partitioned and governed by three empires: the Prussian Empire, the Austro-Hungarian Empire and the Russian Empire. Warsaw, the main urban centre of the Kingdom of Poland, became the cultural, social, economic and political heart of a non-existent state of Poland. For many centuries, it was a multi-ethnic and a multi-religious city with ethnic Poles, who were mostly Catholics, and Jews constituting the two largest groups. Warsaw retained its diverse character throughout the nineteenth and first half of the twentieth century. In the 1880s, Catholics made up around sixty per cent of the population of the city, while Jews were approximately thirty-five per cent. By 1914, the percentage of Catholics decreased to about fifty-five per cent but rose for

Jews to about forty per cent. In a major metropolis of the Russian Empire, where the continuously growing population of the city reached almost 900,000 by 1914, such demographic balance was of major significance. Warsaw was the shared home of both Poles and Jews.

The years of Stefania's and Korczak's childhood and youth coincided with important changes in the Russian Empire as a whole and in the Kingdom of Poland specifically. Industrialization, which began in the second half of the nineteenth century, turned the Kingdom's cities such as Warsaw, Łódź and Białystok into migration destinations as poor landless gentry and peasants searched for ways to make a living. The former filled the ranks of the intelligentsia – writers, journalists, teachers, petty officials and clerks – while the latter searched for employment in factories, workshops, and homes of the wealthy as maids, laundresses and cooks. This process of urbanization, in turn, exacerbated problems typically associated with the rise of large cities, in particular the inequalities between the rich and the poor. These became more pronounced and visible, and social ills were commented on by writers, journalists and intellectuals more broadly, who were actively searching for ways in which the misery of the urban poor could be ameliorated. Amidst the heated discussion, the wealthy were not spared criticism either. Since positive involvement on the part of the imperial authorities could not be counted on, educated society took upon itself the task of improving the lot of the majority of the inhabitants of the cities. In Warsaw, this was particularly manifest.

Changes of a political nature followed in tandem. The era of mass politics was beginning as new political forces, soon to become parties, entered the scene. In the Kingdom of Poland, the lack of national freedom was among the most pressing issues, which new political movements sought to address. The underlying aspiration was the ultimate formation of an independent state of Poland. Independence would allow the cultivation and free expression of national culture: language, literature, arts, customs and religion. It would give Poland economic freedom and national prosperity. It would allow the development of local governments, social institutions and services to ensure the welfare of all citizens, education for all, protection of civil liberties, development of cities and the countryside. The list could go on. Out of these aspirations, political activists created competing conceptions of what independent Poland would look like, and they bitterly fought for the support of the masses. As a result, the political landscape of the Kingdom of Poland became quite diverse. The two most important movements, however, were embodied by Józef Piłsudski and his Polish Socialist Party and Roman Dmowski's National Democratic Party.

Józef Piłsudski, born in 1867, hailed from the borderlands of the Russian partition. These borderlands, once part of the Polish-Lithuanian Commonwealth, experienced particularly harsh Russification policies on the part of the imperial authorities. The aim was to eliminate any attachment to Polish culture and turn its multi-ethnic and multi-religious population into loyal Russian subjects. Piłsudski, however, yearned for a Poland which would reunite all of the former lands of the Polish-Lithuanian Commonwealth, encompassing parts of today's Poland, Lithuania, Belarus and Ukraine, and retain its diverse character. He was attracted to socialism, and his early connections with Russian radicals made him a target of pursuit by imperial authorities. He sought to combine Polish national independence with socialist ideals, such as economic, social and political equality, social welfare for all and the positive role of the state. He argued that once an independent Poland emerged, it would do so on a socialist foundation.

Roman Dmowski was born in 1864 in the Kingdom of Poland. As a university student he became involved in a clandestine youth organization, which sought to resist the severe Russification policies within the Kingdom. He grew close to nationalist thinkers and activists, and soon he himself occupied an important place in the nationalist camp. He opposed socialism and any other form of loyalty that threatened national cohesion. Dmowski also spoke in favour of an ethnically Polish nation, one which had to struggle against internal and external threats in order to survive, expand and prosper. In his nationalist ideology, Jews occupied a central place as Poland's most worrisome threat. Thus, while Piłsudski and the Polish Socialist Party hoped to fashion a large, multi-ethnic state based on principles of socialism, Dmowski and the National Democratic Party preferred a smaller but ethnically homogenous Poland, with antisemitism at its core.

A political process was also taking place within the Kingdom's Jewish community – already shaken by secularization and religious divides – when new political movements began to stir the Jewish street. By the 1880s, proponents of Jewish integration into Polish society were faced with competing ideologies advanced by Jewish political activists. There was the rise of Jewish nationalisms, the most important of which was Zionism. It tied the future of the Jewish nation with a state in Palestine. Alongside it, socialism was gaining in popularity. On the one hand, Jews proposed joining the international socialist movement, which promised a world without prejudice, social inequality or the constraints of tradition. On the other hand, a specifically Jewish socialism developed as well, one in which the fate of the Jewish working class was of primary concern. Eventually, political Orthodoxy would also enter the political scene. Perceiving the other political ideologies as an assault on traditional Jewish life, proponents of Orthodoxy could no longer stay out of politics. The question of language – Yiddish, Hebrew or Polish – was ideologically tied to each movement but also became a means to attract targeted constituencies. These Jewish political movements began to gain in strength at the turn of the twentieth century, and they would continue to grow.

Jewish assimilation as a political movement – dominant between 1860s and early 1880s – was never fully eliminated, yet its weakness and unpopularity were more evident with each passing decade. While the political programme of the integrationists (assimilationists as they were called) was no longer attractive to most Jews, Polonization and various levels of integration were occurring, reaching their height in Poland between the First and Second World War. Yiddish was undoubtedly the language of most Jews of the Kingdom of Poland, including Warsaw. At the same time, however, according to the Russian Census of 1897, almost fourteen per cent of Warsaw's Jews claimed Polish as their native tongue. This was quite a significant number especially when compared to just three and a half per cent of Jews claiming Polish as their main language in the Kingdom as a whole.

A quite small yet vibrant community of more or less acculturated Jews thus existed in Warsaw. They were the product of the Haskalah, the Jewish Enlightenment, which sought the abolition of the ghetto and an end to Jewish isolation from the rest of society. Secular education was proposed as one of the main avenues through which the process of integration of the Jewish masses was to be pursued. The idea was to shed what was perceived by Jewish integrationists as Jewish backwardness, superstition, 'jargon' (Yiddish) and separatism, and instead embrace the standards of the civilized European society. Between the 1860s and 1880s, this project of Enlightenment-influenced assimilation was pursued by both Jewish integrationists and Polish liberals. The aim was to enlighten the common man and foster Polish and Jewish co-existence and eradicate prejudice by spreading ideals of tolerance, equality and progress. This programme did not achieve expected results, and by the 1890s it was rejected by most on both the Polish and the Jewish side. The rising antisemitism of the last decades before the First World War added to the general disillusionment and struck a serious blow at any meaningful attempts to cultivate positive Polish-Jewish relations.

Yet Jews who embraced the idea of integration remained an important force within the Jewish community and Polish society in general. Their choice of integrating with Polish society – as opposed to the dominant, Russian society – was a conscious one, motivated by many factors. For some, Polish culture was more attractive and such feeling was cultivated in their family homes; for others a feeling of solidarity with an oppressed nation drew them to Polishness. Some remained attached to the Jewish faith, but even those who no longer had any ties with the religious Jewish world sought to address some of its needs, primarily through philanthropy and their influence among the Polish elite. In fact, the 'in-betweenness' of acculturated Jews, the complexity of their identity, their relationship with Polishness and Jewishness, all constitute a fascinating phenomenon of Jewish history in Poland both before and after the First World War.

***

Stefania Wilczyńska and Janusz Korczak belonged to this community of acculturated Polish Jews. They spoke Polish, not Yiddish; while their relationship to Judaism was ambiguous, neither of them identified with the traditional, religious Jewish community. They were both raised in the spirit of Polish patriotism and culture, they (and their siblings) were given Polish names (Stefania and Henryk), and they cooperated with other acculturated Jews as well as with ethnic Poles in numerous social endeavours. In general, Poland, and especially Warsaw, was their home; they navigated it with ease, worked on its behalf and cherished the ideals shared by the progressive intelligentsia of the time. At the same time, they never lost sight of the needs of those Jews faced with poverty and struggling to make ends meet – in particular, the youngest victims of destitution: children.

In the last decades of the nineteenth century, Warsaw, along with other cities in the Kingdom, experienced a flourishing of associations – Polish and Jewish, many of mixed character – which hoped to address the needs of the city and its inhabitants in all spheres of life. They were an indication of an active and resourceful civil society, facilitated by an increase in secular organizing. This civil society developed despite the lack of a supportive state, and it demonstrated that social involvement on behalf of the common good was increasingly perceived as an obligation, a civic responsibility. The associations thus filled an important administrative gap when cities in the Kingdom of Poland lacked a municipal government and imperial authorities attended to the needs of the cities reluctantly and often inefficiently.

Children occupied a central place among social concerns of the *fin-de-siècle* Kingdom of Poland, particularly in the cities. Public opinion grew alarmed at the plight of orphaned children and children without appropriate parental care, the so called 'children of the street'. The influx of people into the cities, shortage of proper housing, poor working and living conditions among the lowest strata of the population and lack of institutional support for impoverished, working-class women – all exacerbated the situation of the neediest children in the cities of the Kingdom. Warsaw was no exception. The press stressed the acute need for the establishment of care and educational facilities which could counteract the neglect such children experienced. Not all children who ended up in such facilities were orphans; some were half-orphans while others had parents who simply did not have the means to provide their children with the care they needed. The Orphans' Home on Krochmalna under the auspices of the Orphans' Aid Society served as this kind of an institution. It cared for the neediest Jewish children of Warsaw and, more importantly, it raised and educated them. At the same time, the children maintained some contact with their families and at the age of fourteen they were free to leave the Orphans' Home entirely.

***

When the First World War erupted in 1914, the Orphans' Home was just two years old. Korczak left for war, conscripted into the Russian army, where he served as a military doctor. Wilczyńska was responsible for the survival of the Orphans' Home, which was her home as well. As she struggled to keep things running smoothly, to feed the children under her care, to prevent sickness and disorder from creeping into the world of 92 Krochmalna Street, Europe unleashed the hell that shook the foundations of the old order.

The Russian army and authorities fled Warsaw in 1915 only to have their place taken by the German army and authorities, which were to remain in the city and run its affairs until 1918. The Kingdom of Poland was divided between German and Austrian zones of occupation (the two empires were allies in the war), with the larger, northern one – called General Government – taken by the Germans. Refugees streamed into the city where tensions between ethnic Poles and Jews already ran high. Violent attacks on the Jewish population by non-Jews, known as *pogroms*, were not uncommon in other parts of territories that would soon constitute an independent state of Poland. Yet no such unleashing of anti-Jewish violence occurred in Warsaw.

Polish subjects of all three partitioning powers fought in the First World War. They often fought on opposing sides because while Germany and

Austro-Hungary were allies, the Russian Empire was the enemy of both. At the beginning of the war, thanks to Józef Piłsudski, a Polish military force called the Polish Legions was established in the Austro-Hungarian Empire. Its goal was to fight against the Russian army and ensure that after the war Poland would be granted national independence as a result of Poles' active role in combat. While Piłsudski and his soldiers fought for Poland on the ground, Roman Dmowski sought support for the Polish cause abroad, taking a role in diplomatic negotiations regarding the post-war state.

The First World War ended in November 1918, and in June 1919 the Treaty of Versailles established peace, new states and new borders, along with new grievances that would occupy the politics of the post-war years. The Minorities Treaty – signed by Polish delegates at Versailles – provided official protection for minorities within the borders of the multi-ethnic state. The Russian Empire – transformed by the 1917 Bolshevik Revolution and the ensuing Civil War – became the Soviet Union in 1922; the Austro-Hungarian Empire disintegrated into multiple independent states in Central and Eastern Europe; the German Empire, reduced in size and severely punished as the loser of the war became the Weimar Republic. A new world grew out of the ashes and misery of war, a world in which Poland reappeared on the map of Europe.

The Treaty of Versailles established Poland's western borders (to the dismay of Germany), but the situation in the east remained unclear and soon a new war – the Polish-Bolshevik War – began. During this war, Janusz Korczak served as a military doctor again, this time in the Polish Army. Wilczyńska, once again, was left alone in charge of the Orphans' Home, longing for peace to return. After the Poles launched an offensive, hoping to capture the city of Kyiv, Soviet troops counter-attacked with such force that they pushed the Polish army all the way back to Warsaw. The war could have ended in a disaster for Poland, yet thanks to an army offensive in Warsaw, dubbed the 'Miracle on the Vistula', Poland emerged victorious. The Peace of Riga, signed in March 1921, established the borders of Poland and the Soviet Union; the territories of today's Belarus and Ukraine were split between the two signatories. By 1923, with Poland's official conquest of the city of Vilnius (unrecognized by independent Lithuania), the question of borders was, for the moment, settled.

The first years of Poland's independence were not easy. Faced with the destruction and misery left by the war – to some extent ameliorated by international aid organizations such as the American Relief Association and the American Jewish Joint Distribution Committee – the new state began an ongoing process of integrating the lands hitherto divided between the three partitioning powers. A constitution was adopted in March 1921, and the Second Polish Republic officially became a parliamentary democracy with a strong lower-house legislature (Sejm) and a weak upper-house legislature (Senate) and executive (President). Between 1921 and 1939, the population of Poland increased from about 28 million to over 35 million; Jews made up over 2 million of the population in 1921 and over 3 million in the 1930s. According to a 1931 census, Warsaw's population exceeded 1 million inhabitants of whom more than thirty per cent (over 352,000) were Jewish. The city – as the capital of the new state – was the hub of political, economic, social and cultural activity. There was active public debate on all issues facing the new republic as press organs of all political persuasions and in all languages proliferated. Hopes for the new state – at last sovereign, with so much potential – were plenty, and everyone seemed to be recruited to work for Poland, its prosperity, well-being and prestige. Amidst this exhilarating mood of intense and creative work on behalf of building a new Poland, a new world, the Orphans' Home continued its own reformative work. Korczak and Wilczyńska wanted to change the world too, investing all of their knowledge and energy into raising the poorest Jewish children into happy, independent and valuable citizens of the Second Polish Republic.

Yet behind the optimism and enthusiasm of the early 1920s, conflicts and disappointments already began to emerge. The December 1922 election of Poland's first president – Gabriel Narutowicz – was greeted with aggressive opposition from the nationalists and their sympathizers. Gabriel Narutowicz was educated in Western Europe and led a successful career as a hydro-electric engineer before he was invited to return to Poland from Zürich to assist with the rebuilding of infrastructure destroyed by the war. In 1920, he became the Minister of Public Works. Shortly after, in 1922, he became Poland's Minister of Foreign Affairs. He was also a friend and sympathizer of Józef Piłsudski, who respected him and his work on behalf of Poland. He was a reputable gentleman, a freemason and a proponent of inter-ethnic solidarity.

Narutowicz was elected president thanks to the support of a coalition of the parties of the left, the peasant party *Piast* and the National Minorities Bloc. The latter was led by and comprised primarily of Jewish deputies. Among the right, that earned Narutowicz the label of the 'Jewish president'. The nationalist right deemed the election an assault on the wishes of the Polish majority, bombarding the parties of the coalition with accusations of betrayal, signalling that the Jews had no right to participate in running the country. Less than a week after taking office, Narutowicz was shot to death at Warsaw's Zachęta gallery by Eligiusz Niewiadomski, a follower of National Democracy, who claimed to act out of a sense of duty and love for Poland. Niewiadomski was sentenced to death and executed on 30 January 1923; he became a martyr and hero to Polish nationalists.

The emotions and rhetoric surrounding the events of that winter eventually subsided yet the damage they caused and the sentiments they unleashed and, in fact, encouraged, never disappeared. There was a retreat from the ideal of a multi-ethnic state of Poland where ethnic Poles and national minorities could equally participate in the affairs of their country, out of fear that the National Democrats' exclusivist, ethnic nationalism was favoured by most of Polish society. In this worldview, Poland was a Polish state, belonging solely to ethnic Poles. In particular, Jews and all of the manifestations of their 'threat' to the Polish nation – Judeo-Bolshevism, socialism, cosmopolitanism, secularism, capitalism and moral degeneration – were to be excluded from the national community. Poles and Jews who rejected this vision and its expressions on the ground found it increasingly difficult to voice their protest and secure the democratic foundations on which the Second Polish Republic was built.

When in May 1926 Marshal Józef Piłsudski, a fierce opponent of the National Democrats, successfully carried out a *coup d'état*, there was a partial sigh of relief among opponents of radicalizing nationalism who saw in him a guarantor of stability, peace and protection of minorities' rights. Piłsudski left much to be desired, for he steadily moved in the direction of authoritarianism. Yet most Jews and segments of the liberal and left-leaning public perceived him as better for Poland than the alternative: either another wave of continuously collapsing governments or, worse, the National Democrats in power. Piłsudski's rule – called the *Sanacja* or purification regime – would last until 1935 (the year of his death). After his death, the *Sanacja* regime remained, yet it underwent major radicalization and embraced exclusivist nationalism.

Despite worsening economic and social conditions among Poland's Jewish population, the 1920s and 1930s saw a flourishing of Jewish culture and politics. Jewish political movements – already visible and growing before the First World War – now actively sought after the Jewish electorate and fought for support for their programmes. To be sure, not all Jews joined specifically Jewish parties. Many were attracted to the Polish Communist Party (which rejected national loyalties, Jewish or Polish) and a significant number of acculturated Jews joined the ranks of the Polish Socialist Party. In general, Jewish involvement in non-Jewish-specific politics was most visible on the left of Poland's political spectrum.

Yet most Jews were tied to any of the vast number of Jewish-specific political choices. These included many different forms of Jewish nationalism, one of which was Zionism, which tied the future of the Jewish nation to Jewish statehood in Palestine. Zionism occupied the left, centre and right of the political spectrum (i.e. Poalei Tsiyon, General Zionism, Mizrachi and Revisionist Zionism) representing different visions of the future Jewish state in Palestine and ways of achieving this ultimate goal. Other expressions of Jewish nationalism included the territorialists, who hoped for Jewish autonomous territory but not necessarily that of Palestine, as well as the autonomists (i.e. Folkists) who sought cultural-national autonomy for the Jews in the Diaspora. Theirs was not a struggle for statehood but the right for the Jewish nation to cultivate its national culture within the states in which most Jews lived. The socialist movement also had its Jewish variant, both in the Zionist camp and outside of it. The Jewish Bund was perhaps the most significant Jewish socialist party of interwar Poland. Its main goal was to fight on behalf of the Jewish worker and reject Jewish nationalism embodied in Zionism, perceived as a betrayal of the Jewish worker (and the Jewish masses more broadly) of the Diaspora for an unrealistic *bourgeois* dream of establishing a Jewish state in Palestine. Finally, the main representative of religious Jews – the Agudah – rivaled the other political movements with its strongly anti-Zionist and anti-socialist stance.

This created a mosaic of Jewish political movements, each of which published their own newspapers, printed pamphlets and created avenues for people to become involved: networks of schools, labour unions, youth groups and more. So rich was this system of Jewish institutions and associations, of activities and organizing, of social support and recreation that it continued to bloom and rally support even in the deteriorating conditions of the late 1920s and the 1930s. Amidst this, processes of secularization and Polonization did not stop as majority of Jewish children attended Polish public schools and encountered Polish culture through language, books, newspapers, peers and politics. To speak of one, monolithic Jewish community in the Second Polish Republic is thus impossible, and in fact undesirable, because it risks simplification of experiences, identities and choices.

Most historians agree that after 1935, the atmosphere within Poland became almost unbearable for Jews as antisemitism intensified, parliamentary democracy essentially collapsed, economic conditions saw no improvement, and the *Sanacja* government increasingly embraced the ideological nationalism promoted by the National Democrats. The future of the Jewish population in Poland looked increasingly bleak, particularly for the Jewish youth, who faced violence at universities and on the streets, whose chances of employment decreased significantly, and for whom immigration to Palestine or elsewhere – often the only chance for starting a better life – was becoming increasingly difficult if not impossible. Fascism was spreading across the European continent – and gaining in popularity – and the example of the Third Reich stirred the fantasies of radicals on the right in Poland as well. The world appeared to have gone mad and voices of sanity were steadily pushed to the margins. Perhaps it is unsurprising that, given the context in which it operated, the Orphans' Home of Wilczyńska and Korczak appeared to many a utopian bubble, a world unlike the one encountered outside its gates. Its emphasis on tolerance, respect, cooperation, common good, freedom and individual dignity clashed with the increasingly hateful and anti-democratic values of the general society. They remained an oasis of sanity, but their nonconformity rendered them outcasts, naïve reformers, hopeless dreamers.

On 1 September 1939 Germany invaded the Second Polish Republic. Just over two weeks later, the Soviet Union attacked from the east. The Second World War had begun. The city of Warsaw fell under the German occupation zone – the General Government – an occupation which rendered Poles sub-humans and stripped Jews of humanity entirely. In November 1940, German authorities established the Warsaw Ghetto and a year later, they announced the death penalty for any Jew caught outside its walls. Physically dividing the city between the Aryan and the Jewish side, cramping hundreds of thousands of Jews in the tight confines of the ghetto, the Germans turned life into a struggle for survival as hunger, destitution and death became the characteristics of each and every day. In July 1942, the Great Deportation of the Jews from the Warsaw Ghetto to the Treblinka death camp began. Between July and September of that year most of the Jews of the ghetto perished in Treblinka, among them Stefania Wilczyńska, Janusz Korczak, the staff members and children of the Orphans' Home.

Karolina Kołpak
History Department, Yale University

Notes

1. Singer's quote in Polish and information about Krochmalna street come from a 2012 online article in *Gazeta.pl* (Podróże section) by Jerzy S. Majewski, entitled 'Warszawa

żydowska. Ulica wielu zapachów- Krochmalna'. Agata Tuszyńska's *Lost Landscapes: In Search of Isaac Bashevis Singer and the Jews of Poland* (New York: William Morrow and Company, Inc., 1998) has been an inspiration for depicting Krochmalna as well.

2. This quote by Korczak comes from a 1904 article 'Pogotowie ratunkowe' published in *Głos*. It can be found in Lewin, A., Kirchner, H., Wołoszyn, S. and Ciesielska, M. (eds), *Janusz Korczak: Dzieła*, vol. 3 part II (Warszawa: Oficyna Wydawnicza Latona, 1994), p.31. Korczak's comment a few lines above comes from 'Luźne myśli', an article which appeared in *Krytyka Lekarska* in December 1906, and can be found in vol. 4 of *Janusz Korczak: Dzieła*.

She would come – people said they never knew when or from where.

One, two, right, left, three, four, five, six, seven, eight, fourteen – and now she's inside, even though she's just turned off Krochmalna Street into the courtyard. The steps here creak, even when the shift workers have polished them carefully before Shabbos.

So do the doors – to the dining room, the auditorium, the quiet room where you could hide from the world. Even if you open them very slowly, they always creak (hinges not always oiled, heavy door handles, when you push them they're noisy too).

For everyone, but not for her.

Noiselessness, appearing and disappearing unexpectedly – this they remember clearly. They would later wonder how they didn't notice, didn't hear her footsteps, didn't catch the shadow of her silhouette. Their amazement would last long after.

It was the end of the 1920s and the older children were putting on a New Year's play. It included a little joking around, but someone made a potentially serious suggestion: let's sew little bells onto the apron Pani Stefa always wears over her dress. The gentle tinkling, they thought, will let us know she's coming.

1

'To Ramla?'

'Afraid so.'

'You want a ticket? But why go all the way there?' asks the bus driver. 'And just before Shabbat too. You won't get back in time and you'll end up stuck there forever.'

It's Friday, early November, a steamy morning.

Ramla in central Israel – formerly predominantly Arab, now dusty and transitory – is where Shlomo Nadel lives. A low apartment building at the rear of the main street and the highway that cuts through the city, with corrugated metal siding, satellite dishes and cats. They emerge from all directions and howl, rather than meow.

Nadel, Itzhak Belfer, Yitzhak Skalka. Three house children of the Orphans' Home. The last ones. They aren't hard to find in Israel. They sometimes get invited to schools to tell the children fairytales about a strange time when they spoke a totally different language, didn't eat aubergines for dinner, and after that, didn't eat at all.

I don't manage to speak to Skalka. By the time I reach him, his memory is gone.

So first I go to Ramla to meet Shlomo Nadel. In the Orphans' Home he was called Szlomek and he becomes Szlomek again when he speaks to me in his first language, a Polish as dusty as this city. And afterwards, whenever he phones me to tell me something one more time (he says: 'when I remember something back'), then he's Szlomek too.

But right now it's November 2012. I stand in the pleasantly cool stairwell a little longer than it takes to find the right door (upstairs on the left). Shlomo opens up a crack, then invites me in.

'Just in time.'

I don't ask if he means for Shabbat.

He leads me into the living room, we walk unhurriedly, pausing by his balcony. He moves past it slowly. The apartment is cramped, a narrow hallway leads through the kitchen to the large living room. In one corner stands Frida, Shlomo's wife. She smiles and says in Polish:

'Come on, now, sit down and eat.'

Figs, oranges, cake, wafers, chocolates, pineapple. Coffee, tea, a white table cloth, a photo of Stefania Wilczyńska – Pani Stefa.

'I often wondered: how'd she know where she needed to be?' says Shlomo. 'Whenever I was up to something, she was the first to find out. And the instant you started feeling blue, she'd ask what was wrong. She'd pull whatever you'd lost out of her pocket, and wipe your nose with her handkerchief too. When I got interested in technology I found out that sort of thing is called radar.'

His story has no clear beginning. Not even when we're talking for the first time and he's prepared everything so scrupulously: Shlomo has put on a white shirt, plus a vest – though the weather is hot – and a tie. He had to ask for help tying it. Next to him, on the sofa, sits a box of photos, and newspaper clippings (articles about Korczak) are laid out neatly. Shlomo sits stiffly across the jumbled tabletop and starts telling the story from the middle.

'I remember once Stefa had to hold Shabbos for us. Tradition says to light the candles before sundown, but there was nobody to do it that time, and she was the oldest woman in the Home anyhow. She didn't want to, she kept saying it was an exception, she was standing in. But when the moment came, she knew what to do, what happened when. We prayed and she just watched. For long time, as if looking through us, somewhere out beyond.'

And so sentence by sentence, he goes back to being Szlomek, the boy who was brought to Krochmalna Street, to the Orphans' Home, which for thirty years, between 1912 and 1942, Janusz Korczak and Stefania Wilczyńska ran together. The photo of Wilczyńska that Shlomo prepared for me to see that day usually stands by his bed.

***

'Heaven exists. That's what they say.'

A year later, when I'm at his apartment again, he starts the story differently. He'll tell it to me a few more times. With each one, he tries to force his memory to go back. I'll force him to do so (force nine-year-old Szlomek to go back there). The next time it's November again, and he sits down in the armchair on the balcony, where it's coolest.

'Heaven! I dunno what makes them so sure. I'm the one who can be sure! Because I was there once. Nobody's come back from heaven to tell the tale. Except me. I was in utopia. I lived good. They taught me how it was done. I had a home where I had Stefa for a papa and Korczak for a mama.

Now tell me what you want to hear. What else am I supposed to tell you about her?'

***

Little is known, more is unknown.

There's not much 'for sure', but a lot of 'supposedly', 'somebody said', 'somewhere', 'I suppose'. The scraps don't fit together into a story, they don't support a history. Pages from registry books and mis-catalogued documents lead to dead ends. Months-long searches for email addresses, only for messages to go unanswered or answered with contradictory information. No one noted anything down or heard anything.

On the left I write facts, on the right, hypotheses. The space in between is devoted to insinuations, tempting me to fill it with an assumption that might lend these characters some form, their actions some motive.

Known: That her father was born in 1853 in Nieszawa as Izaak, son of Dwojra (née Barcińska) and Salomon Wilczyński, a stallholder. He died in 1911 in Warsaw as Julian, a salesman, father of Julia, Stefania and Stanisława.

Unknown: Whether he definitely was a salesman. The Warsaw address yearbooks preserve records of a Rafalski trading company. In 1883, Julian Wilczyński runs a small loans agency on Bankowy Square. By 1885 the agency is at 8 Przechodnia Street. (That same year in Nieszawa a certain J. Wilczyński – so maybe the same man – runs a grain export company.) In 1886, when Stefania is born, there are two Wilczyńskis running the loans agency: Izaak is registered on Senatorska Street, and Julian on Przechodnia, in the elegant Janasch Shops building. No trace remains of the fortune that permitted Izaak/Julian to send his children to universities abroad. Apparently his health was poor and had no particular head for business.

Known: Next to her father's signature in the registry (as filled out, at the time, by Stefania), someone has crossed out 'a.k.a. Julian', leaving only 'Izaak Wilczyński'.

Unknown: Who crossed this out and when? Six years earlier, in 1880, Wilczyński had registered Julia's birth.

Wilczyńska's letters contain not a single mention of her father, not one sentence about him.

Known: Izaak/Julian's grandfather, Wilczyńska's great-grandfather, was named Mosiek/Moritz, and her great-grandmother was Szajncha/Ludwika. Both died in 1831 in Nieszawa.

Unknown: Whether they were the ones who started going by 'Wilczyński'. Polish Jews used only given names and nicknames until the time of the Partitions. Those under Prussian or Austrian rule received surnames first; in the Russian partition, the change took place much later. After the Second Partition of Poland in 1793, Nieszawa came under Prussian authority. It is possible Wilczyńska's great-grandfather was born in the mid-eighteenth century. If at that time he was not yet Wilczyński but simply Mosiek (a wool trader, middleman, or milkman); later in life he would choose or be given the surname he was buried with.

From a study by S. Kurzweil for the bulletin of the Warsaw Jewish community, 1937:

> There were four phases of granting permanent surnames to Jews. The first, and simultaneously the earliest, was during the reign of the absolute ruler Joseph II. One of his reforms, introduced by letters patent in 1785 and 1787, commanded Polish Jews in the Austrian partition to adopt permanent surnames. On the basis of these letters patent, by 1 January 1788 every father in a family had to choose a surname that he and his descendants would be required to use permanently and invariably in all activities. The chosen surname had to be confirmed by the kahal and the district rabbi, and approved by the 'Kreishauptman'. According to one very probable version, uncontested to this day, beautiful-sounding names composed of precious metals, flowers etc. were the most expensive, while a somewhat cheaper category was said to consist of names from combinations of ordinary metals, stones and objects; while surnames drawn from the names of animals were entirely free.[1]

Wilczyńska's great-grandfather may have been among the first who were assigned or chose their own surname. Maybe he came from Wilczyn or another village with a similar-sounding name in the area around Nieszawa.

By Stefania's time, the name is no longer new – hers is the third generation to bear it. It is popular – at least, so says Kazimierz Snopek in 1935, when he publishes the essay 'Changing Surnames'. He sat down with documents from *Monitor Polski*, Poland's official government gazette, and made a thorough analysis of altered last names. Like every nation of European and Christian civilization, notes Snopek, Poles have constructed their surnames in accordance with social conditions and linguistic requirements. A beautiful Polish surname, he continues, is of increasing importance, as a ticket to the broader arena of community life. It testifies to its owner's Polishness. Snopek suggests that a noble-sounding Kurkowski, or even a more common Kurek, is a different person from a more Jewish-sounding Kurower.

> Everyone he encounters will know straight away this is someone who has come out of an environment alien to our own, that he possesses a different mentality, and likely will conduct himself in professional situations according to alternative moral norms. The various Kurowers whose business demands close contact with the Polish community find their current names unsuitable and are therefore changing them *en masse.*[2]

One of the particularly attractive, ennobling, and in-demand names for those whom Snopek calls 'New Poles', is the name 'Wilczyński'.

The author proposes the revision of ('our') citizens' surnames to reflect ethnicity, 'so that no one might suspect a Pole of having Jewish descent'. 'Until such time, which we hope will come soon, records of changed names may prove useful to society.'[3]

Known: Her father had many siblings, the registries of Nieszawa record. Stefania had aunts, whom she never mentions, and uncles, whose names do not appear in her letters. They were: aunt Paulina, who married Izrael Peretz and died young; Blima, who married Chaim Barciński, and Berta, who married Segal. There were unmarried aunts: Gitel, Tyne, Hana, Lechna and Lina. There were uncles: Marek, Ojzer, Jakub and Mosiek, then Abraham, who was two years older than Izaak and the youngest of the family, and Dawid. And also uncle Lejb, who later became Ludwik and would have shares in the Łódź Tricot and Knit Goods Company (there were also Wilczyńskis in Łódź, but that branch too, which I initially circle with a thick line, will have to be erased, because it leads nowhere further).

Unknown: Whether this large family kept in touch, whether relatives visited Stefania's parents in their Warsaw apartment on Świętojerska Street. Whether Wilczyńska ever saw Nieszawa, the granaries on the Vistula River, its sandy bank, and the stone sphere that stood on it, a hunk of granite that local legend say holds the entire world locked inside. Whether someone told her why grandfather Salomon Wilczyński came there in the 1830s from nearby Waganiec. And whether he definitely was trading in wool there, not long after the new Prussian authorities withdrew the privilege granted to the town back in the sixteenth century by King Sigismund II Augustus: *de non tolerandis Judaeis*. To not tolerate Jews.

Known: The given name 'Sura' appears in the registry books and 'Sara' in the land registry, yet to her daughter and the world, Stefania's mother was Salomea Wilczyńska.

Unknown: When Aron Walfisz – owner of the tenement with registry number 1769 and the neighbouring square, at 16 and 18 Świętojerska Street, respectively – signed over his real estate to his daughter Sara. He had to pay off many brothers and sisters to make that bequest.

Known: Salomea's mother was born in 1853 or 1854, and died in Warsaw in 1929.

Known: Every Wednesday evening, Stefania went to visit her mother. It was the only time off she was never willing to give up.

Known: She called her 'my dear old girl'.

Known: Salomea Wilczyńska wanted to travel. She lacked money or the opportunity for longer trips, so when she could, she rode around the city on buses. Alone.

Unknown: Where Pani Wilczyńska would go. Whether she inspired her daughter's conviction that, as women, they had many opportunities, in fact more than their less-emancipated peers who hadn't been sent abroad for university to study the hard sciences, which at that time were seen as unsuitable for women.

Known: Salomea supported the Orphans' Aid Society. She made donations. She was thorough, she started getting to know a person by inspecting their buttons (whether they were all fastened and how carefully). She liked the Russian saying 'the slower you go, the faster you'll get there'.

(Did Stefania get her scrupulousness from her mother? At Krochmalna Street, she sometimes chided children with her mother's saying when they were sloppily folding their clothes or doing a careless job dusting.)

Unknown: Anything more about this part of her family.

I search for information in the files at the Korczak archive. It's located at Warsaw's Janusz Korczak Children's Home no. 2, at 6 Jaktorowska Street – formerly 92 Krochmalna Street, the site of the original Orphans' Home. The building survived the war and although it was repeatedly renovated afterward, the topography of the area hasn't significantly changed. A wide gate, a walkway through the square, a spacious, bright building with large windows in the two rooms upstairs, to left of the door where the Home's administrative office once was. Nowadays, to the right of this the Museum of Warsaw operates its research centre – the Korczakianum.

Downstairs, the kitchen hallway is still floored with classic pre-war hourglass-shaped tiles. They've survived the renovations. Upstairs is where the children live. They run around the hallway, laughing, shouting, crying. I come here often and some, the youngest, call me 'auntie'.

In one of the files documenting Wilczyńska's life (the grey cardboard volumes tied with white ribbons take up less than one-third of a narrow shelf), there is a letter. Mary Marley, currently resident in Florida, recalls: 'my mother's mother and the Wilczyńska girls' mother were sisters, the whole family comes from Warsaw, that's for certain.' She hand-signs the typewritten letter: 'Marysia'. I write to her. An answer comes a year later. By then Marysia is 101 years old and in paragraph after paragraph keeps repeating the same sentences. Information about Stefania mixes with information about her sister Julia, their mother, and Marysia's parents. Wilczyńska at one point has a twin sister, then on the other side of the page she's older than her. Mary Marley promises in her next letter to do her best to remember better. A few months later she sends the same typewritten letter again.

Known: Wilczyńska had a sister, Julia, who was six years older.

Unknown: Whether she really had two more: Paulina (Idzikowska?) and Emilia (Kahane?). Were they stepsisters? In her father's obituary, his 'sons-in-law' are overcome with grief, the only indication that Izaak had other daughters.

Unknown: Anything more about these two other sisters. Apparently they died during the war, in the ghetto.

In her letters, Wilczyńska writes about her sister, in the singular and with tenderness.

Known: Julia Wilczyńska graduated from university in Zürich, she was a geography teacher (at the Felicja Buka Coeducational Grammar School at 11 Orla Street). She also ran a children's home outside Warsaw in Śródborów, of a type that we might call a 'sanatorium'. The Jewish women's weekly *Ewa* wrote in 1930 that it was a modern facility for childcare and education, but expensive by the standards of the Depression – it cost 400 złotys for a child to stay there (though discounts were available for the working intelligentsia), and therefore had plenty of vacancies. Julia says: it's because times are bad.

Unknown: What Julia looked like, whether she was as tall as Stefania.

Known: Stanisław, Wilczyńska's brother, was ten years younger than her and drove around Warsaw in a black Chevrolet. He liked riding up and down the new asphalt road from Marymont district to Młociny district and to Kampinos, outside the city. He was very tall (Jarosław Abramow-Newerly writes in his memoirs that he was 'gigantic'). The only son of Izaak and Salomea graduated from an eight-year secondary school – the boys' St Adalbert's Grammar School – run by Wojciech Górski (on a back street behind Nowy Świat). He studied at the polytechnic in Zürich from 1914 to 1918 (getting his best grades in maths and physics, but doing worse in French), and got an engineering degree. People who knew him called him 'Stach'.

Unknown: What his voice sounded like when he spoke and when he laughed (apparently he liked to joke). He had a short temper. For instance, while at friends' for a luncheon, an unexpected guest arrived and struck up a conversation with the man of the house, and everyone present had to pause their meal. The conversation went on so long that Wilczyński, irritated, said with a snort: 'you either come in or you get out'. The descendants of those friends use that expression at home to this day.

Known: He served in the Polish Armed Forces and participated in the Polish-Bolshevik War of 1920.

Unknown: What exactly he was in charge of as a member of the board and trade director of the Kabel Industrial Society. In 1930s Warsaw, his position, title, and Chevrolet suggest success; the dinner he scheduled every week with a couple he was friends with at the Europejski Hotel was far too expensive, but the man and his wife didn't know how to turn it down.

Known: On Friday evenings after Shabbos dinner, he would visit his sister on Krochmalna Street. The children remembered more than the elegant car. He played with them, using his long giant's legs as a bridge stretching across abysses in the faraway lands he told stories of.

Known: Her brother married Irena Eliasberg, daughter of Izaak and Stella, sister of Anna (who supposedly committed suicide in the ghetto during the war), Marta and Helena, who would marry Szymon Syrkus and design housing projects – which she would call 'social housing'. The assimilated family of Dr Izaak Eliasberg occupied an apartment at 99 Marszałkowska Street. They did not speak Yiddish at home and never got used to having money. Dr Eliasberg would see anyone, the waiting room (hallway) of his office was always teeming with people, he never sent anyone away without seeing them. In post-war documents submitted to the Union of Fighters for Freedom and Democracy, Irena (a liaison officer in the Warsaw Uprising, pseudonym 'Stasia'), gives her father's name as Ignacy, her mother's as Elżbieta, and also uses the family name Niemirowska (her mother's maiden name).

Unknown: What Stanisław's attitude was to the dividing line between Jewishness and Polishness.

In the 1980s Irena Wilczyńska spoke to the American journalist Betty Lifton, author of the book on Korczak *The King of Children*. Lifton didn't pry, she didn't grill her about Stefa. Irena talked little. About the smell of the polish the floors were scrubbed with just before Shabbos (which put her off visiting her sister-in-law on Fridays). When she sat in Stefania's room (empty, so different from the wallpapered and picture-decorated interior of her own apartment), she marvelled at how little a person could want. At how little her sister-in-law needed and how similar this made her to her mother-in-law, Izaak/Julian's widow, who had refused all gifts or help when a real estate sale went wrong (unknown: what real estate) and lost most of her money. Instead of giving her envelopes of cash (she would have handed them right back anyway), the siblings made a deal with their mother's sub-letters, for them to pay her more in rent. The family gave a wink, pretending there was nothing going on.

Irena told Lifton: we'd have never gotten away with that with Stefa.

Known: After the Uprising, the POW camps and the War, Irena works in the office of the Warsaw Housing Cooperative architectural and urban design studio. She claims she was the secretary of Poland's future communist leader Władysław Gomułka, but her autobiographical statement for the Society of Fighters for Freedom and Democracy says not a word about it. She is a Party member and practising Catholic, and gives money every month to the Care for the Blind Association in Laski, near Warsaw.

Unknown: Whether Irena contacted her mother (who went into the ghetto during the war and survived) and her sister Anna (supposedly she refused to leave, supposedly she didn't want to leave her lover behind, supposedly she was as stubborn as her mother and nothing – not even the will to survive – could force her), whether they ever phoned Stefania (even in the ghetto that was possible), whether they sent care packages for the Home.

I find a note in one of the files in the Korczak archive: the renowned poet Father Jan Twardowski was in contact with Irena Wilczyńska and the architect Helena Syrkus, and (evidently) personally prepared them for baptism and performed the ceremony. In the note's final sentence, Father Twardowski remarks unprovoked: 'Stefania Wilczyńska was a wonderful woman.'

Unknown: What Father Twardowski knew about Stefania and how. For the rest of her life Irena Wilczyńska didn't ask anyone about her husband's family. Not a single photograph of Stanisław survives. Other documents do survive.

Known: The tenement on Świętojerska was three storeys (the top floor was much lower). There was an entryway in the middle, four cast-iron balconies (two each on the first two floors), two streetlamps, a view of a small section of the Krasiński Gardens.

Unknown: whether the (two? four?) Wilczyńska sisters, on their way to school on the other side of the Krasiński Gardens, took a shortcut through the park. Whether they definitely rented an apartment on the middle floor (the Warsaw address registry of 1908 says only: Julian Wilczyński, citizen – 16 Świętojerska Street), how many rooms it had (supposedly six, most likely facing the street, spacious, bright). What the view was from the window of her room (did she have her own?). There are no details that could be expanded into a story about the place.

Known: The family was assimilated.

Unknown: What their home was like, what furniture there was in this first, closest world of Wilczyńska's. Whether they had a mezuzah at the door and separate dishes for dairy foods to keep kosher, volumes of poetry by Norwid or patriotic mementoes – like a photo of a son in a Polish uniform.

Known: Her sister Julia will be killed in the ghetto in 1942, probably during the *Großaktion* liquidation.

Known: Her brother will not put on an armband with a Star of David. He will live with his wife on the Aryan side, in Żoliborz district. He will die in 1943, of cancer (supposedly), and be buried in the Catholic Old Powązki cemetery. Irena will have carved on his gravestone: 'ZÜRCHER'.

Known: Wilczyńska neither runs away from her Jewishness nor seeks it out. She will need to learn Yiddish.

Unknown: Why and at what moment exactly Izaak became Julian, how his Polish sounded, how Salomea spoke. Did they think (and what did they say?) about themselves as Jews, or Poles of Jewish descent, or maybe of Jewish faith. Perhaps unbelieving Jews? Because that was a possibility too. Or maybe Varsovians? Citizens of the city?

***

Photographs:

of her parents,

of her sisters (how many?),

of her brother,

of the interior of the house where she lived,

from her childhood (with her parents, with her siblings, with her grandparents, in various configurations and settings),

from just before going to boarding school,

from school,
from university;
her diary,
her letters to friends from school, from university (did she have any?), to relatives…
These I do not have.

***

I do have:
the given names of her paternal grandparents from the registries in the Włocławek branch of the State Archive;
the given names of her maternal grandparents: Aron and Hinda, found in land registry documents;
two obituaries of her father, bereft of details, and one funeral notice for her mother;
her parents' grave (broad, with columns, in black marble) on the main pathway of the Jewish cemetery on Okopowa Street;
a register of teachers at colleges and secondary schools in 1926 with her sister's name on it;
her brother's university graduation certificate;
his grave in Powązki;
a slim folder of his wife's documents;
the letters Stefania wrote later on, a few of her articles, statements recorded in minutes of meetings;
a list of locations. 16 Świętojerska Street, 2 Franciszkańska Street, 92 Krochmalna Street, though none has the same address as it did before the war, nor does it look now as it did then.

And also: an email address for the son-in-law of Gerszon Mandelblat, a former house child in the Orphans' Home. The son-in-law lives in the United States. I write to him, asking to get in touch. He writes back a few weeks later and says to call as soon as possible, because 'he can't wait for you to call, he remembers Wilczyńska really well'.

The voice on the phone is clear and strong, it's hard to believe Gerszon is ninety years old. For a long time, he tells me about Korczak. About the pants he got in the Home, the roast chicken he ate for the first time in his life on Krochmalna Street. I ask about Wilczyńska.

He gives a long pause.

'Thank you for writing about her.'

He weeps into the phone.

'But I can't remember anything anymore, not a thing, kiddo.'
He apologizes.

***

The State Archive in Warsaw has preserved a registry from 1886, filled out in Russian. On 2 June 1886 at 11:00, Izaak Wilczyński, a thirty-three-year-old merchant, and two witnesses – Berek Wald, a cattle farmer from Twarda, and the salesman Moszek Dreszer – record 'an infant of the female sex', born in Warsaw on 26 May. They give her the name Stefania. 'The delay in filling out the birth certificate was due to negligence on the part of the parents.'

Known: in 1914 the United States Congress establishes Mother's Day on the second Sunday in May. The idea quickly catches on and further countries honour mothers.

Unknown: who decided that Poland should celebrate Mother's Day on 26 May, coinciding with Wilczyńska's birthday, and why.

Known: Stefania was born on a Wednesday. The weather was sunny, though not overly so, typically warm for May. It was very early in the morning.

***

Shlomo remembers something back.

'The way she lived, we didn't know much about her, she was sort of...' He searches for the word. He's very careful to make sure his Polish, frozen in time in Warsaw's pre-war street markets, is correct. 'Sort of...un-existing. She left nothing behind, as though she was never there.'

Notes

1. S. Kurzweil, 'Nazwiska żydowskie w Polsce', *Głos gminy żydowskiej* 1937, no. 4.
2. K. Snopek, 'Zmienianie nazwisk', Warsaw 1935, pp.4–5
3. Ibid., p.24.

2

There are almost no details and barely a couple pieces of information about her childhood and early youth.

She is twelve, maybe thirteen years old. The nineteenth century is coming to a close as she enrols in Jadwiga Sikorska's girls' boarding school. I search in the school's records and stories from its graduates.

A few recollections from a memorial book published in 1927 for the school's fiftieth anniversary:

> She was tirelessly hardworking, had iron stamina, and her full awareness of the goal before her made her seem simply intimidating. She knew no fatigue, at least she never acknowledged any. She was everywhere; she would appear suddenly, quietly and unexpectedly, both in classrooms during the day and at night in the dormitories. Work that in other institutions would be spread across four or five people she performed herself, alone.[1]
>
> Anyone able to work like that is also able to demand such work of others. She also demanded it from her colleagues and the children. Moreover, she knew how to arouse in them a feeling of and respect for justice – if not infallible, for that would be utopia, then at least as perfect as possible under human conditions.
>
> The farther their school years are from them, the more they value their teacher, the better they understand the motives for her actions, the fundaments of her system of child-rearing and the aims for which she strove. What for the young – impatient for life and the freedom of their natures – was sometimes a disagreeable and needless constraint, in light of later experience and deeper familiarity with people and life, would reveal itself to be a rational, consistent, well-considered plan for shaping young personalities and arming them against influences that might warp them. They understood that while at times their principal's will seemed hard and rigid, life was

> significantly harder, and anyone wanting to emerge victorious against it had to cultivate in advance the internal capacity to focus their energy and avoid distraction.[2]
>
> In these times I often wondered when our principal slept. At twelve at night she would be walking around the dormitory with a candle in her hand. Sometimes when she said, 'Hania, are you sleeping?' I would not speak up, for I knew it would trouble her if I was sleeping poorly.[3]

They aren't talking about Wilczyńska.

This is how the schoolgirls remembered Principal Sikorska, whose private girls' boarding school adhered to the official tsarist curriculum for girls' lower-secondary schools. We don't know what impression she made on young Wilczyńska (was she a role model, did she inspire her?).

For six years Wilczyńska attends the boarding school in a building with a small turret at the corner of Marszałkowska and Królewska Streets. The school is located on the third floor and has thirty-four windows. She can peek out at the nearby Saxon Gardens and the intersection. The pupils most frequently get notes for 'staring out the window and daydreaming'. (What did fourteen-year-old Stefania daydream about?)

The authors of the memorial book write:

> Parents entrusting their children to Jadwiga Sikorska's knew that no one would flatter or indulge them there. Study, work, duty are at the forefront; joy, play and amusement are left for free time and are handed over to the individual initiative of the girls themselves.[4]

(What did Stefania do on her free afternoons?)

Most of the pupils are daughters of affluent, white-collar Jews. There are plenty of them, for the school is located in the northern part of the City Centre, a neighbourhood of Jewish families; yet the girls are not required to take part in community prayer.

Uniforms are compulsory at the boarding school – the principal is careful to make sure girls from wealthier families don't stand out with fashionable clothes. Photographs have survived: dark dresses, white collars reaching as far as the upper arms, girls bent over implements, turning the small metal elements in their fingers, noting their observations down in notebooks. This is the physics lab, practical exercises. In science classes the uniform is looser: kilts with woollen capes thrown on top. The pupils stand at long tables, deep in focus. The reverse of these school photos show the school motto, from a poem by Adam Asnyk about cultivating internal courage, 'Not the just-one-day kind, bursting forth in desperate endeavour, but that which, with its head held high, firmly stands its ground forever.'

In one of the former pupils' recollections, we read: 'at school they instilled ambition in our minds, and God forbid we should be parasites living at the expense of others.'

Classes always begin at eight. At boarding school Wilczyńska's subjects include French and German, natural science, and physics – which is taught despite being illegal at this time for Polish women. The lab has access to formalin solutions, herbariums and taxidermied animals. They are able to demonstrate to the pupils any kind of experiment using fluids, magnetism and optics. Their history teacher is the renowned scholar Władysław Smoleński – the girls joke that, with his enormous beard, he looks like a knight of the Polish-Lithuanian Commonwealth. Before his lectures, they stand in the hallways and nervously flip through their notebooks. For geography they have another well-known expert, Paweł Sosnowski – who, whenever he can, uses blank maps without labels, since officially schools can only teach using maps in Russian or German, and he didn't want the girls to internalize names written in a foreign alphabet: Висла, Варшава, Карпаты.

Other things preserved in the girls' memories: colourful carpets, the principal's lounge with armchairs upholstered in green plush – this is where she holds her most important conversations. They also remember the lesson plans: one for the Tsarist authorities and another with more hours of Polish language and with lessons in the banned history and geography of Poland.

At the entrance is a loud bell, and a window hidden in the panelled doors; the girls have guard shifts – they have to warn everyone if a tsarist inspection is on its way.

(Did Wilczyńska also stand guard?)

When the alarm goes up, all the Polish teaching materials are hidden and the girl with the best Russian is picked to answer questions. For instance: Maniusia, head of her class in 1879, who feels greatly embarrassed later, but languages and all the other subjects simply come easier to her. After the boarding school and a state grammar school, Maniusia also attends lectures of the underground Flying University – secret 'girl' classes for women who were not yet allowed to enrol in colleges and universities. Then she goes to France to study in the mathematics and natural sciences faculty of the Sorbonne. Even later she will discover the chemical element with the atomic number 84 and the Latin name Polonium, and become known to the world by the name Marie Curie.

After graduating from boarding school, Wilczyńska also leaves the country.

***

Jadwiga Sikorska, on herself:

> What have I done? I have always fulfilled merely my simple, everyday duty, nothing more. And if my actions have proven good as such it is because I have loved my work very much, I have been champing at the bit for it since my early youth, I have idealized it and, strangely, not felt that it was a profession. And when terrible times have come, when I thought the ground was shifting beneath my feet and my lungs were gasping for air, that was when instead of despair, or perhaps alongside it, a peculiar strength has manifested itself, a voice that whispered that I could not possibly give in. And that is when I have felt truly needed.[5]

***

In Europe, higher education is increasingly open to women. University after university grants them the right to enrol. The Jagiellonian University in Kraków reluctantly begins in 1894 by permitting women to hear lectures. Three women, who by law cannot take exams to earn a degree. Three years later women will be allowed to study philosophy, seven years later – pharmaceutics and medicine. The University of Warsaw will not open its doors to women until 1915.

Perhaps this is why she goes abroad – Wilczyńska does not explain her decision anywhere. First to Geneva (though her siblings chose Zürich), where the university has accepted women since 1872. Here name is there, last on the list of auditors for the summer semester of 1906. The University of Geneva's archive confirms: 'Miss Stefania Wilczyńska was accepted as an auditor for a course in natural science.' According to the lecture lists, she took organic chemistry with Professor Carl Gräbe and botany with Professor Robert Chodat.

Next stop: Liège, Belgium. She is not alone – the list of students is full of names appended with the letters RdP: *Royaume de Pologne*, the Kingdom of Poland. Christian women and Jewish women, not all from wealthy homes.

At this time the college was encouraging young women to 'take up new subjects'. Maybe that was all it took for her to choose Liège. Her listing on the register of studies: 'Stefania Wilczyńska, born 26 May 1886, studied at the University of Liège 1906–1907, 1907–1908, natural and medical sciences.' And then a mark by her name indicating she was a good student. The register does not say why she didn't finish her studies. A response comes from the university: 'We know nothing more about the lady in question.'

The archive preserves a photograph from this period, a group of women in light-coloured hats and long dresses. Their bodies, though squeezed into corsets, and bent over in a boat; their faces wear broad smiles.

Wilczyńska is not among them.

In one of her later letters, she also says: 'I did Fröbelian courses' (from Friedrich Fröbel, a German pedagogue and creator of the first programme of pre-school care). A short mention, without a date or any elaboration (when did she do them? After returning to Warsaw? And why?).

A typical training programme included:

Pedagogy – 3 hours per week: the most essential details of physical and mental education, educational measures as applied to kindergarten, the relationship of kindergarten to the family home and school, goals and duties of the kindergarten teacher.

Practical exercises – 8 hours per week.

Polish language – 6 hours per week: reading poetry and prose passages appended with factual explanations and drawing attention to proper language and presenting a train of thought, memorizing stories with potential application in the kindergarten, exercises in storytelling and description, drawings – 2 hours per week.

Teaching of forms – 2 hours per week: candidates are acquainted with materials, tools, and shapes as well as methods allowing them to develop skills and dexterity in creating various objects appropriate for entertaining children.

Singing – 2 hours per week: learning songs and developing skills for singing with children.

Gymnastics – 1 hour per week: easier slow exercises and the simplest ones with apparatuses, instructions on the proper way to lead and pick up small children.[6]

***

But this isn't the only way it could have happened.

We need only go back in time: the end of the nineteenth century is one again more than a decade away. Somewhere in the Russian partition of Poland, or in Galicia under Austrian rule, four girls are born to four different families. What they share is that their grandparents were named Salomon and Dwojra –and not, say, Stanisław and Kazimera; Hersz and Chaja, not Henryk and Anna; Jehuda and Ryfka, not Józef and Radosława; Szmul and Estera, not Aleksander and Elżbieta. The first girl is born in a wooden house on Tannery Street or Short Street, in a shtetl like Łomża, Izbica or Góra Kalwaria. People speak to her in Yiddish and she knows no other language, except maybe a few words in Russian. Her mother wears a headscarf, her father studies Torah. The girl has four brothers and two sisters. She studies at home. When the time comes, her parents will marry her off to a boy, Aron or Srul, who, like her father, will be bent over the Holy Book. She will put on a headscarf. If she is prematurely widowed and needs to support her home, she will open a small spice store or become a travelling trader. She will not read the socially-conscious writings of Bolesław Prus, and maybe will never even hear of him.

The second girl grows up in the family of a rabbi, who won't shut down the discussion when young people come to him and ask: is it a sin to send your children to a public, non-Jewish school? He himself speaks Polish with a strong accent, but he's glad – though he would never admit it – that his daughter's accent is practically gone. For the same reason he won't be angry when she says she wants to keep studying and enrol in a boarding school, or when she reads Prus's 'Weekly Chronicles' in the Polish-language *Warsaw Courier*, nor even when one day she declares she will be a governess in a Polish family. He only requests – and she agrees – that she does not work on Saturdays.

The third girl lives in Solec district in central Warsaw, in a basement shared with two families of strangers. Her mother died young and her father dropped out of cheder long ago, and in general rarely turns his thoughts to the past. He has no time to remember. He works three shifts, plus in evenings he goes to rallies where the speakers persuade him to join forces with the whole proletariat. But even so the two of them are going hungry, he and his beautiful daughter, who in a few years' time will get a job in a factory. Though she liked learning Polish in school, she won't have time to read Prus. She will join the socialists and campaign herself. She will be exiled to Siberia.

The fourth girl is born in an assimilated family. She doesn't know Yiddish, doesn't have an accent, goes to a Polish boarding school, studies abroad, and returns to Warsaw; it's 1906, maybe 1907. The Russian Empire is still finding its feet after the failed revolution of 1905. Poland, which is still officially absent from the maps, has little to offer a young woman of Jewish descent.

But emancipation, a fashionable word at the time, has an effect on her as well. As a Jew, for some time now: in Russian-ruled Poland, by 1862 the Jews' special legal status was abolished and four years later Jews were allowed into the civil service. More recently as a woman: in fact, the first signs of equality are just appearing. It's still not enough, though more, at any rate, than the three previous girls have been able to enjoy. She has her own choice (of a slightly enlarged set of options).

If she decides to marry, it will be to a man who probably doesn't study Torah, and if he goes to synagogue, it's to the reformed one on Tłomackie Street; he wears a fashionably trimmed beard like Henryk Sienkiewicz's and an elegantly-cut frock coat and hat. She will be able to get involved, as befits a fairly well-off married woman, in philanthropy and myriad aid committees, throwing fundraisers and organizing balls.

If not marriage, then maybe teaching? That will be harder, but certainly possible by now, especially if she maintains her Swiss, Belgian, and university contacts abroad. Not only Marie Curie, but also others before her have paved the way – like Józefa Joteyko, who also studied in Geneva and laid the foundations for special education in Brussels, or Maria Grzegorzewska, another pioneer who also studied in the Belgian capital.

And once she is looking for practice rather than theory, maybe there will be a position waiting for her a governess or a teacher – but in a Jewish school (her set of options is only *slightly* enlarged, after all). There are many of these in Warsaw, as well as orphanages where she can work as a caregiver.

Maybe this is exactly why our fourth girl, the granddaughter of Salomon and Dwojra, twenty-three-year-old Stefania, with her unfinished Swiss degree, now a kindergarten teacher, sets off one day – it's 1909 – down Franciszkańska Street. 'Stone,' goes the chorus of her favourite song, 'is what your life's to be'. She isn't sentimental, she doesn't get soppy. It's crowded – after all this is one of the most important shopping streets in Warsaw. She passes Szmul Nierenberg's upholstery workshop, Mosze Rubinstein's store, and Zysia Landoberg's colonial imports store, as well as Judka Neuman's tobacconist's (across the street). She can't read all the signs, they're in Yiddish. She stops at no. 2, which houses the orphanage run by the Orphans' Aid Society. A Jewish society, for Jewish orphans in the northern (in this case, a synonym for 'Jewish') district of Warsaw. It's not far from here to Świętojerska Street – she may have passed it many times before.

She knocks (no, in fact she goes straight in).

***

> When you beat down the fruit of your olive trees, do not go over them again; that shall go to the stranger, the fatherless, and the widow. When you gather the grapes of your vineyard, do not pick it over again; that shall go to the stranger, the fatherless, and the widow.[7]

So says the Torah.

(Did she ever go to synagogue?)

She surely knows the verses of Holy Scripture.

In Judaism, caring for the weak is a religious imperative. If the Wilczyńskis were well-off, they would have to donate money to the poor. In the late nineteenth century, secular organizations to aid the poorest also began being formalized. The Haskalah, the Jewish Enlightenment, secularized many areas of Jewish community life in the second half of the eighteenth century. Compassion and good deeds, meant to hasten the arrival of the Messiah, were steadily enveloped in motivations of utilitarianism, humanitarianism, and solidarity. A Tzadik, a just man in Hebrew, who wished to please God became a welfare activist, a pragmatist. He felt an obligation to help not only for humanitarian reasons, but social ones as well – to modernize society through education. To make this task easier, kahals – Jewish communities – formed charitable divisions concentrated in a single institution: Tzedakah Gedolah, the Great Charity. They aided orphans as well. When the authorities of the Russian partition dissolved the kahals, these charitable divisions transformed into smaller, independent organizations, societies, and councils, which sometimes also operated illegally.

One of the organizations that gathered these welfare activists was the Orphans' Aid Society. It entered the registry of the societies and unions of Warsaw Guberniya in December 1907. It was founded by people with diverse views, some of them religious and conservative, but others secular. They paid membership fees, made donations and drew up by-laws. They convened a board and committees, and everyone held their positions unpaid. In the first year of the Society's activity it numbered 1,500 members. These were mainly made up of representatives of the learned professions: doctors, lawyers, but also businessmen. They were mainly drawn from – or were forming – assimilated families.

I check the register of members: it includes Stefania's mother Salomea Julianowa Walfisz. Her sister Julia, too.

A similar organization to the Society was the Fraternal Aid Association for the Support of Small Merchants, Shopkeepers and Artisans, which in 1903 provided support to more than 200 orphanages. It ran a shelter at 5 Dzika Street. The conditions were hellish. A large apartment held a gang of filthy children: there were puddles of urine under the beds, faeces in the stoves, children left without care. A new organization was needed to take up the challenge – the shelter was handed over to the newly-formed Society. The children were quickly transferred to a house in suburban Grodzisk, and then back to Warsaw in 1909, to a specially renovated and adapted location at 2 Franciszkańska Street. A lease was signed with the landlord for three years.

In those days, a dozen or more such charitable organizations were operating in Warsaw alone. Maybe Wilczyńska appreciated the fact that the Society was taking in children – and only children – regardless of gender and origin, which at that time was a rarity. Other facilities divided residents by sex and sometimes the family's economic status, or also accepted adults or the elderly. Maybe it suited her that the Society gave the staff a relatively free hand and did not interfere excessively in educational matters. Maybe she saw these as necessary conditions to be able to successfully change the world. Education, child-rearing – enlightenment, as it was called, because it was with education that change started. The moral imperative to selflessly assist the weak, to perfect the world through aiding those in a worse condition – this is what people talked about as they read socially conscious literature by Stefan Żeromski or Eliza Orzeszkowa.

(Did Wilczyńska talk about this too? With whom?)

We have no evidence of what's going on in her life between graduation and the day she arrives at Franciszkańska Street. We only know for sure she is met by Stella Eliasberg, an activist at the Society. Wilczyńska asks for an unpaid position. 'I agreed, though I didn't trust her much. She was young, accustomed to comfort, coddled by her mother, and after studying in Belgium she was going to work enthusiastically with filthy cellar children?'[8]

Wilczyńska arrives at work punctually, loaded up with mugs of broth for the sick children. She organizes the daily schedule and duty shifts, washes diapers and combs out lice. She will take a special liking to one of the house mothers, Estera Weintraub, who will help with her work. Wilczyńska will organize some money for her so she can go to Switzerland to study.

It is also here that one day Stella Eliasberg brings Janusz Korczak (great-grandson of a glazier who installed windows in a shtetl, possibly Hrubieszów; grandson of Hersz, who went both to cheder and the University of Lemberg medical school; son of Józef Goldszmit – a lawyer who writes stories about Jews and Poles as 'inhabitants of one land'[9] – and Cecylia Gębicka). This young paediatrician, already a veteran of the Russo-Japanese War and author of a well-received début, is focusing more and more of his attention on the issue of early childhood education. He is meant to listen to an evening of recitations – poems by Maria Konopnicka (Wilczyńska is teaching them to the children), and reportedly he's thrilled.

***

Or maybe what brought her to Franciszkańska Street was mere curiosity, or ordinary happenstance?

The older girls in the Orphans' Home would later gossip that it was unluckiness in love, disappointment, emptiness, the need for a change.

Maybe sensitivity alone was enough. The kind she had and no other, at that time and in that place.

She was twenty-three years old and made up her mind: she was going to work for orphans. Jewish ones, in a Jewish orphanage.

She stayed.

And he stayed.

The choices that make up a life can only be seen once it has run its full course.

Notes

1. K. Król, I. Moszczeńska, *Szkoła Jadwigi Sikorskiej w Warszawie: wydano w celu uczczenia 50-lecia pracy jej przełożonej* (Warsaw: 1927), p.61.
2. Ibid., pp.73–74.
3. Ibid., p.88.
4. Ibid., p.102.
5. Ibid., p.209
6. Report of the Directorship of the Imperial-Royal Women's Teaching College in Kraków for the 1903 school year.
7. Deuteronomy 24:20–21, Jewish Publication Society, 1985.
8. 'Pani Stefa', recollection by Stella Eliasberg, manuscript, Korczakianum – research centre of the Museum of Warsaw, inventory number 0616.
9. Joanna Olczak-Ronikier, *Korczak. Próba biografii* (Warsaw: 2011), p.39

3

Israel, 2013.

'And do you remember your home, Shlomo?'

'On Krochmalna?'

'No, the one before. Your mom, your dad?'

'I was born in Warsaw in 1920, as the first child of Gela Nadel and Josef Rotbard.' This first time he tells the story of his life in order, like a recitation. 'I was four when my father died. My mother was left with me and Samek, my newborn brother. She found a job as a live-in maid, but she couldn't stay there with the children. She handed me over to distant relatives, outside Grójec. There used to be orchards there, are there still?'

'Yes.'

'They had no children of their own. They were just a little less poor than my mother. My aunt, I can't recall her name, I don't remember…She was nice, but my uncle had a habit of beating her with a thick belt. After a few years my mother managed to get me a spot in the Orphans' Home. My little brother wasn't so lucky, because they had a rule that of not taking two kids from the same family. She had to leave him on the street and believe someone would take care of him.'

'On the street?'

'On the street. At the shelter door. Well, what was she supposed to do with him?'

***

The Orphans' Aid Society wants more. Children shouldn't merely survive, they ought to have full lives. And Korczak and Wilczyńska are just the ones to make their goal a reality. The two of them find support for their plans in the Society. And then there's Dr Izaak Eliasberg, who joins them. Since 1910 the Society has been raising funds to build its own building. The first donation (12,000 rubles) comes from Chaim Krawcow and his mother Sara.

For 24,000 rubles, the Society buys a lot on Krochmalna Street (at number 92). The full cost of the construction will be ultimately come to

114,000 rubles, all financed by private donors. At this time, one pound of bread costs three kopecks and skilled workers earn less than twenty rubles a month.

Korczak will become Director of the Orphans' Home, while Wilczyńska will be Matron. She will have room and board included in her salary.

The construction – Korczak consults on the design – will run long, but finally in the autumn of 1912, fifty boys and girls from the orphanage on Franciszkańska Street and thirty-two new ones will move in. The decision to accept new the children is made by the Orphans' Home Childcare Committee. The letters of application have not survived.

In the Korczak archive, in one of the grey folders, is a typescript. In this anonymous survey of former house children, conducted in the 1980s by Ada Poznańska-Hagari, I read memories of their family homes.

> My father died when I was born. There were eight of us: six daughters and two sons. My mother worked here and there. She was 'enlightened', she read a lot. She knew a man from her younger days who wanted to marry her, but she didn't want to burden him with eight children. She didn't see any way of keeping us fed, she committed suicide.

> Our food supplies were low, but it was warm at home in winter. My mother earned money sewing and it had to be warm in the apartment when customers came.

> Until the age of seven I lived with my mother, who worked very hard and would leave me alone on the street. It's all hazy in my memory. Out of four children, we two sisters were left. My sister was seven years older and went to work very young. Because of the tough conditions at home she got married when she was sixteen. By then I was already in the Orphans' Home.

> My mother worked very hard, on her way to work she would leave me alone on the street, because I couldn't go with her or stay in the dark and cramped place where we were living.

> My mother worked in someone else's home, she couldn't keep us with her and she handed me and my brother over to a childless older aunt and uncle. We were all right there, but they died after a short while. When I was in the Orphans' Home I couldn't visit my mother, we would see one another at my grandfather's.

There were three of us children – the two older ones were in orphanages, I stayed with mama. I remember being hungry for bread and collecting bits of it on the street. At the age of 12, I would get up early, at four, five o'clock, and deliver papers. I wasn't a distinguished student, since oftentimes I was thinking about bread and not about learning. We lived in severe poverty. The hardest problem for me was that I was born after my father died. When I heard a kid on the street calling out 'papa', I'd get a lump in my throat, I couldn't bear it.

We lived in extreme poverty. My mother was always moving from one workplace to another. When she was widowed, there were four of us children. My older sister was already self-sufficient. My mother wanted my brother, who was two years older than me, to get into the Orphans' Home, but they took me, because I was in bad health. My brother got taken in at another orphanage and it was so bad there that he ran away and would move around with our mother. My younger brother was still a baby. My mother couldn't keep him and gave him up to an orphanage, where he suffered badly. Mama got married once I was already grown. They lived in the attic of a filthy, abandoned house, but at least they had a roof over their heads.

Mama was pregnant when my father died. I was born in sadness. My health was poor, I kept getting pneumonia. Mama sold everything off and moved in with some people as a seamstress. My mother's father didn't want anything to do with us and we had nowhere to live anymore. We rented a tiny room to live in: mama, my sister, and I. There was no coal, it was freezing cold. There was a sawmill nearby where I'd collect wood shavings. I'd light a fire and put a bucket of water over it. A woman, a house mother from the Orphans' Home, saw me and asked what I was cooking. 'Just water, if my mama brings something then we'll put it in,' I said to Pani Stefa [...].

Pani Stefa took me in.[1]

***

Their homes are cramped apartments in tenements where there are brothels on the upper floor and thieves meet on the roof; or a temporary place with extended family. Mouldy basements shared with strangers. Wooden shacks (the wood rotting and decaying). Instead of floors, pounded dirt sprinkled with sand from the Vistula River, purchased once a year (if there was money for it) in Solec district. Bedbugs falling off the walls, and rat infestations. Windows overlooking the gutter, sewers flooding the apartment after heavy rain. One bed or sleeping pallet divided into three. Or not even a pallet, a shake-down with rags to cover it. A table, maybe a cupboard, nothing more. A bucket for waste in the corner. Only the clothes on your back. If you have any more, they hang them on a nail on the wall, near the stove (if there is one), to dry. Either an oil lamp burning or, more likely, sitting in the dark. A consumptive's cough coming from the other end of a hovel. Father's wheezing (tuberculosis, typhus, infarction) before he dies. Mother's weeping when it happens. The landlord screaming to get out. Horses neighing in the courtyard where you sit all day, and night, and another night, before mother finds a new place to stay. Before you end up at Krochmalna Street. One of seven, or ten. In mouldy shoes (if any). With a job (maybe for several years already). With lice, scabies, bad eyesight, too thin, with bones sticking out. From homes where Yiddish was spoken and the kitchen (if there was anything to cook in it) was kosher.

They come to the Home, which has central heating and a tiled floor (which the philanthropists were afraid the children might damage). To beds in a large dormitory with white, starched sheets. Everyone has a separate bed, their own. To the dining room, where they can ask for seconds (and there are seconds to give). To bathrooms with tubs and showers. To the auditorium with swing doors, with books, toys, a piano. To swallowing fish oil, listening to records, looking at microbes under a microscope.

But a new home also means fear. A long hallway, a ceiling so high. White walls and cold floors, squeaking floorboards. The first nights in a new place: the shadows of trees moving on the ceiling, on your right someone mutters in their sleep, in the corner they're snoring, fidgeting. They're all seven or eight years old. Wilczyńska knows most of them from back on Franciszkańska Street. She leads them to bed when they lose their way. She explains how to use the bathroom, which most are seeing for the first time.

Their new home is set up differently from what they know. They can master the layout of the rooms quickly, but the house rules are trickier to understand. Some children are hearing for the first time that they must do something. And that they are allowed to do something else. The ones who aren't used to crowds want to hide, but there's nowhere to hide. They get something that belongs to them and they don't know what that means. Everything amazes them.

They rebel.
They're afraid.
They miss their loved ones.
It's hardest on Saturdays, when they come back from visiting family.

***

Back to the survey.

> When I arrived, they cut my hair. Short. I cried because I'd had long, beautiful hair, and I hid in a corner. Suddenly I could feel someone stroking me. Pani Stefa. She said it would grow back, and that she herself preferred it short, it was prettier that way. And I was embarrassed, I didn't want to go home. But I missed my family a lot. After my visits, I didn't want to go back to the Home. It was a year before I started to like it.
>
> It was my first time sleeping without my grandmother.
>
> For the first time I got my own underwear.
>
> They gave me a bath in the tub and I ate breakfast, for the first time in my life.
>
> I got sick with mumps, they asked my grandma to take me for two weeks so I didn't infect the rest. My aunts were so happy, they spoiled me, but I was waiting for them to take me back, I was afraid they wouldn't let me back into the Home.
>
> I was incredibly scared, because until then I'd only known my mama, papa, and little brother, and suddenly here were so many new people, all the time. Talking, running around, sleeping next to me.
>
> 'What have I got at your house, mama?' I asked. 'Over there I study, they help with my lessons, I can already speak Polish. I'm going to stay.'
>
> I knew I had a home, that I was here, on Krochmalna, temporarily.[2]

***

Israel, 2013

'You know, once I was walking back from school – we either went to the public school or the Jewish one, depending – through Grzybowski Square and I saw my grandma on the street. My mama's mother. When mama, Samek and me had to leave our apartment, she didn't have anywhere to go either, and my mother couldn't find a place for her to live. She noticed me too. She called out: "Shoymele, Shoymele." I sometimes dream about that, her saying "Shoymele, Shoymele." I looked at her from the other end of the street. I didn't know: to go to her, not to go? After all, she couldn't help me, and I couldn't help her. I turned my back and walked away. What do you say to that?'

'How old were you then?'

'Nine, I think.'

***

Korczak and Wilczyńska teach them too. He has already decided not to have his own family. 'A slave has no right to have children.'[3]

(What about her? Did she make the same decision? No letter has survived where she explains it, I don't know if anyone ever asked her. Years later she will only write: 'And don't rush, go slowly, carefully with the reforms. And don't be angry if life punishes you harshly for each mistake, don't be angry if the punishment proves disproportionate to your guilt. That is how you learn. This comes hard to young educators – I remember how hard…')[4]

***

A kilogram of peas,

37 meters of rope,

hair clippers – 1 set,

5 second-hand dresses, toys and books – donated by little Irenka,

gloves worth 10 rubles,

a sewing machine,

2 kilograms of toffees,

41 dolls, 32 puzzles and 14 chimes,

18 pairs suspenders,

delivery of ice in the summer months,

goldfish for 13 rubles,

200 mugs from Irena and Stanisław Wilczyński,

2 dozen girls' undergarments,

5 crates of oranges (this is many years later) from First Lady Maria Mościcka

and other gifts in kind as well as monetary donations for the children and the Home are noted (by Wilczyńska?) carefully in the reports.

She rarely leaves Krochmalna. She feels like she lives in the provinces, since she so rarely visits 'real Warsaw'[5] She misses the Sports and Industry Exposition in Łazienki Park – the hit of winter 1912, thanks mainly to the ice slides. A year later, the hit is Zygmunt Krasiński's classic *Irydion*, the most popular show in the repertoire of the newly-opened Polski Theatre. Nor does she have time to visit the annual Salons of the Zachęta Fine Art Society or the Iluzjon Kultura movie theatre at 125 Marszałkowska Street. She doesn't have the chance to see how quickly – in response to an order from city hall – street after street in Warsaw is cobbled, nor to see the completion of a third bridge over the Vistula River, which in the second-to-last year of the World War is renamed from the Tsar Nicholas II Bridge to the Prince Józef Poniatowski Bridge.

She herself later recalls that era in a letter:

> Nothing so stupefies and dulls a person as a perpetual stay at a boarding school. You did not know me before, but please believe me that I have become so narrow-minded, I've coarsened in this barrack life. And I know more than anyone how hard it is to tear oneself away from the boarding school for a few hours, but you must, for the good of the cause in the future, so as not to become deaf and blind to what is happening all around. You must simply learn to foresee everything that could happen during your absence, put everything in order, and teach the children and the remainder of the staff to wait with non-urgent business until your return.[6]

(How does a person learn to foresee *everything*?)

***

The children do not get long to enjoy the calm of their new home. Two years after its official opening, in 1914, the First World War breaks out. Before Korczak leaves for the Front – drafted, like Eliasberg, into the military – he writes a letter to Estera Weintraub. He asks her to return to Krochmalna Street to assist Wilczyńska.

From the Orphans' Aid Society report for 1914: 'Who knows [what would have happened] if the helm had not been bravely taken from the Director's hands by our Matron, who with all dedication and understanding is continuing with the system and task that our Doctor Goldszmit has created and loved.'[7]

A hundred-odd children and not enough food. A hundred-odd children and typhus. A hundred-odd children and a shortage of fuel.

(Esterka is there, the laundry woman is there, other helpers are there too, volunteers from the Society. What does she herself do? Does she wait in the lines that cut across Warsaw's streets? Does she arrive by four in the morning, clutching ration cards for bread and sugar? Does she wait twice a week in front of a store with meat in stock, since it's only sold two days out of seven? Where is she in line when they start giving out fuel, since there was generally only enough for half the people who needed it?)

She definitely leaves the city to get food, bringing her haul back in full sacks. She wraps a blanket around a sick child, tying it around their neck, and carries them on her back to the doctor. She walks home through dark streets (the Front is near, blackouts are enforced, gas and electricity are limited, kerosene is expensive and rationed), she passes homes with damaged fences, devastated gardens and parks – people are ripping out anything that can be burned for fuel.

In 1913 the total 'cost per child per institutional day' is 34.9 kopecks, but by 1914 it's nearly 40 kopecks. That's how much it costs to feed the children, according to the pamphlet *How to Eat in Wartime*, published by the Bolesław Prus Society for Practical Hygiene in 1915, on the eve of the German occupation of Warsaw. The Food Commission has estimated what a full-value meal should look like, one that ensures 2,100 calories for adults and 525-1,575 for children, depending on their age. The Commission also recommends that, in addition to breakfast, lunch and dinner, children should also receive an afternoon snack consisting of a glass of milk and a roll with – if possible – butter or lard.

In the budget for 1915, now anticipating 135 children, Wilczyńska calculates that they will require 11,250 rubles for food, 1,500 for fuel, 450 for lighting, and yet another 300 for laundry. The funds from gifts and donations are not sufficient and there will be a deficit of nearly 1,000 rubles.

The budget's predictions turn out to be wrong. They take in another fifty-odd children at Krochmalna Street, they must also give at-home support to those the Orphans' Home does not have space for, and equip fifteen children who have turned fourteen – the year they graduate from the Home. The Russian Front, the German Front, the war, none of that matters, the children need layette sets: three shirts; three pieces of other undergarments; three pairs of socks or stockings; three handkerchiefs; three bed sheets; the same number of pillowcases, bedspreads, and towels; two sets of clothes, including dresses and petticoats; a coat; two pairs of shoes; a pair of suspenders or three pairs of camisoles; a cap or hat; a sleeping pallet; a bed; a comforter; a basket; a padlock; a brush; a comb; a mug; a toothbrush and a sewing kit.

In the first year of the war, they receive twenty-four applications to place a child at Krochmalna Street – in the second year, 143.

The Society appeals to the consciences and wallets of its donors so that in the next year, 1915, the Home doesn't close due to a calculated deficit of 28,000 rubles. The appeal is successful thanks to considerable sums contributed by, among others, the Religious Community Board's Jewish War Victims Assistance Society.

By the third year of the war 160 children live at Krochmalna Street. Food rations have been cut further back, there are no potatoes at all, and fuel is also harder and harder to come by in the city. Workers are striking, including at the waterworks, because even if they're being paid, they still can't afford to feed their families. The city is also facing a rising epidemic of typhus and typhoid fever, born of poverty and filth. The death rate from typhoid fever and additionally tuberculosis has increased threefold during the first three years of the war. It's impossible to compare deaths from starvation – in 1913, the final year before the war, city hall tracked no such category.[8] The Warsaw Ambulance Service notes increasing instances of people fainting from hunger.

The Warsaw City Council sets up kitchens for the most impoverished, giving larger subsidies for meals served to Christians. They take away Jews' permits to sell on main streets and refuse to hire them for municipal public works projects.

***

Every year the Home summarizes (she summarizes?) the number of illnesses among the children:

1914

January	1 tonsillitis
February	1 tonsillitis, 1 favus [mycosis], 1 appendicitis
March	8 mumps, 1 measles, 2 tonsillitis, 1 chickenpox
April	1 scabies, 1 favus

May	2 scabies
June	2 favus, 2 tonsillitis
July	0
August	0
September	3 tonsillitis
October	1 dysentery, 1 lung disease
November	2 tonsillitis, 1 scabies
December	1 typhus
1915	
January	0
February	2 tonsillitis
March	0
April	0
May	0
June	4 hives, 1 smallpox, 1 measles
July	1 tonsillitis, 1 dysentery
August	0
September	epilepsy
October	1 tonsillitis, 1 enteritis
November	2 tonsillitis, 2 lung diseases, 2 scabies
December	2 mumps
1916	
January	0
February	1 mumps, 2 dysenteries
March	2 scabies
April	2 scabies, 2 tonsillitis, 1 whooping cough
May	0
June	3 scabies
July	0
August	0
September	0
October	1 dysentery
November	1 tonsillitis
December	1 tonsillitis

***

In 1916, her office receives 130 applications to take in a child.

The New Gazette writes: 'The Orphans' Home has established a reputation as an exemplary child-rearing institution. The entire system of classes, the division of labour, and the daily schedule are based on principles of modern pedagogy and deliver excellent results.'[9]

A year later, the same publication: 'As a result of the forced absence of Dr Korczak, who is detained in Russia, the directorship has been temporarily taken over by Panna Stefania Wilczyńska, who completely selflessly and with true love dedicates herself exclusively to raising the orphans.'[10]

This is the first time Wilczyńska wants to leave Krochmalna Street.

The revolution is starting in Russia, in Warsaw the city government's food and heating departments are battling speculation and supply shortages. Children in Warsaw are losing an average of two kilos a month. The Society – and Wilczyńska – successfully organize summer camps for sixty-four children from the Children's Home. In a rented house in Anin, on the outskirts of Warsaw, the children lounge on deck-chairs on two verandas in the sun. They come back weighing on average a half a kilo more.

***

Wilczyńska didn't record her memories from the time of the war. No one remembers her complaining. However, we do have a diary by an anonymous pupil of the Orphans' home, 'girl no. 56'.

> **26 January 1917**
> Today we had an unusual day: Esterka came.
>
> We are going to have to listen to her almost just like Panna Stefa. […]
>
> Esterka is 20. Neither homely nor beautiful. But her smile lights up her whole face.
>
> All the children threw themselves at her, but I stood to the side and looked her over carefully. So this is the famous Esterka, who I've heard so much about.
>
> She was a house child at the Orphans' Home. A house child just like me, Surka, Łajcia, and Helenka, and just like us she wore numbered dresses, shoes, and stockings.
>
> She always dreamed of becoming a house mother, like Panna Stefa, and work her whole life with children. When she grew up, she went to Switzerland. Panna Stefa thought life in a boarding house

was like living in a convent. So first Esterka should learn a lot and get to know the world.

The older girls, the ones of her generation, almost her same age, say that over in Switzerland Esterka was not living in paradise at all, that she even had to scrub stairs. […]

19 February

I haven't written for a few days, because I'm so hungry I can't focus. When the Russians were here we didn't feel poverty, but now the Germans have really made our lives miserable. […] I mean, we have never even received field peas. These are a sort of pea, but completely black, and cooking can never turn them soft. Beniek says before the war they used these field peas to feed horses. But now even the field peas taste good to us.

Or for instance the Germans have invented cocoa with water. It looks like tea, but smells like hot chocolate. You just have to close your eyes when you drink it. Surka told me that before the war the children often had real cocoa. But I wasn't here then.

Surka laughs and calls me a baby because I don't know what cocoa looks like. But why should I care about that? Better to have soup with plenty of potatoes, so we don't have to fish around for them, as Fulek says, and to get more than two ounces of bread for supper.

23 February

God, such freezing cold now! 1917 has arrived and nothing has changed. The war still goes on […]. Panna Stefa says she cannot remember such a harsh winter in many, many years.

On our street we have a bakery and a coalyard. People are endlessly standing in line. They hold vouchers in their hands and huddle up against one another, it's 10:00, and they have been standing there since six in the morning. They warm one another up, so that they don't freeze in this cold too.

How happy I am that although I'm still hungry I don't need to wait in long lines. […] We look at them and think that each of us over a single day would be able to eat a sack of kasha. Panna Stefa was sad when she came into the office today. Apparently they sent half as much as she'd expected.

Is my sister standing in line too? Is she also huddling up against strangers, warming her hands and chest, does she have the same sad eyes when she sees a store that's still closed?

I asked her. She says she never stands in line. Then she smiles, but very sadly. She doesn't want to worry me, and maybe they really are sparing her. She's so weak and gaunt.

27 February

I would be very happy if someone loved me the way Panna Stefa does Esterka. When she hugs and kisses her, it makes me think a mother could not be more attached to her child than Panna Stefa is to Panna Esterka.

When I watch them, I don't feel jealous, but I also wish I had a mother, even not a real one.

5 March

Sad days have arrived. I'm starting to feel like a real orphan. I'm suffering, often not so much for myself as for my friends. I don't blame Panna Stefa for that, since she wants the best, and if she doesn't manage it, she gets agitated and her anger spills out on us.

Today while handing out stockings she lost her temper with Estusia and Surka; she told them to look for a job, because they were too big to stay in a boarding school. I know she didn't seriously think that, but it was painful to hear.

The cold snap is continuing, but we're only burning enough to keep the boiler for the central heating from cracking. [...]

We've gotten some turtleneck sweaters. They're very warm, but sleeveless. Unfortunately there weren't enough for everyone. We're also getting mittens, these gloves without fingers, which we're even allowed to wear inside.

Because how could they have enough for everyone? After all, besides us another 50 children have come as half-boarders. They're with us all day, and then at night they go home to sleep. Gee... I don't envy them. In this cold!

12 March

Today Panna Esterka told us stories about Switzerland again. Listening to her memories, we forget we're hungry. We don't look as often at the clock to check how many hours there are to go until our afternoon snack or dinner.

We like listening to songs. They're actually in German, but Panna Esterka translates everything [...]. The most beautiful one is a song about a storm at sea and a sinking ship. Panna Esterka sings so emotionally that I feel as though I can see that awful night and the waves breaking on the sea, and the ship sinking deeper and deeper into the water, and the captain preparing people for the worst.

28 March

The older children keep telling stories about the two doctors who are at war. One is the chairman of the society caring for the Orphans' Home, the second is the director.

The first doctor is apparently very irritable and will raise his voice about anything at all. He's even capable of yelling at Panna Stefa (well?), but he has a good heart, he's just so short-tempered and impatient. He always inspects the girls' heads and most often says to get a haircut. He has no mercy and there's no changing his mind!

And right now I've ended up with mine cut short. I can still part my hair and tie it together on both sides with ribbons. It still sticks up a little, but it always looks like pigtails.

That other doctor is apparently bald, with a red moustache and a pointed beard. If he likes someone, he calls them 'dummy' and 'dolt' and pretends the child doesn't matter to him at all. But everyone knows perfectly well that out of the older children he likes Regina the most, and of the youngest, Natka. This doctor is apparently just as important, or even more important than Panna Stefa. Is it possible that someone could have more say than Panna Stefa?

12 April

The cold has eased off, spring is coming, and awful rumours are coming with it. Our little store, which until now has been selling, or rather giving away for free, notebooks, pens, and pencils, now is selling raw rutabagas and carrots for a few pennies. Anybody who gets some money from their parents runs to the store. Of course the lines are longest on Sundays, because the children are at their parents' just the day before.

Panna Stefa warns everyone not to buy rotten herrings or horse meat at Kercelak market, because it can make you sick. That must be why she prefers selling in our little store, so no children eat those dreadful things from the market.

20 June

Since the 13th I've been in the countryside, in Anin. I belong to a lucky group of 60 weak boys and girls who finally had to be sent to the country. Since the site here is small, our group of thirty will only be here a month, and then the second set will come.

Panna Esterka is with us. She's weak too, and ought to be in the country.

It's my first time seeing a forest, fields, and meadows, I can hear larks singing and trees rustling the window.

It's beautiful here. I can almost forget that there's a war, that my friends in Warsaw have no idea what the countryside is and are still suffering hunger.

Here we eat practically just like we did before the war. We get stew, vegetables, and sometimes even an egg. Bread is often short, so instead we get a double portion of cottage cheese. Panna Esterka brought a dish from Switzerland called *pudding*. It's made of farina and sugar. You pour the farina into mugs and leave it out in the cellar. On the second day the pudding is so hard that you can slice it with a knife. We think it tastes yummy.

But the sun is the best thing. [...]

24 June

[Esterka] often take me in her room, sits me on her lap, and cuddles me almost the same as Panna Stefa does.

'You're my little daughter. My lovely, sweet, little daughter...'

8 July

Today the second group arrived and we're going out for dinner. There wasn't enough food, so they've cut our stay short a few days. [...]

17 July

This afternoon I was sitting on the lawn in the front yard. Panna Stefa now lets us go out to the yard there and enjoy the grass. Before the yard was sacred, we were only allowed to walk across it; the playground is located on the other side and never gets any sun. Now it's different. There's nothing to eat anyway, so they're letting us at least enjoy the sun.

I lay down and plucked at the grass. I put one blade in my mouth and sucked out the juice. It's bitter, but tolerable. And I thought: maybe if you added something to this grass and boiled it up, it would be perfectly edible. It used to be that horses ate field peas, now we eat them without complaining at all. [...]

25 July
In Anin they've started up a 'Productive Amusement Club'. Apparently the second group was very bored (it's been raining often), so Panna Esterka had the idea to split the children into two groups: older and younger. The kids from the older group will hold talks with the younger ones and read easy books to them, while Panna Esterka will take the older group. At their meetings they'll discuss various topics, the world war for instance, and will also have lectures and read some lovely books together. The younger club is called 'Brotherhood,' and the older one 'Sunbeam', and all of this plus Panna Esterka is combined under the common name 'The Productive Amusement Club'. [...]

5 August
Panna Stefa went out to Anin to bring the second group home. Panna Esterka told us to give her a lovely welcome. We lined up in two rows by the gate, and the two youngest kids held a tray with bread, salt, and sour cherries. A large garland was made of vegetables, hand-woven by all the children. We heard singing from far off. That was them. We could hear them more and more clearly. [...] The children appeared in the gate. [...] Singing:

'Little white house, how are you?
Friend, we're glad to see you too.
We have missed you very much
Because we love you!'

I saw: Panna Stefa looked away. She had tears in her eyes. I know what that means. Today they also gave everyone a raw carrot for our afternoon snack, so that the second group would not feel hungry right away, but tomorrow...

13 August
Hunger drives people to do terrible things.

Panna Esterka has a weak heart and can't boast of good health. On Panna Stefa's orders, the girl on duty puts more butter on Panna Esterka's food, serves her meat more often and makes her wheat-flour dumplings.

The children, especially the boys, watch this jealously. Because they get cabbage, beets, black kasha, and thin soup, while Panna Esterka get white little dumplings... [...]

Panna Esterka senses that jealousy and it makes her feel really guilty. She often sends her food back, but Panna Stefa gets mad at her as if she were a little girl. No wonder: after all, she loves her more than life itself. […]

15 October

Awful! What a miserable Friday! It got right off to a bad start. We sat down to eat at 4 o'clock, and by five after four the pots still hadn't arrived in the dining hall. The servers on duty looked into the elevator, knocked, phoned, but it was as if the cook was deaf.

To make our waiting time go by faster, we naturally talked to one another. Panna Esterka struck the gong and asked for quiet. For a few minutes it was calm, but then got noisy again. Finally the pots arrived, but Panna Esterka didn't let them serve out the soup, because it had gotten too loud again. Suddenly Panna Stefa burst in from the office and said:

'You all can get up! There will be no lunch today!'

It went so quiet you could hear a pin drop. No one could believe those terrible words.

'Yes, yes – you've got nothing to sit here for'– and Panna Stefa disappeared into the office.

We know Panna Stefa well. Once she had spoken, there was no helping us: we were not getting lunch.

Words of protest rang out and some children, when they saw the pots going back down to the kitchen, sincerely cried.

Little Esterka, who had just been living with us for six months, and as a day student at that, sobbed and wrung her hands:

'Oh no, at home it's the baddest when there's no lunch!'

These honest words cheered us up a little and made us less angry at Panna Stefa, who was probably sitting in her office now regretting the words that had maybe slipped out of her mouth inadvertently and deprived us of our most important meal […].

26 October

In Łódź there's a boarding house for orphans just like ours. Only over there they haven't got anyone like Panna Stefa, Panna Esterka or those two doctors who, even though they're far away, watch over our house. It's awful for the children there, because they don't have any decent care.

So Panna Stefa went to those children straighten things out there. The Home was left under the care of Panna Esterka, who is now our most important person. […]

Meanwhile Panna Stefa has now been in Łódź for two months. Here everything is continuing as usual. Panna Esterka is on top of everything, and the kids listen to her just like Panna Stefa herself.

A few times a week we get a visit from Samek, the brother of one former house parent. Pan Samek is very handsome and I like him a lot. The older girls say Pan Samek is in love with Panna Esterka and will definitely marry her, but Pesa explains to me no one who wants to work in a boarding house should marry.

'Why?'

'I don't know. But you must understand it yourself. That's how it is now. Look: the director of the Orphans' Home hasn't got a wife, and Panna Stefa hasn't got a husband.'

18 November

There's been a typhus epidemic raging all over Poland. It's hit Warsaw too and has even snuck its way into our quiet home.

The first victim of this horrible illness was Fryc, and now one child after another is getting sick.

Panna Esterka is running around like a headless chicken. She fusses over the sick children and is terrified the healthy ones might get infected. [...]

1 January 1918

Today is New Year's. 1918. Our awful '17 is finally over. God, if you're out there, make sure we have no more years like that. Hear us, because we can no longer bear the freezing cold or the hunger. God grant us more bread, potatoes and coal. Because as for the war ending, I no longer believe it. I've already forgotten what the world looked like without war and orphans. But at least let there not be such hunger, let this horrible typhus epidemic, which sends another child to the hospital every day, pass.

11 February

Today Panna Esterka didn't come down to see the children. She has a headache, so Panna Stefa asked her to lie down. Could it be typhus? There's no way, after all, the epidemic has nearly ended. Panna Stefa is worried. After coming back from Łódź she begged Panna Esterka to move in with her mother until the epidemic is over, but Panna Esterka insisted on staying on at the boarding house. We aren't going to our schools. Anyway us studying isn't worth much. Panna Stefa split us into two groups and she gives us lessons herself. They're even more fun than school. [...]

12 February
Panna Esterka's got a high fever. We're not allowed to make noise in the auditorium, because the sound reaches up to her room.

I'm on duty in the hallway. This is right where Panna Esterka's room is. I wanted so badly to see her that I couldn't resist any longer: quiet as a mouse, I moved the stepladder over and peeked into her room through the upper windowpanes. [...]

Now I know for sure: Panna Esterka is gravely ill.

13 February
Doctor Gutman came. She said Panna Esterka has typhus. I'm not allowed to tidy the hallway anymore. Panna Stefa cut Panna Esterka's hair herself and called the hospital.

Right in the middle of class we heard rattling. It was the typhus ambulance coming for Panna Esterka. Panna Stefa left the classroom as fast as she could and we all stood by the window. About fifteen minutes later we noticed two men in white aprons, carrying Panna Esterka to the ambulance on a chair. Her face was pale, her eyes sad, and she looked as tiny as a little girl in that chair. [...]

17 February
Panna Stefa spends almost entire days sitting with Panna Esterka in the hospital. The doctors don't let her come here so she doesn't infect us, but Panna Stefa is deaf to everything. She's only cut her hair to make it easier to keep her head clean.

Rózia K. is sleeping in Panna Esterka's room. She's caught typhus and wants to become a nurse in the future, so she's now keeping vigil with Panna Stefa in the hospital.

Every day Panna Stefa brings us news from the hospital, it doesn't look good. The fever isn't going down. Panna Esterka isn't regaining consciousness.

When early in the morning Panna Stefa comes into the dormitory to tell us 'good morning', it frightens me to see her face pale with dread.

26 February

At six in the morning, as soon as the alarm went off, Panna Stefa appeared in the dormitory with a handkerchief at her eyes:

'Panna Esterka has died…'

And she went into her room in tears. It went quiet, then we could hear sobs from one corner of the dorm. That sobbing set the others off crying, until finally the whole dormitory, 56 girls, was bawling. Some buried their face in a pillow and let the tears flow that way, but some were wailing out loud. […]

The whole time, Panna Stefa sat in her office with a handkerchief at her eyes.

27 February

The funeral was today. In the morning, Panna Stefa gathered us together in the classroom to choose who was allowed to go to the funeral, since many of us have been through the disease, and today the weather was bad and cold.

Panna Stefa called us out by number. When she spoke Panna Esterka's name, she burst into tears, and we all cried too. The windowpanes rattled with hail and the trees in our garden rustled quietly.

When Panna Stefa got to number 56, she said:

'You're frail, but you may go. Panna Esterka liked you very much.'

I covered my face in my seat and cried quietly.

'Well, in fact,' I heard Panna Stefa's voice, 'you may all go…' […]

Panna Stefa walked just behind the hearse, walked along by her sister, then the caregivers at our institution, and finally us. The hearse moved slowly, the hail pounded our faces, our clothes blew in the wind and hats flew off of heads, but we walked on and on. […]

Doctor Gutman went up to Panna Stefa:

'That's enough crying now. Go on back home. Why, the children are freezing.'

Hearing these words, Panna Stefa came to her senses, gave us a tender look, and for the first time in many days, said softly:

'Come on children, let's go home.'

25 March

Today is one month since Panna Esterka died. Panna Stefa has come back from the cemetery. Pan Węgierko, the gardener, said he'd try to plant a spruce on Panna Esterka's grave, but he can't be sure it will work. Because he's planted spruces so many times and so far none has taken root at the cemetery...[11]

***

The tree in section XVII in the Jewish Cemetery on Okopowa Street did take root. 'The Productive Amusement Club' remained at the Home permanently.

Hanging on the wall of the reading room at the Home, next to a portrait of Poland's leader Marshal Józef Piłsudski, was a picture of Herbert Hoover. In 1919 US President Woodrow Wilson sent a mission to Central and Eastern Europe under the aegis of the American Relief Administration, created by a special Act of Congress after the Versailles Conference and headed by Hoover. The delegation was to assess the post-war material needs of Europe's newly-formed countries, with particular attention to the condition of children. The delegation calculated that the number of orphans on Polish territory was 75,000. In May 1919, the delegation summed up: thirteen million people, excluding children and adults from the Eastern Borderlands, remained without any kind of food resources. To meet their needs it was essential to provide 360,000 tonnes of rations a month. In 1919, the Hoover delegation visited Krochmalna Street. In the courtyard the youngest boys, in paper hats, were playing war. Hoover would later send the children some balls.

Next to the portraits of Piłsudski and Hoover in the reading room, a third also appeared. The caption under it read: 'Esterka had neither a father nor a mother. She grew up with us, got a job and went far away to Switzerland. She liked it there, but later we had war, hunger, illness. She wanted to help with the work here, because she knew how bad and unhappy things were. She returned to the Orphans' Home, she nursed sick children, fell ill and passed away.'

The diary of girl no. 56 was printed many years later by the children's newspaper *The Little Review*. Wilczyńska, its co-editor, didn't cut the passages about her despair or outbursts of anger.

***

It's 1918, and the war is now over. The children are dressed in their Sunday best, are standing in rows under Wilczyńska's leadership, and are shifting their weight impatiently from foot to foot. Many of them have never seen the doctor everyone talks about. When he arrives in the courtyard (he walks up, shakes Wilczyńska's hand, they exchange glances), the joy is endless. He's returning to his post.

A year later, an article appears in the *New Weekly*:

> Among the Jewish philanthropic and welfare institutions, one that deserves special positive distinction is the Orphans' Home, conducted under the enlightened and skilful direction of the well-known doctor, pedagogue, and writer Dr Goldszmit, with the active collaboration of Dr Eliasberg and Panna Stefania Wilczyńska. This institution, in its use of the latest developments in pedagogy and hygiene, is the equal of the finest child-rearing institutions of Europe.
>
> In Dr Goldszmit's view, 'a child is the only expert, law-giver and judge of the child-rearer'; it is in accordance with this principle that the Orphans' Home is run. We need only state that 2 adult persons suffice to maintain law and order in these children's world in order to understand the profound rationality contained in this distinguished pedagogue's outlook.
>
> This utter freedom granted to the individuality of the child, who has the opportunity to exercise constant self-control over his own behaviour, delivers unexpectedly beneficial results.
>
> It must be emphasized that children do not fall into the Orphans' Home warped by concepts of duty owed to the society that has put a roof over their heads and is raising them, yet nonetheless the children realize on their own the duties that social care places upon them.
>
> A religious spirit pervades the Orphans' Home, the ritual to which the child was accustomed in the domestic atmosphere is maintained, yet here too, the freedom of individuality is left entirely to the child, who has the opportunity to shape his own world-view.
>
> Despite the salutary influence the Orphans' Home exerts on children, the staff cannot perform their civic labour as they would wish, for the institution's existence rests on terribly shaky ground.
>
> [...] The Matron of the Orphans' Home Panna Stefania Wilczyńska, who had so many obstacles of a material nature to combat during the war years, is hopeful that society will feel the children's distress and will not permit the liquidation of an institution of such tremendous social significance.[12]

The new, young Polish state is only just being built, still unsure itself of what exactly independence means. Its citizens of Jewish origin don't know either, but keep up their efforts for civil equality. Orthodox, assimilationist and socialist Jews are joining the process of making Poland whole. It's not easy – it requires the erasure of over a hundred years of differences between the formerly partitioned regions of the country. It's increasingly obvious how poor the workers are, and also how politically impatient with the lack of prospects for change in their situation. This impatience is cultivated and fed by the nationalist parties. The open letter published by the Ministry of Internal Affairs in February 1919 does not come from nowhere:

> I am compelled to remind you that the Jewish population enjoys the rights of Polish citizenship on an equal basis with the indigenous ethnic Polish population and should not be the object either of violence or abuse. In a free Poland there is no division of citizens into categories. All are equal before the law [...]. I therefore warn you that all acts of lawlessness and anarchy directed harshly against the Jewish population, carried out by administrative bodies or private persons, will be investigated and punished with the full impartiality and severity of law. In a free Poland there is no place for injustice, violence or lawlessness.[13]

The international situation is still fragile as well. Within two years of declaring independence, a new war breaks out, against the Russian Bolsheviks. Korczak registers at the City Defence Office, is called up during the mobilization and works in war hospitals. Wilczyńska runs the Home on her own.

***

Israel, 2013

Shlomo takes from of his box a laminated piece of paper with a stamp.

The letters read: 'Matron of the Orphans' Home and Hostel'– barely visible, the ink has faded. No name, only this. But that's enough. She used this stamp for documents, reports, bills and souvenir postcards like the one Shlomo is showing me.

Notes

1. All quotes from: A. Poznańska-Hagari, 'Janusz Korczak i Stefania Wilczyńska w oczach ich wychowanków', *Rocznik Seminarium Kibuców* 1982, pp.9–10.
2. Ibid., pp.11–12.
3. Letter from Janusz Korczak to Mieczysław Zylbertal, March 30, 1937, quote from H. Mortkowicz-Olczakowa, *Janusz Korczak* (Warsaw: 1978), p.98.

4. Letter from Stefania Wilczyńska to Fejga Lifszyc, undated letter from 1925. The originals of all letters to Fejga Lifszyc are in the Ghetto Fighters Kibbutz Archive.
5. Letter from Stefania Wilczyńska to Jakub Einfeld, 26 March 1934.
6. Letter from Stefania Wilczyńska to Fejga Lifszyc, undated letter from 1925.
7. Report of the Orphans' Aid Society for 1914, Korczakianum – research centre of the Museum of Warsaw, inventory number 0388.
8. J. Zawadzki, *Warszawa w czasie okupacji niemieckiej. Ze wspomnień osobistych* (Warsaw: 1928), p.62.
9. *Nowa Gazeta*, 13 June 1916.
10. *Nowa Gazeta*, 11 April 1917.
11. 'O choince na cmentarzu żydowskim', *Mały Przegląd*, 4 October 1935.
12. 'Dom Sierot', *Tygodnik Nowy*, 21 June 1919.
13. Quoted from M. Fuks, *Żydzi w Warszawie*, Poznań 1997, p.273.

4

One day, Shlomo phones me, agitated.

'A microscope! We had two of them in the Home, donated ones. Sometimes she let me look in it but I was more curious about how it was built. But she didn't let me take it apart. She also gave me this book on microbes to read, about how they got discovered.'

The book was *Microbe Hunters* by Paul de Kruif, published in Poland in 1932. I borrow it from the National Library.

> The title of that letter was: 'A Specimen of some Observations Made by a Microscope contrived by Mr Leeuwenhoek, concerning Mould upon the Skin, Flesh, etc.; the Sting of a Bee, etc.' The Royal Society was amazed, the sophisticated and learned gentlemen were amused – but principally the Royal Society was astounded by the marvellous things Leeuwenhoek told them he could see through his new lenses. The Secretary of the Royal Society thanked Leeuwenhoek and told him he hoped his first communication would be followed by others. It was, by hundreds of others over a period of fifty years. They were talkative letters full of salty remarks about his ignorant neighbours, of exposures of charlatans and of skilled explodings of superstitions, of chatter about his personal health – but sandwiched between paragraphs and pages of this homely stuff, in almost every letter, those Lords and Gentlemen of the Royal Society had the honour of reading immortal and gloriously accurate descriptions of the discoveries made by the magic eye of that janitor and shopkeeper. What discoveries! When you look back at them, many of the fundamental discoveries of science seem so simple, too absurdly simple. How was it men groped and fumbled for so many thousands of years without seeing things that lay right under their noses?[7]

***

Korczak and Wilczyńska were neither first nor unique.

In the eighteenth century, Johann Heinrich Pestalozzi – building on the Enlightenment idea of development tied to education, not only of a formal, intellectual character, but a moral one as well – worked on elementary children's education, saw children as members of society, and gave them the right to join in building it. Józef Babicki in the 1920s developed a model for bringing up orphan children that included space for the child's right to privacy and for the biological family to participate in care-giving. Anton Makarenko, two years younger than Wilczyńska, wrote *The Pedagogical Poem* (published in English as *The Road to Life*) and coined the saying: 'There are no bad children, only bad teachers.' Maria Grzegorzewska was a co-founder of special education. Maria Montessori granted children a wide scope of freedom in their development.

They all scrutinize the child, note down observations, create projects, systems, principles. Paedology, the study of children, is only just taking shape. It's a novelty to recognize a child's right to develop, discover what influence the outside world has on them, define their capabilities. Anthropometric measurements are zealously taken and then compiled in tables of indicators: height, weight. The child is an object of observations and experiments that bear the fruit of new knowledge, whose guidance, however, is not entirely clear.

Yet Korczak sees something different. The gentleness with which a child must be treated in order to connect with them, the partnership they must be granted, the unconditional respect they deserve. Only now has Wilczyńska started to notice this too (or maybe earlier, back in college?), at the same time – maybe inspired by him. Maybe he shared his thoughts. Maybe their similar sensibilities came together and that was all that was needed to start working together.

Neither he nor she ever described when they met.

Note

1. P. de Kruif, *Microbe Hunters* (New York: 1996), pp. 6-7.

5

He left his goldfinch in a cage at home, his mother said he didn't have to worry about it. She held his hand on the way there. As they were coming down Krochmalna Street, he anxiously kept an eye out for number 92. The gate was tall and iron. When he walked through it he did his best not to let his mother notice how scared he was and how little he wanted to live there. The courtyard of the main building (two storeys and with long rows of windows) was empty.

He didn't notice when Wilczyńska came out, nor when she started walking toward them. He didn't hear her steps, only the clinking of the iron keys she held in a bunch in her hand.

'And where's your "hello?"' she began. 'Did you leave it at home?'

He wanted to answer louder, more formidably, as was fitting for a big boy who doesn't whine and is ready any minute to give her a piece of his mind. He gathered up his inner strength, but only a murmur came out.

'And what's your name?'

He answered quietly.

'Are you so embarrassed you can't lift up your head?' She placed her index finger under his chin and pushed upward. 'That's really a beautiful name, Srulek, but we already have two boys by that name. We'll call you something else.'

The crows stuck in his memory – large, black, circling over the square. They were cawing just as he was trying so hard not to burst into tears.

Tall, a black skirt, a black sweater, a black cape. Short, dark hair and a mole on her cheek. That little dark spot started growing and growing until it made his head spin. He thrust his clenched fists even deeper into his pockets.

'Why isn't his hair cut? Didn't they tell you, ma'am, that his head was to be shaved?'

Srulek wanted to shout that it was his fault, his mother had even given him money to go to the barber, but he hadn't let them cut off his bangs.

'Never mind, we'll clip off the rest ourselves.'

He's assigned number 41, and so that he doesn't get mixed up with the other boys named Srul/Izrael, he becomes Staś. He settles into his new name quickly, but it takes longer to get him out of the habits of the backstreets of Praga district, where he grew up, and the mustiness of the shack he lived in before he came to the orphanage. And also to get the lying out of him – one day he wrote on a piece of paper: 'I, Staś, the undersigned, hereby commit to the Doctor, the whole staff, and all the children to speak only the truth for period of one month, and for all that time not to lie even once, not even with a single word.'

These sorts of wagers were often made in the Orphans' Home: not to doze off, not to be late, to get a better grade. Korczak invented this system.

Staś, whose full name was Izrael Zyngman, didn't like Wilczyńska. That is, until the day she called him into her office.

'This Friday you'll be on the panel of judges, just do your best not to have any cases before the end of the week.'

Him, a judge? Who'd have believed it, but look, here was strict and demanding Panna Stefa herself telling him so. If she weren't so big, he'd probably have dared to hug her with joy. And maybe he'd even apologize for being so spiteful when he thought she was being unfair. And what if he could get through not just this week, but the whole month and more, thought Staś, without any violations?

'It will become the habit of a lifetime,' she said, he remembers.

***

'When you came to the home, everybody got a number, you know that already, right?' Shlomo asks me in November 2012. It's our fourth meeting. This time I stay for dinner. Vegetable soup, then a second course of potatoes ('with no pork cracklings'), fried fish ('good thing it's not herring'), cucumber salad and home-made apple juice.

'Do you remember yours?'

He looks at me like I'm crazy.

'What a question! Five. So that our clothes didn't get mixed up, each of us got a number, just for that. Or if there was scabies going around, to keep the sick and healthy kids' clothes from getting mixed together, so you could tell whose pillowcase to wash in boiling water. The boys were numbers 1 to 51, and the girls went up to 56. But no one ever called me "Five", Korczak and Stefa both remembered my name. And the other kids too, it was only to keep things organized. And you know, to this day I bet on number five in the lottery? And I'll tell you something else, but you won't believe me. Here, in Eretz, it wasn't until I'd racked up five Nadels that I felt like I could relax.'

'I don't understand.'

'Well, that there were Nadels again. Nadel is my mother's maiden name, after the war I decided to use it because that whole part of the family was killed, and the name along with them. At first I didn't want to have children, then I met Frida and she encouraged me to live life more fully. I have sons, my firstborn I gave the name Yossi, after my father. I have grandkids. Now there's more than five of us, I'm not scared we'll disappear again.'

***

I also get to know boy number 43. Icio Belfer was in the Orphans' Home in the 1930s, Itzhak Belfer invited me to at his Tel Aviv studio in 2012. His business card reads 'artist, painter, sculptor, drawing teacher'.

'I was ten by then. Pani Stefa once came up to me and said: "Icio, you like painting. I'll give you paper and paints and on the ground floor, in the little room by the recreation room, where the store is, if you want you can take the key hanging in the office and do your art in there. Take it whenever you want." I was over the moon. How lucky. Pani Stefa suggested it herself, meaning she knew I liked to draw, meaning she was thinking about me. And I saw just me, you know, nobody, nothing special. Neither she nor anybody else ever asked me what I was drawing, and they never asked me to show them. I know if they had, I'd have stopped using that room. But instead I relished the solitude, the work I loved, and the secret that existed between us.'

Itzhak Belfer invites me into his studio. Pastels: the house on Krochmalna, Korczak and the children in Treblinka, portraits, sculptures. In Itzhak's paintings, Stefa has large and warm eyes. Velvety ones, he says.

'That's how I remember them, somehow. And that they were deep violet. Definitely just like that. You couldn't look into those eyes for long. How should I know why?'

***

Their memories clash.

Shlomo calls early one morning.

'She couldn't have violet eyes! Don't listen to what that guy's telling you. Hers were different, dark.'

***

Post-war Poland was rebuilding itself out of mismatched pieces: the legal systems of the former partitioning powers did not align, there was a need to unify the rules and to create new ones in those areas that had so far been entirely unregulated. It wasn't until 1923 that socialist-sympathizing parliamentarians managed to get a social welfare bill through the Sejm. Some of the people the government was to take under its wing were orphans, children who'd been separated from or lost their parents in wartime, and ones suffering neglect in their families. The act stipulated providing for their essential needs in life – for clothing, for food and for shelter with heat and light. This task was delegated to local governments and also the Ministry of Labour and Welfare, which was also to exercise control over private institutions. Yet in reality, it was still mainly societies, foundations, and religious orders providing childcare, with the government's participation remaining symbolic. That included financially: national and city grants were limited, and with the onset of the Great Depression, they shrank more and more each year.

Since it's impossible to help everyone, they have to choose: they will accept only physically and mentally healthy children. The society explains: 'we are focusing our labour and material capital where we expect the maximum social benefit.'[8]

The Home is now over ten years old.

Korczak devised its principles and institutions back when the war was still going on.

(Does he inform Wilczyńska of his ideas? Or does he consult with her?)

A rule book has been drawn up, a code of rights and responsibilities for all the children, for the staff, for him and for her. Its basic values are: respect, trust, responsibility and freedom, the limit of which is where it harms another. A council has been founded, meaning a self-government (with electoral districts, representatives, the right to set principles that were binding for everyone). A court has been founded.

***

There were ninety-nine articles of acquittal.

If a defendant received one of them, the no trace remained of the charges – or there remained a commitment not to behave that way anymore.

There were ten articles of conviction:

§100

The court says [the defendant] is not at fault, offers no reprimand, doesn't get angry, but, regarding §100 as the minimum punishment, includes it on the table of court verdicts.

§200

[…] He has behaved inappropriately.

Tough, it happened. It can happen with anyone. We ask him not to do it again.

§300

[…] He's done a bad thing.

The court condemns him. If in Article 100 and Article 200 the court asks him not to do it again, here it demands that it not be repeated.

§400

[…] Serious guilt.

[…] [Y]ou've done a very bad thing, or: you're behaving very poorly.

Article 400: this is the final attempt, the final willingness to spare the guilty party shame, the final warning.

§500

[…] 'Whoever has committed such an act, whoever is so indifferent to our requests and demands, does not respect himself or does not care about us. Thus we, too, have no opportunity to spare him.'

The verdict is announced with his first and last name on the newspaper's front page.

§600

The court posts the verdict for a week on the court notice board and announces it in the newspaper.

If Article 600 has been handed down because someone repeatedly does the same thing, his behavioral chart [of prior sentences] can be posted for a longer period, but instead of his full name only his initials are provided.

§700

In addition to the consequences provided in Article 600, the content of the verdict will be sent to the family.

For it may be that he will have to be expelled. Thus one ought to warn the family. If you were to tell them right away, 'Get him out of here,' the family might complain that they hadn't been given warning, that it had been concealed from them.

§800

[…] 'The court is no help.' Maybe punishments that were once used in pedagogical institutions would help, but we don't use them anymore.

We offer one week for reflection. During that week, he can neither bring a case to the court, nor will we bring him to court. We'll see whether he straightens out and for how long.

The verdict is announced in the newspaper, posted on the notice board, and the family notified.

§900

[…] 'We have lost hope that he will straighten out.'

This verdict says:

'We do not believe him.'

Or:

'We are afraid of him.'

And finally:

'We don't want anything to do with him.'

In other words, Article 900 expels him from the institution. He might remain, however, if someone assumes responsibility for him. Expelled, he might return if he finds a tutor.

The tutor answers for all his faults before the court.

The tutor can be a [house parent] or one of the children.

§1000

[…] 'He is expelled.' Every expellee is entitled to request re-admittance after three months have passed.[2]

With a sentence of Article 100, the court states that: child A did that of which he stands accused, 200 – A acted inappropriately, 300 – badly, 400 – very badly, 500 – so badly the sentence will be announced in the newspaper, 600 – and on the notice board, 700 – and conveyed to A's family. 800 – A is also stripped of his rights for one week and his family is summoned. 900 – a tutor is sought, if one is not found in two days, the child must leave the Home. 1000 – the child leaves.

As they announce a sentence, the court thanks the defendant for their truthful testimony, asks that the behaviour not be repeated, and expresses the hope that A will grow into a courageous person.[3]

Sittings take place on Saturdays. Charges can also be filed against a house parent. Korczak is taken to court numerous times, and is once sentenced with article 100.

None of the children ever take Wilczyńska to court.

Shlomo:

'But she deserved it! For what she did to me at least.'

'So why didn't you take her to court?'

'You listen and listen and you still don't get it! Stefa? To court?!'

***

One of the Society's reports reads: 'the transformation of 100 children into 100 workers, each of whom, according to his age and reserves of strength, his quality and degree of skill, and his desire, is obligated to work together in a common abode, an immeasurably difficult task, has been successfully achieved thanks to our head house mother, Panna Stefania.'[4]

So she transforms them. She sets about it methodically, according to a plan. Living permanently at the Home are fifty-one boys and fifty-six girls. Over a hundred children is a huge amount of work. They have to be divided up: half an hour is one unit. Assessments for performing chores are calculated in these units. Fifty units means a commendation and a commemorative postcard.

Shlomo:

'Here it is, look. "To the best letter carrier – Stefa".' He recites from memory, the ink on the commemorative postcard has faded.

Wilczyńska splits up work units in shifts, she divides responsibility for the Home's functioning among everyone. The boys and girls perform the same chores on an equal basis. There are easy ones, like cleaning up papers, and harder ones for the older children, like operating the elevator in the kitchen. There are morning ones and evening ones, daily ones and weekly ones, summer ones, winter ones. Keeping things tidy (sweeping, dusting, washing the floors); work in the kitchen and dining room; caring for the sick; helping out in the sewing shop, the bookbinding shop, the carpentry shop; helping with studying; handing out and keeping track of carpentry tools; work in the school and homework. The children volunteer on their own – Wilczyńska hangs up a shift list, after approval by the council, once a month.

Each of the four floors also has its own duty officer. The duty officer can recruit additional assistants. Furthermore: there is a duty officer for the kitchen (this includes helping serving lunch, collecting cutlery, operating the freight elevator between the kitchen and the dining room), and a duty officer for the laundry room. These three most important jobs come with payment. Even during the war, in 1915, the budget dedicates 255 rubles for duty officer pay.

(Wilczyńska dedicates it?)

Toward the end of the month she accepts applications: a child has the right to extend their current job or switch to another one.

***

Korczak occupies a room in the attic of the Home. Wilczyńska's room is situated on the third floor, next to the girls' dormitory. It's long, ill-proportioned, poorly laid out. A narrow bed always neatly made, as if no one ever touched it. A table with a freshly-pressed tablecloth. A dresser, a washbasin in the corner by the door, a wardrobe. A few books, nothing more. The duty officers were later surprised that Pani Stefa cared so much for order when her own room was such a mess. Papers scattered everywhere, spectacles, an apron thrown over a chair.

The children got money to tidy it up.

(Did she leave a mess on purpose?)

***

Wilczyńska also invents a system of categories of personal cleanliness. There are four. The children in the first category get the best clothes (donated, or also sewn in the Home's own sewing shop, or purchased, but even so there are not enough for everyone); those who take the least care of their possessions are the last to receive clothes. The only thing everyone gets new are shoes, so that the children's feet don't get deformed. The categories are not permanent – a child can improve and advance to a higher one.

Korczak and Wilczyńska want them to believe they can.

Wilczyńska also looks after the notice board. It's hung low so the youngest children can see it. It holds the list of chores, the newspaper written by the house children, drawings, current announcements and messages (who found my key? who wants to switch spots in the dorm?).

Itzhak Belfer: 'The notice board was a guidepost for us. What was, what would be. Order. Peace. After all, we were coming from a world where no one explained anything to us. On there, everything was laid out.'

One day, maybe in 1928 or maybe later, Wilczyńska posts a piece of paper on the board regarding titles. So far she has gone by 'Panna', the title for a young woman. But she says: a woman who has so many children cannot be 'Panna'. She asks them, from now on, to use the title of a mature woman: to call her 'Pani Stefa'. She finds room for this announcement alongside scraps of paper where she corrects the youngest children: 'not "cleening shoes" but "cleaning."'

She also accepts (once a week) records of bets, like the one Staś made. These are commitments – to oneself and others – that something will be done, something will change. Will improve. The commitments are public, meaning the children take them very seriously.

She also records votes in the plebiscite.

Itzhak Belfer:

'Do you know what that was? The children voted on you, after you got to the home you, after six months and after a year. Plus, minus, zero. "Like", "don't like", "indifferent". And the plebiscite made you a comrade, a resident, or an indifferent resident. They used to have "troublesome", but they got rid of that. Do you know how proud it felt to be promoted? Everyone got categories, our house parents too. I remember once, when Stefa told one man who'd gotten nothing but minuses from us: "it's possible you'll be a good child-rearer, it's possible you're a good person. But given how our children have rated you, you can't stay here now."'

Wilczyńska checks the lost-and-found box. And the letterbox, where you could can express anything (distress, sorrow, a request, a question).

***

The day is always too short, so she has to get up before everyone else.

Wash her face, brush her hair (fix it, it won't lay flat), put on her glasses, a black dress.

Go to the dormitory, first one, then the other, wake up the children (they make their beds, get dressed – a few need help).

Give out the fish oil. Make sure they drink it. Change bandages and give medication to the sick ones.

Wait for them to finish prayers (those who want to).

At seven, strike the gong (which came from a donor), let them know breakfast is ready. Breakfast is milky tea and two rolls.

Send off to school the ones who go for the morning shift (check if they're cleanly dressed – people will call them 'Pani Stefa's dolls').

Itzhak Belfer recalls:

'Now breakfast is over and the kids are leaving for school. Stefa stands in the door, alongside her are two baskets of sandwiches. She remembers who gets what. The kids at my school were jealous of me because I was the only one who brought something. There were these two brothers, they would take turns going because they had a single pair of shoes, so I used to share with them.'

At eleven, call the remaining ones for second breakfast. Serve the children bread and butter.

The first round of lunches is at 1:00 and the second at 4:00: take the eighth place at one of the tables. In the middle of the room, to see all the children. Get up to help those having trouble, spilling food, spitting it out. Lunch is soup and meat (six times a week) with vegetables. She always tastes the tomato soup. They don't put together a menu, but they make sure that bread is always available between meals; if a child gets hungry, they know where they can get it. When one philanthropist sniffs at the thick slices, Wilczyńska replies: 'you serve your children butter and meat on their slice, ma'am, so it can be thinner. The most I serve mine is jam.'

Unless it's Saturday.

Then: they can get up later, they don't go to school. She accepts applications for bets (who with whom, about what and when), then she gathers them all in the auditorium to read the newsletter (she reads, or Korczak). Open the gathering by announcing that this week no child was hit by any of the house parents (if that's true). Send them off home to their families.

If a holiday or celebration is approaching – find time to prepare for it.

Organize a field trip – the Botanical Garden, the Old Town, the movies (get money, buy tickets, divide up the groups, send them off).

Every day of the week – stop by the office (a desk, a chair for inquirers, a cabinet for documents, a plaque with the names of funders – here, not where the children live and play every day, nor on the front wall), answer letters, receive guests, register the incoming mail, answer the phone (number

624-01), sort the expense lists (one line item: 'tips for workers'). Go to school, if the principal summons her about something to do with a house child. Still find time to: accept records for the notary's office (who, to whom, what; sale, loan, debt), make sure the menu is hung on the notice board, collect testimony for the Home's court (listen, ask, confirm). If it's Saturday – oversee the court session. At the end of the week: help weigh and measure the girls (Korczak does the boys: they are researching the connection between weight and children's well-being and health). A dozen or so times a year comb out lice, order the laundress to wash the pillowcases and hats in boiling water (they're numbered, so it's easier). Once a month, compose a shift list. Consider applications, do her best to divide them up fairly.

Once a month, post sign-up list for prayers.

Once a year find time for wardrobe inspection and giving the children new clothes (if they come in donations). Choose who gets what.

At seven, strike the gong for supper. Once again two rolls and milky tea.

If it's Wednesday evening, visit her mother. If it's Friday – help the girls wash. Sometimes – get a visit from her brother.

Read the children a fairytale (taking turns with Korczak, instead of him, alongside him).

At ten – lights out (she doesn't have to remind them, the pupils know the rhythm of the day).

Then her night rounds (one, two) and she can go to her room (and maybe also: talk with the Doctor). Read? Definitely write letters. Maybe if there's enough time: observe microbes under the microscope.

She doesn't have to do everything on her own. There's the staff to help, and the Hostel residents have their own duties as well. The newspaper, the plebiscite – those are often the Doctor.

But don't forget: limits. She has to maintain order. Someone has to.

(I – does she keep telling herself? – have to.)

***

There isn't too much time for academic work, but there are indications that she occasionally managed to find some. In 1928 *Dos Kind*, a Yiddish journal dedicated to pedagogy, publishes an article by her. This is an account of two months of observing a ten-year-old boy, Pinkus, who returned from Palestine and ended up in the Home.

Wilczyńska writes in concrete terms, not muddling her description with unnecessary topics, staying precise and careful. Discreetly ('When you aren't looking, he's gentler and quieter'.)[5] She notices every detail of her new charge's behaviour.

In a foreword, the editors emphasize: 'this observation was conducted by one of the most talented and diligent collaborators of Dr Janusz Korczak.'[6]

***

Israel, 2013

Shlomo: 'I've got a lot of grudges against her as well. You want to hear about that too?'

The first.

'That cobbler whose house I lived in, he always had a belt with him. But his wife, I called her "auntie", she didn't let him beat me, she took the whippings for me. She used to not buy shoes for herself because she preferred to get me something. And one day she came to the Home, I'm sure to see if I was doing well, because you never knew with the orphanages back then. Stefa saw her. "Now, ma'am, we've told you that you can't see the children on any day but Saturday. You can't bring the children anything to eat." "But I've just got a couple pears and apples." "Please leave here at once!" And she left. And I cried my eyes out. Then I found out she went home and right away her heart gave out and she died.'

The second.

'I went out with a letter. She would often send me out on important errands. Many times I was the best duty officer. One day she got a call to send someone to pick up gifts for the children. Toys. And she picked me. Me, not somebody else! I had to go pretty far, and since it was fall, she gave me money for the streetcar. But I wanted to keep the twenty groszy for myself. (Even though afterwards she could tell if I'd taken the streetcar or not, I don't know how, but I knew she knew.) I take the stuff back to the Home, about half an hour later Pani Stefa comes up to me and says: "Aren't you ashamed? You asked them to give you a toy just for yourself." "I did? I'm not a little kid anymore, what would I want with one? Go ahead and call them, you'll see I'm telling the truth." "I don't need to call them, I know. You won't get that toy unless you make one yourself." I begged her to believe me or at least call them and check that I was telling the truth. But forget it, she wouldn't hear a word, she'd made up her mind. That really hurt me. You're not gonna believe me? But I went down to the wood shop and made a copy. A little top, the kind you spin. Out of spite. And her response was: "See, I knew you'd make one." "So why didn't you want to believe me?"

"There's nothing more to say about it," that was all she'd say. "You've made one, so you'll have something to give your little brother when you go visit him."'

(To make an exception – just one. But why this time? Children would come to the Home with no knowledge of discipline, routine, prohibitions or rights. To make an exception for one child and not another? To let in one aunt, then tomorrow a father, the day after tomorrow a grandmother? What if they bring something with them and the other children get jealous?)

'Korczak,' says Shlomo emphatically in Ramla, 'would have told my aunt: "You don't know our rules. But you've come a long way, so I'll make an exception and let you in for a moment to see him." I'm sure that if he had met her at the door, that's how it would have ended.'

Yet Shlomo misses Stefa just as much as the Doctor.

Notes

1. Report of the Orphans' Aid Society for 1914, p.3.
2. J. Korczak, 'How to Love a Child', translated by Benjamin Paloff, in *How to Love a Child and Other Selected Works*, vol. 1 (London: 2018), pp.211-213.
3. Adapted from Ibid., pp.217-218.
4. Report of the Orphans' Aid Society from 1914.
5. S. Wilczyńska, 'Pinkus. (Notatki z obserwacji dziesięcoletniego chłopca)', in *Słowo do dzieci i wychowawców*, B. Puszkim and M. Ciesielska (eds) (Warsaw: 2004), p.58.
6. Ibid., p.56.

6

You'll never hear the word 'pleasure' when people talk about Wilczyńska. Pleasure would prompt a smile, which doesn't fit her either.

'It's not that she didn't smile,' explains Shlomo. 'At times she did, at times she'd even laugh. Except the smile wouldn't feel at home, it'd be a guest of Stefa's that had come a long way and didn't know what to do with itself.'

It was strange to see her laugh.

It was good to see her laugh.

'Understand us: big, deep-set eyes, a large nose, wrinkled cheeks, short wisps of hair surrounding her face, a black mole, a furrowed brow. Tall, sturdily built, in a black dress. In her hand, always that bunch of keys, heavy, jangling.

No setting for 'pleasure'. But one day Shlomo calls me, clearly delighted:

'There was something! Those microscopes I was telling you about. On evening I saw her taking one up the stairs, to her room. She gave me an embarrassed look and from then on we had a secret.'

She also enjoyed passing the children botany textbooks to read, with large, full-page illustrations. She enjoys talking about Darwin's discoveries. Or, once the Little Rose summer camp is founded in 1921 in Gocławek (at that time just outside of Warsaw), she likes taking the children for walks, showing them a meadow and telling them how 'during the day, cows graze here' (one of the girls whose last name means 'cow' is furious: 'I'm gonna take you to court!'). So she also explains cows, rivers, forests. For some children, it's the first time in their lives seeing so many trees.

Supposedly she also likes speaking French, and when she's annoyed, she mutters to herself in it so the children won't understand.

(Maybe as she's planning the expenses, and seeing the funding from city hall evaporating?)

At the start of the 1920s the Orphans' Aid Society requests financial support from the city authorities, not wanting to maintain itself exclusively on donations and the goodwill of benefactors. It's on the lookout for new ways of raising funds. Other institutions will pay to use the summer camp. The Society leases an additional piece of land and sets up agricultural plots.

In a few years, they will build a boarding-house there for children awaiting a space in the Home and for house children who've had to repeat grades, and then in 1928 construct a pre-school as well (run by the former Hostel resident Ida Merżan).

(To add – does Wilczyńska remember? – to the schedule: keeping an eye on the pre-school, answering the young staff ladies' questions, enough time to take hundreds of children out to Little Rose in the summer, dividing them into groups, equipping them, leaving with them).

At first the children don't know what to do with themselves away from Krochmalna Street. Icek Cukierman, a house child later transferred to Gocławek, recalled: 'the only thing that kept us connected to the Orphans' Home were Pani Stefa's weekly visits, which we looked forward to.'

***

Shlomo: 'She demanded a lot from everyone, and the most from herself.'

Sara Kramer, a former house child, recalled in an interview with Betty Lifton: 'I missed my mother very much. On Saturdays when I was home, I'd cry that I didn't want to go back to the orphanage. But my mother would say: "Stay, it will be good for you." And she was right. My mother was always my mother, but I developed differently than I would have if I had lived with her. She couldn't give me the knowledge and values that Stefa did.'[1]

Hanna Dembińska also lived in the Home. She said of Stefa: 'I think Stefa may have been jealous of my mother [...]. Whatever Stefa did for me, she could never be my mother.'[2]

Seweryn Nutkiewicz: 'Korczak and Stefa were less than parents and more than parents. They were pedagogues. [...] A father looks at a child subjectively, [...] a pedagogue [...] objectively. They led us neither from the beginning nor to the end. With family, a child encounters the real world from day to day. The Home on Krochmalna was a closed world.'[3]

An unsigned recollection:

> Korczak appears briefly and then the children run to him with their business, pull him into their play, and he doesn't refuse. Stefa was the mother of the house, often severe out of necessity, and it was not hard to understand that among 107 house children and others that they might have grudges against her. She was tough and it did happen that she would punish someone for nothing. They gave us warmth, but it was the warmth of a pedagogue, only a pedagogue. But anyone can

> be a father or a mother. A pedagogue for other people's children, only a few.[4]

Ida Meržan remembered: 'Once, when someone once asked me how many children Pani Stefa had, I joked: fifty girls, just as many boys, twenty in the Hostel and one older one, the most difficult one, because he's too independent – Korczak.'[5]

Jochewed Cuk: 'Korczak was that beloved papa, Stefa was the nasty mama who was always there, twenty-four hours a day.'[6]

Samuel Gogol: 'I don't think she was cold. The Home couldn't have existed without that remarkable woman with the serious face. Every detail interested her. The Doctor didn't look after things like clothing, clean hands, tidying up. I think for us she took the place of both mother and father, you see, someone had to lead us with a strong hand. In my memories, the Orphans' Home was Pani Stefa, and Pani Stefa was the Orphans' Home [...]. As far as material things, she was mainly the one who took care of them. It was Pani Stefa who made sure I had pants, that I put on my slippers. It wasn't talked about, it *went without saying*'[7] [emphasis mine].

***

In Ada Poznańska-Hagari's anonymous survey in the 1980s, they also said:

'She was like a mother, but one who held you tight.'

'She was capable of yelling at a child so loudly it would terrify them.'

'As a kid I thought the Doctor was better, but in retrospect I think Stefa played no smaller role in my upbringing.'

'The Doctor was very sensitive, tender. She had to be tough.'

'Korczak was like a mother, the father was Stefa.'

'When she was mad at me, she wouldn't speak to me and wouldn't answer back. I understood she was mad but I didn't understand what about.'

'When the girls started having their periods, she took special care of them. She'd let them have an extra bath. She'd have a talk with them. I was embarrassed. Stefa explained to me exactly what was going on.'

'There were children she didn't like. She threw me out of the Home for nothing.'

'Why did she love me so much when I was so awful?'

'When I turned seven, she threw a birthday party for me, though that wasn't our custom in the Home. She asked who I liked and she invited those children. There were snacks, songs. I had a great birthday.'

'We were sick and lying there in bed. Korczak examined us and declared we had gotten better. We stayed in bed. We waited until Pani Stefa came and let us leave.'

'I was secretly meeting up with a boy. Stefa came in and turned the light on. After that she came every time to check if I was in bed. If Stefa was like a mother, then why didn't she believe me?'

'She said: I know there's something wrong with this method. Direct contact with the child is better. But she didn't change it.'

'Once I got a slap from her, I don't remember why. We were alone. I said: I've got hands too and I can hit you back. She looked at me, amazed, and – hugged me. She didn't apologize, but she hugged me, knowing she'd made a mistake.'

'There was no discussion with her.'

'I didn't like her.'

'I loved her.'[8]

***

Stand-offish, tough, unyielding, blunt, unfair.

(Shlomo: 'She played favourites. She liked some children more than others. The talented, good-looking ones more.')

A stickler for rules, a grudge-holder. Words like these keep coming up in house children's recollections, sometimes arranged in a litany of still-fresh resentment, or an indictment: she wasn't like Korczak.

But alongside these words, sometimes running alongside them, others appear too: instead of unfair – honest; not strict – demanding; not overly serious, but pragmatic and down-to-earth. They (one, a third, a fifth) remember her face over the bed when they were sick. A hand on their forehead when they had a fever. Cheering them up after coating their throat with iodine.

***

A letter from the second half of the 1930s that Wilczyńska writes to a former, now grown-up, house child (her name has not survived):

> My darling child, I will neither cheer you up or persuade you. Nor will it help you that Julek worries along with you, that others feel sorry for you. No one and nothing can cheer you up on this occasion. Only time and work will see you through. We observe this with

> others around us who've experienced similar losses. I know from my own experience, as I've said farewell to some of my loved ones at the cemetery.
>
> People won't help anything. No one has anything but themselves along with their pain. And no one can grasp it, no one can cheer you up, even the most loving person.
>
> What I'm telling you is difficult, my darling child, but it's so. And even the thought that, after all, someday you will have another child, even that will not soothe you.
>
> The only good thing is that you have your Julek by your side, and he has you.
>
> I want so much to see you, but I truly don't know how that will be. [...]
>
> I send a big, big kiss for you, like when you were little and worried.[9]

***

Shlomo:

'The Home used to get free tickets from donors. To the movies, the circus. I went to the circus in my first year on Krochmalna Street. We split into groups, I was in the one Stefa was leading. I really liked the animal acts, but the acrobats terrified me. I was afraid they'd fall. Really afraid. I wet my pants. Stefa stroked my head and said: "Szlomek, something like this could happen to anybody."'

***

In 1926, Korczak starts up *The Little Review*, a newspaper co-created by children and for children, a weekly supplement to the Jewish daily *Our Review*. He becomes the *Little Review*'s editor. Wilczyńska also joins him in setting it up.

(She adds to the lesson schedule: find time to read letters to the newspaper, choose questions from the youngest children, editorial meeting. She sends articles back with corrections: 'from extreme to extreme: this time too concise').

In one issue, I read:

> Everyone believes that, since Szlojme really did invent the 'glass home-cinema,' he should sign his name in a foreign way: Schloyme.

Because great inventors mainly have strange names.

The boys were very interested in Schloym'e's apparatus, they have even formed three companies that work and make movies. The largest company, called 'Kroch-Film,' with 16 partners, is run by Heniek, Szymek, Wolf, and Mojsie.

The second partnership is named 'Jakób-Cyn-Film,' because it is run by Jakóbek and Cynamon, and the third, 'Kołek-Film-Man,' is run by Piekołek and Herman.

The chairman of all these companies is the inventor Schloym'e. This is how he made his invention:

'At school,' says Schloym'e, 'they showed us slides about plants on a projector. These machines have always interested me. I wanted to get a close look at it, but I could barely get near, the boys shouted: "Get away – you'll smash it – I'll tell teacher!"

'It wasn't until recess, when everyone had left the classroom, that I could stay and investigate it. While they were projecting I sat in the front row and saw how a slide gets put in and taken out. I noticed that strong light passes through the slide, then through a magnifying glass, and then the image hits the wall. Now I knew.

'I told Karolek and Sorka we had to make a movie theatre. That Saturday Karolek got 40 groszy, so he bought some cardboard. We had to make a long, square box. We cut the sides off the cardboard with scissors (they were dull, which is why they left jagged marks on the carboard). We put the sides together and Srulek glued white paper onto them. Karolek said it looked awful, so he tore it off and glued on black paper.

'A friend had given me a magnifying glass, so we glued it to the opening of the device. On the sides we made three elongated openings for different-sized slides, but we didn't have any slides yet.

'[...] We made a screen out of an old, torn shirt that we nailed to two sticks, so we could roll it up. In a dark room we hung up the screen, put the device in front of it, lit the small lamp inside the device, put in a slide, and waited. Only the round spot of the magnifying glass appeared on the screen. It was obviously getting in the way, so we removed the glass and there immediately appeared on the screen a girl feeding a bird, 5 times bigger than the picture. Everyone wanted to see. It was like a miracle: pictures appearing on the wall!

[...] The first presentation took place on Saturday at 6:30. We invited children from the whole house [...].[10]

'I'm sure that was me, not some other Shlomo! I'll tell you how I'm sure. See, all that started with her. It was a sunny day, springtime, these yellow bushes were growing.' Shlomo tries to remember the word *forsythias*, 'and just coming up were both holidays, the Polish and the Jewish ones. She found me in the courtyard. She'd had an errand to run in the City Centre. She took me along and a girl as well, I think she was called Tobcia. In the streetcar she gave us each a piece of candy. It was strange, it looked like a chunk of marble. I asked if she wanted me to break my teeth. She said: "Try me." And she laughed, which was rare. I did, the marble was sweet and you could suck on it for a long time. Here, in Eretz, I spent a long time looking for candy like that but I didn't find it. Maybe they've still got it somewhere in Warsaw? From the streetcar, we walked through the streets and she held my hand. Until we went all the way up to an enormous palace, at least that's how it looked to me back then, which turned out to be a department store. I think at the time it was the largest in all of Warsaw.'

'The Jabłkowski Brothers' store?'

'I don't know, maybe, I guess so. It had a several floors, wide steps, enormous windows. And a toy department. What especially caught my eye were the models you could build, Meccano, a well-known company. Big and little ones, cars, ships, various constructions made of metal pieces, these flat plates with holes, screws, joints. In the middle of the room stood this tall, enormous model, it looked to me like it reached all the way to the ceiling. I stood in front of it with my mouth hanging open. "What do you say to that?" asked Stefa. I said it was the most beautiful thing I'd seen in my life. "We can't afford to buy one like that, but the Home got a small set as a present. Take a look and see what you can build out of it, how it all works." Afterwards when I was taking apart an alarm clock at school and it went off in class, the teacher called her into the room and she only yelled at me a little bit. Like I was saying before, I used to do repairs in the Home. Stefa would sometimes leave me alone with broken equipment, she wouldn't tell me how to fix it, she'd just bring me the broken object. For instance, a beautiful thermometer that I had to get the mercury out of. She'd only say: "I'm relying on you." Do you know what that meant, for her to rely on me? I mean, I was just this poor little nobody.'

Notes

1. B.J. Lifton, *The King of Children: The Life and Death of Janusz Korczak* (New York: 1988), p.156.
2. Ibid.

3. Ada Poznańska-Hagari, 'Janusz Korczak i Stefa Wilczyńska w oczach ich wychowanków', *Rocznik Seminarium Kibuców,* 1982, p.82.
4. Ada Poznańska-Hagari, 'Janusz Korczak i Stefa Wilczyńska w oczach ich wychowanków', *Rocznik Seminarium Kibuców,* 1982, p.82.
5. I. Merżan, *Pan Doktór and Pani Stefa. Wspomnienia* (Warsaw: 1979), p.52.
6. 'Okruchy wspomnień', Materials from a session of the Board of the International Janusz Korczak Society (Warsaw: 1984), p.55, manuscript (copy, Korczakianum - research centre of the Museum of Warsaw).
7. Ada Poznańska-Hagari, *Janusz Korczak i Stefa Wilczyńska...*, op. cit., p.105.
8. All quotes from A. Poznańska-Hagari, *Janusz Korczak i Stefa Wilczyńska...*, op. cit.
9. Letter to unidentified addressee, from the 1930s, Korczakianum – the research centre of the Museum of Warsaw, inventory number 0644.
10. *Mały Przegląd*, 29 April 1932.

7

Her day has been getting even shorter, ever since two rooms on the second floor were designated for the Hostel, a boarding house for children over age 14 who can't stay in the Home but wish to continue learning there. They do a few hours of work a day for the Home. Later the Hostel will also accept university students and future pedagogues wanting to gain experience at the Home.

She also receives new duties connected with running the Hostel (introducing young house children to the routine of the Home, getting together in the evening for a talk, checking their report notebooks, reading, answering questions, giving notes).

The children compare her to Korczak. They find his past, his wartime service and his publications impressive. To them, he's the mighty 'Pan Doktór'. Some think Wilczyńska has nothing to say and that's why she doesn't write. She simply (and that sounds like 'only') is there, non-stop, arranging, checking, overseeing. In the Home, they remember, she's everywhere.

She doesn't stop working even when she's sick (unless it's something infectious, then she can be persuaded to rest, out of care for the children). Influenza arrives, and an ear infection too. It hurts. She works without ceasing.

The Korczak archive has Hostel residents' notebooks – little diaries, observing the children and their own responses to them.

The first belonged to Miriam Greblich. A violet cover, blue graph paper, inside – the red ink of Wilczyńska's fountain pen, her notes. She responds to the trainee's conclusions briefly, she explains, she rarely gives advice. She praises her forgetting to know the children well.

A note of Wilczyńska's: 'This is a delayed issue. They won't make up the difference now. Here's a little information around their lives. They know how to read, do some arithmetic, write. It's not a lack of schooling that will hold them back in life. Dawidek congenitally sick (heart), Gołda – mentally underdeveloped.'

Wilczyńska encourages her to get the children to tell stories: 'Children tell so many interesting stories about school, about their lives before they came to the Home, and some enjoy having a listener.'

In one sentence Miriam writes 'all the children'. Wilczyńska asks: 'All? You cannot generalize that it's all of them.'

She answers the trainee's question about whether to exert influence on the children: 'Before "exerting influence", you have to spend years examining what kind of person this Gusia is.'

She corrects her Russianisms.

She replies to the effusive comments of one Hostel resident who is exaggeratedly moved at the sight of the sleeping children: 'The dormitory does bring the pedagogue much closer, but I've never known it to have such a magical effect after only 5 minutes.'

The workbooks of Różka Sternkac have also survived. For 20 and 21 December 1933 there are no notes. Wilczyńska, in the margin: 'flu'. On 25 December, Różka writes: 'Thank you very much for looking after me while I was sick.'

One of Różka's opinions: 'Our girls are little women in miniature.' Wilczyńska: 'Not in miniature, truly.'

Under one of Różka's entries, Stefa explains:

> I didn't have the slightest intention of causing hurt or criticizing. I can remember similar things that happened to me and the feelings they caused me twenty-odd years ago, and changing my mind after a week or a month. I can't compare your mindset with mine now, because the power of experience is just as harmful as it is helpful in self-criticism. That's why I'm so careful giving advice.

Różka complains that the children haven't memorized a poem on time. Wilczyńska replies: 'There was a special announcement that they shouldn't leave it to the last minute, but don't you remember your own schooldays…?'

Różka: 'During quiet time the boys were looking at an encyclopaedia. When they saw their teacher, they started laughing and quickly closed it.' Różka took a look at what was making them laugh – embryology. She started looking at it with them and telling them ('very, very generally') about how frogs reproduce. Wilczyńska:

> I know from long-standing experience that if you don't let your nosey curiosity provoke them, don't pester them with questions, don't smother them, they themselves will happily tell one another and inform themselves. Former house children have told me they didn't like talking to adults about sexual matters until the subject had

> already come up among themselves. They were put off by younger house parents who acted like they wanted to tell them about the birds and the bees, but were actually poking around to see what kind of understand they had of these issues.

In her notes to Różka: 'They often want to squeeze advice out of me when they don't want to decide for themselves (grown-ups, too). But I want to force them to make an independent decision. It's better that way.'

Różka: 'the method of "you will be held responsible", "that's the rule," is really very useful. The girls wanted to move their pillows to the other side, but "Pani Stefa won't allow us", because their beds stand by the wide aisle and it's not healthy to lie head-to-head like that.'

A note from Wilczyńska: 'I've explained to them many times my motivation for not allowing that. It may be permitted "until lights-out", if they police themselves.'

Różka:

> In the OH [Orphans' Home] a certain straightforwardness arises, a directness, an openness toward life. Above all: if someone's stolen something, then a punishment weighs on him for a certain period, his lockbox is taken away, and then nothing, he's a colleague again, a friend, an upright person, without the label of a 'thief'. Next: the general meeting, the newspaper, or in the auditorium: Hania sits quietly, and without Felcia being embarrassed at all, picks nits out of her hair – that's normal. I'm sure you find it very simple too, and maybe you're surprised at my amazement, but I remember when I was in elementary school it was embarrassing to have lice: tears and name-calling. Beyond that: if someone was red-haired, had a big nose, a squint – they'd never hear the end of it. The words they often use in conversation! Yesterday Szajuś was sitting next to me at breakfast, Bronek came up and said, as if in reproach: that Szajuś! I've got to lace up and polish his shoes. Szajuś smiles. I ask: Why doesn't he do it himself? Bronek: he's crippled. Szajuś: I can't bend my legs. Both of them simply and clearly, without pity and without anger. Why, how unusual that is!

Wilczyńska notes: 'these are the greatest pluses of our life, unappreciated by the opponents of the system we've created'.

She herself comments on some children's behaviour: 'wily', 'crafty', 'ambitious', 'an interesting person', 'talented',' she acted very brave'.

Różka: 'How do I explain to children who ask what it means to be eight years old?'

Wilczyńska: 'In the latest issue of *Literary News* there was a lovely description of time in memories of childhood: "This was in days when time was not yet counted..."'

When she reads about the young pedagogue's plans, she asks 'Aren't you taking too much on, Pani Różka?' When she wants to know more about a child she asks: 'What kind of person is he?'

***

Łucja Gold, a resident of the Hostel, recalls: 'one time [Wilczyńska] brought me some galoshes. [...] "Listen, Lunia, you've caught a cold [...] you've got such pathetic shoes. So maybe you'd... I got these from the donations. They're good quality. Maybe you'd put them on." I was so happy [...]. When my sister was meant to come visit [...], we're sitting, talking, Pani Stefa comes in, with a plate full of these fresh sour cherries. "It's so hot. You two must be stifling. Offer some to our guest."'[1] That '*our* guest' moved Łucja. She felt so important.'

From one of Łucja Gold's letters: 'Now I'm at the Hostel, I watch, I'm amazed, and I try to work. [...] In my heart I promise myself that when I'm in an independent position, I'll follow in Pani Stefa's footsteps. But first I must get to know children well, work hard and absorb everything so I can equal her even a little...'[2]

Gold returns to the Home many years later. On the way she passes through the Łódź ghetto and an orphanage she runs there; through Auschwitz, Bergen-Belsen, Dachau; back in Łódź to work in the Helenówek home for Jewish children who survived the Holocaust. When she ultimately finds herself before the familiar old building, she will set up a government children's home there. For fifteen years she will be a house parent there. The children will call her Pani Lunia.

The letter quoted above was addressed to another Hostel resident, Fejga Lifszyc. Wilczyńska befriends her as she once did Esterka. The two exchange dozens of letters.

Notes

1. *Żywa pamięć. W 75 rocznicę otwarcia Domu Sierot przy ul. Krochmalnej 92*, B. Puszkin (ed.) (Warsaw: 1989), pp.78-79 [photocopy, Korczakianum – the research centre of the Museum of Warsaw].
2. Letter from Łucja Gold to Fejga Lifszyc, 10 January 1936.

8

Not a single hair on Fejga's braid is out of place. If she isn't pleased with how it comes out, she unbraids it and starts over. Twice, five times. When she decides she doesn't need to fix it anymore, she ties it with a ribbon. She always pulls the strips of hair tight.

***

Fejga Lifszyc was not easy-going. She was stubborn, they say to this day in Ein Harod kibbutz. Difficult. Devoted to our cause. But very hardworking, you can't deny that.

From a commemorative brochure that the kibbutz publishes whenever a member dies: she is born on the holiday Tu BiShvat, marking the end of winter and the start of the rainy season, in 1905 in Zhytomyr. The eldest sister of eight siblings, she helps her mother at home. Her father studies great tomes and has long conversations with Fejga, but does little in the home. He is eternally hunched over Torah commentaries; he sometimes forgets to open his store and their money disappears. It's her mother who makes sure they don't go hungry. To the end of her days, Fejga will feel resentful toward her father. But she'll remember her mother fondly, even on the kibbutz: every day Fejga's mother sent eight children to school fed, clean, well-behaved. Their home was tidy and warm.

When in 1914 her mother falls ill and dies of typhus, Fejga must take her place. She boils milk, sends her sisters off to school, helps them with their lessons (she herself sometimes oversleeps and is late for school).

We don't know when exactly she joins Dror ('freedom' in Hebrew), a Zionist youth organization. She feels the need to leave home. She starts thinking about emigrating to Eretz.

She sets off travelling when she's 16 years old. She hides her slim braid under a cap while she does fieldwork for a bowl of kasha outside Rivne. She takes every job and saves up money. In the evenings she discusses with Zionists (she pins up her braid at the back of her neck, to look more serious).

We don't know how she ends up in Warsaw. She studies at the Tarbut teacher's seminary, where she meets Korczak. She goes to his seminars and moves into the Hostel. As the future pedagogues inundate him with questions and discuss theories of child-rearing, she stays quiet. When asked her opinion, she only has one question for Korczak: 'Do you happen to know a way of treating children for lice?'

She works at boarding schools on-and-off for several years. She thinks she's doing everything wrong and writes to the Orphans' Home for help.

Korczak writes back:

> Giving advice casually or from a distance is impossible. Here, much time is needed – to familiarize oneself, much individual effort to give a remedy. I can imagine how difficult you're finding things, and here is what I suggest: split yourself in two – be an actor and an audience member. Alongside her work and current unpleasant feelings, a young pedagogue must understand that she is preparing herself for future work, that she is achieving for the future, that she is toughening up and growing. […] When it comes to our student pedagogues, the Orphans' Home is free of the sin of giving prescriptions.
>
> We ourselves are constantly trying, searching, unsatisfied with things as they are, gazing inquisitively toward tomorrow. Wanting too much right away means wearing oneself out too swiftly and then seeing only with drowsy eyes, working with tired hands, battling obstacles with exhausted energy.
>
> To want too much is to be angry at oneself and at the children.
>
> Is there scabies? – very well, there will be more; messes were made – they will happen without me, too.
>
> It will be better in a year.
>
> Not soon.
>
> Not immediately.
>
> Not everything.
>
> Panna Fejga, you will not bring Warsaw to Białystok – that can't be helped. You must come to terms with this – and calmly, soberly, untremblingly do what you can, what is possible.
>
> PS sleeping 8 hours a night is obligatory![1]

Wilczyńska's reply:

> Please believe me, for those three months [in Białystok] you did a great deal. A very great deal. Eradicating mycosis and scabies, even

> if in individual cases it will still occur, [...] not counting many other things that haven't caught my eye. You are a brave person and that puts you under obligation, dear Fajgusia. [...] [T]he weight of responsibility rests on your young shoulders. After getting back I spoke [...] with the Doctor. He is of entirely the same view as I: remain in your current post, anything you could learn in the Orphans' Home you have already learned; staying with us can't offer you much now. PS For scabies, the best is Wilkinson ointment, over the counter at any drug store. 4–5 times a day rub it over the whole body, especially get it under the armpits, on the joints, under the knees, not too strong, a bath after three days, boil the underwear, change everything from the shirt to the sleeping pallet. Mycosis isn't so infectious when there's hair on the head. You have to take the most care when the hair falls out after diathermy, that is the most dangerous period. Number the caps, pillows, and towels so they don't trade them and borrow them. All my love, Stefa W.

Fejga works in Białystok, Kraków, and Warsaw. She falls in love. Frequently, intensely, unhappily. She belongs to no one and nowhere, she says.

She writes letters, she laments.

From a response of Wilczyńska's, 1925:

> As I read your letter I recall the first months after Dr Goldszmit went off to war. It was hard to stay on my own – it's true my working conditions were a hundred times better than yours, but my responsibility was a hundred times greater not to ruin what the wise teacher had wrought. And then the hard years: war, hunger, the Germans, typhus, scabies, mycosis – and me all alone. God helped me not to give it all up [...]. Go ahead and cry quietly at night, then in the daytime continue what you have to do.[2]

(And she herself, did she cry at night?)

***

In 1929, Fejga arrives in Palestine. She ends up in Ein Harod, one of the new type of agricultural settlements that even the Zionists in Warsaw are now talking about. She intends to leave after a few years. Maybe with Chaim Biber, who wants to go with her, or maybe alone. Biber loves her stubbornly and won't hear a word against her. He goes to Wilczyńska for help, persuading her first and Fejga only afterward.

Wilczyńska and Biber try to find her a job. Anywhere, she asks, just not where she is now. She comes to Poland, but after a few months she returns to Ein Harod and never leaves it again. She marries Biber, they have a son, Neta, and later a daughter, Hana. In the late 1940s, Biber falls ill. For more than ten hours a day, Fejga nurses her husband, washing him, giving him his medicine. When he dies, she's left with two small children, and before long her son gets sick.

From the memorial pamphlet again: 'Many things which now seem obvious, established, long set in stone, in actuality were introduced by her and with her assistance: the technique of labelling clothes, the changing rooms in the bathhouses, the organizers for sorting underwear, the shift system for children's chores.'

For a long time Fejga refuses to work with the children and sticks to farming, though she has no real passion for it. Planning and organization are what come most naturally to her. She arranges and rearranges objects, reorganizes, streamlines. She works more than ten hours a day. It never occurs to her to do otherwise. At kibbutz members' meetings she doesn't ask questions, she announces results.

She is demanding and a harsh judge. The floor, her daughter remembers today, must sparkle. The grades her daughter brings home have to be the best. Her work – always done on time and with no errors (if there is one, she has to do it over it until she gets it right). Fejga rarely smiles. She doesn't let anyone hug her.

In the 1960s her own health weakens. It's her joints. She's in danger of not being able to walk. She locks herself in her room. Hana drops out of school to care for her mother, who often doesn't speak to her for entire days. Fejga dies in 1971. Before her death, she donates copies of her letters to the archive of the kibbutz Lochamei HaGeta'ot, the Ghetto Fighters. But not all of them, and not all complete: from some she removes paragraphs or pages, or erases dates.

I read them for the first time as photocopies in the Korczak archive in Warsaw.

Now, in Israel, I hold them in my hand. The pages are brittle to the touch. Fejga's cuts mean the letters don't make sense. Smudged traces (spilled water? tears?), unclear handwriting.

I don't know how Fejga came to donate to the Ghetto Fighters kibbutz not only the letters from Stefa that she'd saved, but her own outgoing letters as well. Did she ask Stefa to return them to her? If so, when? Or maybe someone (who?) kept them?

These are the only texts where Wilczyńska writes about herself. About her desire to be needed. About yearning for that feeling. She writes with tenderness, yet without sentimentality, with care. She accepts Fejga's confidences and rarely – cautiously – offers advice. She worries about Fejga's health, about her being alone in Palestine. She listens hungrily. She wants to know everything. To see.

***

In a photograph from the memorial pamphlet, Fejga sits stiffly in a chair. Her hands lie on her immobilized legs, the sun is shining in her eyes, she doesn't have the energy to shade them.

Someone has done her braid tightly.

Notes

1. J. Korczak, *Pisma rozproszone. Listy (1913-1939)* (Warsaw: 2008), pp.165-166.
2. Undated letter from Stefania Wilczyńska to Fejga Lifszyc, 1925.

9

'Shlomo, what did you all think about Korczak and Wilczyńska?'
'Well what were we supposed to think?'

***

On a bookshelf in the Home stood a small, green volume – *The History of Arab Literature* by Julian Święcicki, published in 1901. In it is the story of Imru' al-Qays, a poet who wanted to avenge his father's death. Imru' al-Qays travels to see Emperor Justinian and ask for help. Unhappily, Tammah, whose father was killed by Imru' al-Qays himself, sends the poet a poisoned coat, to disgrace him before the ruler. Imru' al-Qays puts on the jacket with the poisoned fabric and his body is immediately covered in wounds. He falls at the feet of Asib Mountain, just beside the grave of a princess buried there.

O neighbour, fate has driven us together,
And here we'll stay, like Asib's rocks, forever!...
Though we two find ourselves on foreign ground
All wanderers' hearts in brotherhood are bound.[1]

Igor Newerly, a child-rearer and Korczak's secretary who wrote about this green volume in his memoirs, asks: 'these four verses were underlined there. When did she do this – in 1901 or afterward, many years later, at Krochmalna Street?'[2]

***

There were several possibilities.

Number one: 'Wilczyńska loved Korczak.'[3] In accounts from pupils and those closely connected with the Home, we hear again and again: 'everything pointed toward' and 'without a doubt.'[4] Stefa once said to the former house child Bella Cytryn-Miodowska: 'I fell in love for the first time when I was ten years old.'[5] In one letter to Fejga, Stefa mentions the young woman's husband has moods similar to Korczak's. Nothing more.

Maybe she expected reciprocation, was waiting for it, or chose close friendship instead. Maybe she felt all this at once, or none of the above.

The period of their work together was not an era when emotions were spoken of or shown openly, and in the house where they lived they were constantly interacting with boys and girls all day and night. It was a house where doors were not locked. Where Korczak and Wilczyńska measured and weighed children, bathed them. Korczak was an expert witness in the 1930s and included in one of his works the results of court cases about molestation and paedophilia, with appeals for children's protection. Maybe fear of accusations stemming from the Home's innovative methods heightened his self-control in personal relationships.

Korczak's own views toward women are ambiguous. While he displayed support for equal rights and emancipation, he also showed distance, reticence, coolness. Ida Merżan wrote:

> We Hostel girls held a grudge against Korczak [...]. We thought he preferred the boys to us. He dedicated more time to them, went on walks with them, spoke with them more often, invited them into his room. He ran most of his errands with them. If he occasionally made spitefully sarcastic remarks aimed at young people, it was mainly at the Hostel girls. [...] We told ourselves he was probably afraid of gossip, cheap sensation, pious hypocrisy, people sniffing around for unwholesome affairs. Or maybe he also feared gushiness and oversensitivity from the girls?[6]

Korczak:

> I have a difficult time with girls – it is easier with boys. Conversations with them are more concrete. For instance: 'Tell me, young man, what has gotten under your skin, what on Earth made you lose your temper?' I know: being young is, to some extent, a mental illness. (Someone said: I broke out of my youth like from a madhouse). Well yes, but eliminate conflicts in more favorable periods, to leave no traces behind. A storm? Even better, because after that you can get it off your chest. Parents – they too, we too have our woes, difficulties, eccentricities and caprices. We must somehow resolve the contradictions on the common territory of the family.

> Well, that is with a boy. But what of her?[7]

Yet his whole life he was surrounded by women and worked with them.

There was his mother, whom he had a close relationship with (when she died, he fell into depression). There was his sister, Anna Lui – a translator. She would visit the Orphans' Home and bring presents for the children. He lived with her in the 1930s, after moving out of Krochmalna Street. He wrote: 'Here on earth, she's the only one who calls me by my name.'[8]

He had an acquaintance from his student days with the author Zofia Nałkowska, he had professional contacts with the pedagogues Maria Grzegorzewska and Helena Radlińska, he had a friendship with the modest Maria 'Maniuszka' Podwysocka, 'a fiendishly good organizer in the pro-independence underground.'[9]

Then there was Maria Rogowska-Falska. Korczak got to know her during the First World War. She met him not long after losing her husband and only daughter. In one letter, she wrote: 'An encounter with Korczak. I have beheld His goal. [...] I have grasped it – and I am going.'[10] After returning to Poland she ran Our Home, a boarding house in Bielany district for ethnic Polish children and the orphans of political prisoners. She co-founded Our Home in 1919 along with Korczak and Podwysocka, and for many years they worked closely together. A black dress, a white collar, and time off once a week to visit family. The pupils in Our Home called her Pani Maryna. At the start of the Second World War, when Korczak learns Our Home is having trouble with food supplies, he sends over sacks of lentils. She will offer to help him get out of the Ghetto to the Aryan side.

Korczak again, from his diary (written in the Ghetto, a perspective that influenced everything):

> It's only girls I had no time for, though if they weren't so greedy and wanting all your nights, and getting pregnant besides. Nasty habit. It happened to me once. It left a bad taste for the rest of my life. I'd had enough. The threats, the tears.[11]

And he goes on:

> First anxieties and inconsolations. One moment voyages and stormy adventures, and the next, a quiet family life – friendship (love) for Stach. The principal dream among many, among dozens: he a priest, and I a doctor in that little town. I think about love, until then it had been a feeling; I loved. From seven to fourteen, I was constantly in love, always

> a different girl. Strange, I remember so many of them. [...] I loved for a week, a month, sometimes two, three girls at once. I wanted one for a sister, another for a wife, or the sister of a wife. From the age of fourteen, my love for Mania (in Wawer, that summer) was an integral part of [—] feelings, which lulled and shook me by turn. The fascinating world was no longer outside me. It was within me. – I was not here to be loved and admired, but in order to love and to act myself.[12]

***

Korczak held a deeply-rooted faith in change, which was marked by bravery in breaking stereotypes and defining himself. These were the aims of the rules and principles he invented, and the chores and categories Stefa invented. They both believed in freeing oneself from the extant norm, not only at the community level but also individually.

From the textbook Wilczyńska used to learn microbiology:

> Creationism believes that the species were created separately, successively, and moulded forever into the forms in which we see them currently: *sint ut sunt aut non sint* seems to be, in the eyes of this doctrine's supporters, their unalterable motto. In this theory, the physical structure of each species has a goal, an aim, and this is permanent [...]. Contrary to this doctrine, transformism looks where the facts have led us, and declares that the species are born of their environment, that they are merely varieties temporarily fixed by it, and maintained by heredity. [...] 'The qualities of species,' Étienne-Geoffroy Saint-Hilaire has said, 'are fixed for each species inasmuch as they endure in an environment of the same circumstances. They change if the ambient circumstances come to change.' [...] [H]e added in 1795: 'The species could well be naught but the various generations of one same type.[13]

From Korczak's writings: 'We will build a school where [...] they will learn how people live, why they live that way, how else they can live, what they must know and do to live full of a free spirit.'[14]

In his diary on 21 July 1942, he wrote: 'I don't know what I would say to bid the children farewell. Simply enough to leave them with a sense of complete freedom in their choice of a path.'[15]

***

Possibility two: their relationship cannot be fit into a box.

Wilczyńska could be, at times:

a secretary (when he needed such help),
a collaborator (executing, consulting, giving opinions),
a reviewer (if he gave her a text to read),
a confidante (if he consulted with her on ideas),
an assistant (she organized a trip to Palestine for him),
a caregiver (she would buy him a new sweater and remind him to take change for the streetcar on his way out of the Home).
She could also be: an ally.

There is not a single surviving letter from him to her, nor from her to him. They lived under one roof, so they simply talked. Though surely they corresponded during longer absences.

All that we have is the dedication at the beginning of the first edition of *King Matt the First*:

> To Panna Stefa – boy no. 51 – does not have mycosis – he's lost his certificate in the Country of Bum – Druma is asking for a shift collecting bits of paper – he's clean ('God forbid'). Permanent resident of Warsaw – Goldszmit. 25/10/[1]922.[16]

In the 1930s Wilczyńska sends Korczak's books to Palestine, wanting to know ('for herself') how they will be received. When in 1935 the American author Sinclair Lewis announces a list of the 15 greatest figures of the last 50 years – including Freud, Einstein, Lenin and Shaw – she's outraged that he overlooks Korczak's name.

Arie Buchner, later a house parent in the Home, records in his diary:

> July 15: Tomorrow the Dr is going to Warsaw to get a Medal. [...] July 19: I was in Warsaw. Pani Stefa showed me the Medal and told me she'd only show it to good workers. She also said the Medal probably made her happier than the Doctor.'[17]

'She'll go out and we'll have peace,' Korczak would say to the Hostel girls on Wednesday evenings, when Wilczyńska would leave to visit her mother. That's what he calls her: 'she'. Pani Stefa. In his articles he mentions her barely a few times. He doesn't need to be on his best behaviour for her. He can be who he is – not just the good-natured and cheerful Doctor, he can be himself, with all his contradictions and moods. In her letters she calls him: Pan Doktór. Or, for short: Dr.

***

Possibility three: what if we approach the subject theologically? Look for an answer where it seemingly cannot exist? Although Korczak and Wilczyńska both emphasized their non-religiosity, they came from an environment that, willingly or unwillingly, shaped them. Judaism exempts women from the majority of religious prohibitions and commands (of which there are 613). They have fewer chances to perform a *mitzvah* – their duty, a good deed. They are excluded from the majority of rituals, ceremonies, active spiritual life. Their lives revolve around *gashmiut*, the realm of the physical, also in its most mundane sense: tending to housekeeping, food, children. Men's life revolves around *ruchniut*, spirituality, ideas. The relationship between a woman and a man is less important than the fruit it bears, meaning the family; it lacks a romantic essence, instead containing a great deal of pragmatism.

***

Possibility four, and not the last: a coming together of similar solitudes.

Korczak, in his diary: 'I was terrified of the lunatic asylum to which my father had been sent several times. And so I am the son of a madman. I bear an hereditary affliction. Several decades on, and the thought still torments me periodically.'[18] And also: 'I'm not looking for close friendship, because I know I won't find it.'[19]

Wilczyńska, in a letter: 'The best thing someone can do is to make someone else less lonely.'[20]

(Or the only thing someone can do?)

***

1909

'Doctor Korczak.'

'Panna Stefania.'

1942

'Doctor.'

'Pani Stefa.'

Notes

1. Translators' note: I was unable to identify a direct translation of this poem from Arabic into English, and so I have translated it from the Polish version.
2. I. Newerly, *Żywe wiązanie* (Warsaw: 1978), p.67.
3. J. Olczak-Ronikier, *Korczak. Próba biografii* (Warsaw: 2011), p.141.
4. For instance: A. Poznańska-Hagari, 'Janusz Korczak i Stefa Wilczyńska w oczach ich wychowanków', *Rocznik Seminarium Kibuców*, 1982, p.42.
5. B. Cytryn-Miodowska, *Rozmyślania*, manuscript, Korczakianum – Research centre of the Museum of Warsaw, inventory number 0052.
6. I. Meržan, *Aby nie uległo zapomnieniu* [May it not be Forgotten] (Warsaw: 1987), p.90.
7. J. Korczak, 'The Solitude of Youth,' tr. by Sean Gasper Bye, from *How to Love a Child and Other Selected Works*, vol. 2 (London: 2018), p.187.
8. J. Korczak, 'Letter to Abram Gepner,' tr. Anna Zaranko, from *How to Love a Child* (op. cit.), p.249.
9. I. Newerly, 'Wstęp' in: *Wspomnienia o Januszu Korczaku*, L. Barszczewska, B. Milewicz (eds) (Warsaw: 1981), p.29.
10. Letter from Maria Falska to Jan Pięciński, 29 June 1933, in M. Falska, *Nasz Dom. Zrozumieć, porozumieć się, poznać* (Warsaw: 2007), p.284.
11. J. Korczak, 'Diary', tr. Anna Zaranko, from *How to Love a Child* (op. cit.), p.261.
12. Ibid., p.299.
13. M. A. Bordier, 'Les microbes et le transformisme', *Revue Scientifique*, vo. 41, no. 16, Paris 1888. Quote translated from French by Sean Gasper Bye.
14. J. Korczak, 'Szkoła życia', in *Dzieła*, vol. 4, Warsaw 1998, p.13 (quote translated by Sean Gasper Bye).
15. J. Korczak, 'Diary' in *How to Love a Child* (op. cit.), p.319.
16. Korczakianum – research centre of the Museum of Warsaw, document inventory number 0132.
17. M. Falkowska, *Kalendarz życia, działalności i twórczości Janusza Korczaka* [Calendar of the Life, Activity, and Creative Work of Janusz Korczak] (Warsaw: 1989), p.223.
18. J. Korczak, 'Diary', from *How to Love a Child* (op. cit.), p.312.
19. Ibid., p.300.
20. Letter from Stefania Wilczyńska to Fejga Lifszyc, September/October 1934 [?].

10

In fall of 1929, Wilczyńska's mother passes away. *Our Review* prints a laconic obituary: 'No condolences are requested.'[1]

She has lost her only reason for leaving the house every week, always and without exception. She beings thinking about going to Palestine.

In a letter to Fejga:

> Dear Beloved Fajgusia. Your letter (please, there's no need to call me 'Pani', I insist) arrived here on the day of my Mother's death. You understand what a Mother means, so there's no need for me to explain to you how I'd have suffered for the rest of my life if I'd left with you and not spent these last difficult weeks with Mother. Now I am a free person, my siblings don't need me, the Orphans' Home can also get along perfectly well without me and the thought of leaving is crystalizing more and more.
>
> Just the decision must be made: 1) when? 2) for how long?
>
> Because, you see, I have to be brave enough to declare that 44 is already the start of old age, I'm also worn out and ever since the war my nerves haven't been at their best.
>
> But there's still time for that. You'll get a look, darling Fajgusia, in a few months with your own eyes and write to me, advise me. As if you were practically advising your own mother.
>
> Now I've got to get to my steady work, because it's hard and lonely to lose dear ones one after the other like this. [...] I'm not patient enough to write more today. I want to dash off at least one little page to you so you know that you're on my mind. A big kiss from me, a very big one.
>
> Have you gotten slimmer?[2]

Fejga replies:

> My darling, beloved Pani Stefa,
>
> I opened your letter in the dining hall and couldn't hold back the tears. How badly I wanted to be with you. For so long I haven't been

thinking about writing back, about how things were with the Orphans' Home, with you. But by the time I got your letter I'd begun feeling homesick.

We're both orphans, Pani Stefa. But you were lucky enough to bury your mother when she'd lost her strength. Mine died while we still needed her so awfully much. I know that for you, like any daughter, that doesn't ease the pain. I myself am far from my relatives, my family. I didn't get a letter from home until recently, via a friend. My sisters write that they found out by chance that I'm in Palestine (they must not have gotten my letter). But I'm used to being alone now. Sometimes it's a good thing.

Work here under these conditions isn't easy. I'm usually sleeping on the floor in the dirt and mud people keep tracking into the room. Daily baths for the children, meals and sewing in the workroom, so difficult that the children only put on fresh clothes 3 – 4 times a week. The daily work overwhelms me even with a fairly small handful (25). The conversations are interesting. I observe and am often amazed. They're full of questions. Why, when we believe in showing them goodwill and a great deal of motherly affection (most of the workers are mothers), do the children not show us the same? A child's 'I want' wins out over an adult's 'I want.' They tell me I'll understand a great deal in time. Here, people have renounced their own paths both in life and in child-rearing, have put in work, thought, and ideas and await the results with trepidation and hope. I'm not yet a member of the kvutzah, I don't want to join before I convince them. But I am with them in spirit. Except I'm cut off from the community again. I eat with the children, so I don't go into the dining hall where everyone gathers. Outside those hours, I don't have time to see people either. I guess now I'm the type who has to be constantly overwhelmed with work. I don't rule my work, my work rules me. Still, you know that's when I fee alive. I want badly for you to come, Pani Stefa, but for a year.

The past hardly exists here.

It's spring now, everything's in bloom. The mountains are full of flowers.[3]

Anemones. When they bloom, the slopes of Mount Gilboa – which Fejga writes about – turn red. But on rainy, damp days, the Jezreel Valley transforms into a vast marshy bog and momentarily returns to its state before the arrival of colonists like Fejga. This scenery appeals to tourists, who visit this part of Eretz in increasing numbers because when the wagons they pack onto (the rail board did not foresee such great demand, so small, newly-built Ein Harod station – on the line from Haifa to Samakh, then onward to Damascus – is not large enough to serve them all) get stuck in the mud, the guides can say 'this is what this land looked like, before our brave pioneering work brigades began to drain it.'

Wilczyńska writes back:

> Sweetheart, you don't have to tell me twice to come. I'm very sad here because I can't adjust [...] to not going to my mother's when I have my free evening, and the children don't need me like they used to, because we're so organized our own staff aren't as necessary.[4]

***

(Does she sum up?)

I'm 44 years old.

When the children come back from their families on Saturdays, before they're in the door they're telling me stories, quickly, right away. They come when they need me.

That's all.

I know every centimetre of this house.

I can see Krochmalna Street perfectly through the window, and the roofs of Karolkowa Street further on. I know somewhere out there are the City Centre, the Saxon Gardens, Łazienki Park.

I know what's outside.

We lock the gate for the night.

We lock the gate for the day.

We have a court that is fair and a council that listens to its delegates. We are polite, open, respectful of one another.

We have 107 children, who in a few years will look back and say how naïve they were.

But, you see, we wanted to change young people so they would change the world.

Is what they have here for these few years enough?

You see, we haven't been able to help them all. Some couldn't adapt to the rules (were the rules good?). There was Stasiek, there was Dana who said 'I hate you'. There was Srulek, a difficult boy, he racked up convictions until he was finally expelled from the Home.

The two of us have our moods, our limits. I don't know how to play train with them, like the Doctor does, or run up and down the stairs. I get impatient, I can be unfair.

I don't know how to admit my mistakes. I punish myself for that.

Maybe our accusers are right. Maybe we need to change the world outside the gates? I'm not sure I know how. Or whether anyone would find that necessary.

Maybe a day institution would be better. Maybe smaller ones, little homes with a room for every child. Solitude for them and us. Constantly reminding yourself: don't cross the boundaries, don't get too attached, don't project your own expectations, desires, lack of fulfilment onto the child. Is that enough to not feel empty?

Or maybe they'd be better off staying with their families. Maybe growing up with people who have more patience, who don't need to divide their attention twenty ways, a hundred ways. Maybe somewhere else they know what is best for a child.

***

Twenty years have passed since she walked into the shelter on Franciszkańska Street. Twenty years of participant observation and decreasing certainty. Twenty years of getting up before everyone else, waking them, weighing them, sending them off to school. Reports, operations, planning.

The repetition of activities, scheduled with her perfectionist exactitude, feels wearing.

The increasingly difficult economic situation frustrates her. In Warsaw alone, in the industries that employ the most Jewish workers – tailoring, leatherworking, metal-working –by the late 1920s unemployment is raging, only one in five have work. And the Depression is still to come.

For a few years orphanages have been under the care of the state, but this care is exceptionally modest and dedicated funds are shrinking. Jewish children are not the priority. For twenty years, the Home has supported itself mainly on what the Orphans' Aid Society can raise. The donors are being less generous, but demand is holding strong.

Take bread, for instance. A large amount is needed every day. It costs 40, maybe 50 groszy per kilogram. One kilo is enough for four children. That's twenty loaves – no, better to have too much, but mustn't overdo it, can't afford to waste any. So 30 loaves a day times 30 days. Less than 1,000 loaves, at a cost of several hundred złotys. Their public grant gives them just under 1,600 złotys per month.

When she goes out to the City Centre, she has to pass street sellers with the cheapest wares and shack-stores knocked together from odds and ends and selling odds and ends – there were over a dozen of these on Nalewki Street alone. She reads in *Our Review* of the eighty per cent unemployment rate among Warsaw's Jewish carpenters, bakers and cobblers' journeymen, about businessmen who've lost millions and commit suicide. She doesn't know Yiddish, so she doesn't read in the afternoon paper *Hayntige Nayes*: 'Today11 poor tenants evicted at 9 Stawki Street, Cold -14 Degrees'.[5] but even so she knows about the people being thrown out for falling behind on rent. In November 1932 *Our Review* writes about a renters' appeal to the authorities: 'eviction is currently all the more tragic because there is simultaneously no chance of providing new quarters to those without an apartment [...]. The size of an apartment should be of no consequence when rent is behind due to the economic crisis. No one frivolously exposes himself to eviction [...]'.[6] More than two years later, the same newspaper prints an appeal from the Rescue Committee (headline: 'Save Us, For We Are Dying'): 'Before our eyes, the abyss of poverty is swallowing up a third of Jewish Warsaw'.[7] The committee delivers aid to over 20,000 families living in destitution. Their 'Current' rubrics are full of reports of people kicked to the curb, suicides of laid-off workers and the chronically unemployed, people stricken by exhaustion and hunger dropping dead on the street, suddenly, like a spring shower.

When Poland is hit by the first effects and then subsequent waves of the Great Depression, Wilczyńska is struck by her own crisis. With increasing boldness, she is facing up to her doubts, her questions – repeated in her letters to Fejga – about what she has been doing for so many years. She doesn't wax lyrical, she analyses.

For twenty years she and Korczak have been trying to create conditions for children to mature. The second generation of house children has already left the Home.

On the way they still receive: underwear, a sleeping pallet and a few items of clothing. If money is found, one or two will receive 500 złotys to get themselves on their feet, plus maybe also a letter by Korczak like the one the first children received:

> We give you nothing. We do not give you God, for you must seek Him yourselves in your own souls, in solitary endeavour. We do not give you the Homeland, because you must find it in your own work of the heart and mind. We do not give you love for people, because there is no love without forgiveness, but to forgive is toil, a labour

> each must undertake alone. We give you only this: yearning for a better life that does not exist, but will come one day [...]. Perhaps this yearning will lead you to God, the Homeland, and Love.'[8]

Shlomo remembers: 'When I was leaving the home, they both kept telling me: "don't forget what you had here". My life was never that good again. I gave my own children less.'

***

They are all 14 years old when they leave the home and, at first, marvel at the world. Like Samuel, who works in a store. His boss cheated him and Samuel felt humiliated. Doubly so, because he told his sister about it and she burst out laughing. Life isn't Korczak's Home, she said.

So later they're offended, some by how incoherent the world is, and sometimes, to put it bluntly, at Korczak and Pani Stefa. They walk out of Krochmalna Street into worklessness, poverty, exploitation. They return to mildewed cellars, basements, holes in roofs, holes in shoes, and empty bellies. To families that do not understand them and whom they no longer understand.

For several years *The Little Review* has printed letters from working young people. If anyone hires them at all, the pay is too low to support themselves. It's the same for their parents, sisters and brothers, whom they must once again share bug-ridden sleeping pallets with.

The respondents to Ada Poznańska-Hagari's anonymous questionnaire said:

> 'When I left, I was like a fish out of water. I didn't like it at home. Back there I'd had my own little corner, at home I had nothing and no one to turn to.'
> 'I left at an age that wasn't suitable for anything.'
> 'We went from luxury back to the ghetto.'[9]

They are alone once more.

And so they come back to the Home. Like Seweryn Nutkiewicz, who on Sundays puts on his best clothes and goes to Krochmalna Street. He can tell he's not from there anymore. Another former house child stands for a long time at the front door, but she doesn't dare go in. Years later they'll say: 'Korczak forgot where we'd come from and where we went back to.' They also remember that the Doctor usually wasn't there for them, it was Pani Stefa who made time to talk. Though also not always and not for long.

As this time many are drawn to communism, in search of belonging. Or they emigrate – to Brazil, Argentina, the United States, Palestine. These young people, like the Hostel residents, are bolder in criticizing the child-rearing methods of the Home. They accuse Korczak and Wilczyńska of naïveté. They see what's happening all around, outside the gates of Krochmalna Street: the Depression and none of the prospects that – after all – were meant to be the fruit of study and honest, conscientious work. They see no place for themselves in the existing order.

The equal rights declared in the Constitution of 1921 exist on paper, but not on the streets, in government offices or in universities. The Home's alumni want changes. Beyond what the Home can offer to a lucky few until the age of 14.

At one meeting, former house children accuse the staff directly, saying the world does not wait and is not like Krochmalna Street. Korczak takes it hard. He does his best to explain that they are doing as much as they can, here and now.

We don't know if Wilczyńska spoke up. But when the government authorities order monitoring of outcomes for former orphanage residents, she co-founds the Former House Children's Club. She puts an ad in the press. She recommends alumni to work in offices, stores, factories, workshops. Three days a week, in the afternoons, she accepts applications. She pulls strings and signs references. She writes letters to former house children. And they write back – about work, a new profession, a child.

She has her first 'grandchildren' (that's how she refers to the children of alumni in her letters).

***

Around this time Korczak also starts feeling fatigue, though for the moment it's not overwhelming. He works outside Krochmalna, he writes, critiques himself, and others critique him too, from all sides: he is too secular for the religious, too rooted in Poland for the Zionists, too conservative for the communist-leaning youth, too Jewish for the truly Polish.

Wilczyńska is tangled in the same web. She has good hearing, and when she complains about a dress she commissioned from a seamstress, she can hear the woman mutter, 'Jewish fantasies.' Stefa also knows why, even though she arrived first, she must wait until a colonel's wife is served. But from then on, out of spite, she'll only order from Jewish shops.

***

One of the employees of the Orphans' Home was Pani Wolańska – no one remembers her full name, but they called her 'Wosia'. She was warm, devoted to the children. Another was Piotr Zalewski. They were both ethnic Poles, Catholics. The house children went both to Jewish and Polish schools. They went to see their families or on field trips, but they always came back to where they felt at home.

But such mixed places are becoming rarer.

One day, one of the house children, little Libcia, cried:

'I can't stand any Christians, because they bully Jews!'

'What?' asked Wilczyńska. 'You can't stand any of them? And they all bully Jews? What about Pani Wosia?'

'No!' shouted Libcia. 'I love Pani Wosia.'

'And Pan Zalewski too?'

'But Pan Piotr is so nice.'

Wilczyńska kept on listing until Lubcia changed her mind.

She gave a list because she didn't like to generalize.

The paradise of the Home does not extend beyond its gates. House children graduate into a world of not just poverty and the economic crisis, but violence as well. There are truncheons and stones awaiting them on the streets, newspapers encouraging buying goods 'from our own people', headlines crying: 'Jews taking over'. Those who go to university in hopes of improving their chances face difficulties too. In November 1931, the Central Executive Committee of the Union of Jewish Academic Societies issues an appeal: 'Following the pattern of last year, we have seen a recurrence of incidents provoked at universities by nationalist youths with the goal of removing Jews from educational institutions. Jewish students have been forcibly removed from lecture halls and workshops in line with declarations from nationalist leadership.'[10] The death of a Polish student during a riot in Wilno – tragic and accidental, but at the hands of a Jew – and a similar incident in Lwów add momentum to a wave of anti-Semitic disturbances. Over the following few weeks hunts for 'passersby with Semitic appearances'[11] are organized by the nationalist youth movement in Warsaw, Częstochowa and Kraków. The next few years will also see the arrival of segregated classrooms. These are first introduced at Lwów Polytechnic, but before long the heads of practically every Polish college and university will do the same, having been given a free hand by the Minister for Religious Faiths and National Education. Some departments introduce limiting quotas for Jewish students, some won't accept them at all. Stamps appear on Jewish students' course registration books reading: 'odd-numbered seats only.' Some ethnic Polish friends and lecturers stand during lectures as a sign of protest against discrimination. Not many.

Jewish students also read and pass on news of pogroms ('incidents', 'events'). By the second half of the thirties, these are common enough to make up a topical, very political, map of Poland: Grodno, Odrzywół, Przytyk, Mińsk Mazowiecki, Brześć nad Bugiem…

The message: they are very much not at home.

***

The Little Review gets letters from children all over Poland.

> Leon wants to know if Jews really use blood for matzoh, because the rabbi never said a word about it in cheder.[12]
>
> My sister and I were walking down Nowy Świat. There were piles of dirty snow lying around the roadway. A certain elegantly dressed lady was walking by and said:
>
> 'Out of the way, little yids.'
>
> We just kept walking calmly. But she said it again to a gentleman:
>
> 'Will you look at those little yids just getting in the way here.'
>
> The gentleman said it wasn't our fault, it was city hall's for not clearing the snow. It seems to me that if someone is walking down the street and not causing trouble, there's no need for rude remarks.
>
> Jehuda.[13]
>
> [Abram asks:] 'Does the fact that I'm Jewish mean I have to get beat up?'[14]
>
> Stefcia asks if it's right for Jewish children not to have school because the one Christian school doesn't accept Jews.[15]
>
> 'Although I love this country, it does not like me.'[16]
>
> Jasio goes to a Polish elementary school. At first they shouted 'Jew!' but now they only do it sometimes when they're angry.[17]

I saw a Jewish boy getting beaten up, but he wasn't defending himself, because he didn't know what he was getting beaten up for. He didn't want to fight, because he was in pain, and why should others be too?[18]

'Poland is my chosen homeland. I love her very much, though not as much as Eretz. I cannot feel like I am in my true homeland, because at every turn we're made to remember we're outsiders. With each step I hear the slur "Jew-girl", sometimes even with a hurtful nickname.'

Ewa[19]

'Let's consider what would happen if war broke out. It would take place not on the front lines, but on the home front, the population of the cities and countryside would suffer most. Soldiers would not take the lead, but poison gases and murder Machines would instead. This is what will happen if the young people of all countries do not say: down with war. [...]'

Lutek, from Nowolipie Street.[20]

[Sabcia] knows boys who take off their school badge, so when they're out walking no one can tell they go to a Jewish school.[21]

'I hope my new teacher will be better and won't let my Christian classmates bully Jews.

Alek.[22]

'Christian boys accosted Motuś in a city movie theatre. Motuś doesn't know whether to hit them back.'[23]

'Eda doesn't know what to do when people call her "Jew-girl" on the street.'[24]

'Lolek used to play with Halinka, but now Halinka calls him "you Jew". Lolek is five, and his brother wrote a letter for him, complaining about Halinka.'[25]

'Christian children act disgusted by me, even though my mama washes me every day.'

Wunia[26]

Under the heading 'The Little Corner', Wilczyńska selects letters from very young children: 'Are there separate Polish and Jewish angels?– Kubuś.'

***

So there's anti-Semitism.

So there's the Depression. Wilczyńska is tired of worrying about money. She sighs to the communist-leaning Hostel residents: 'Why don't you get your revolution over with?'

So there's disappointment, that maybe everything she's done so far and what had been her whole life has no meaning (anymore? At all?)

So there's yearning. For a goal she could achieve, though not here. Not in these conditions. And for Fejga. She worries about her, her poor health, her weak constitution and difficult living conditions, the excessive work in Palestine. Stefa races through every letter. She wants to know as much as possible and asks about everything: the climate, the conditions, the job, the kibbutz. She reads publications by halutzim – young Jewish settlers, future pioneers in Palestine. She starts learning Hebrew.

***

Hebrew has no present-tense form of the verb 'to be'. Stefa is learning a language that has no word to describe her own presence. Instead you skip straight to the noun, for instance one describing a profession. On one page of her notebook she writes: 'מורה'. Teacher.

Notes

1. *Nasz Przegląd*, 15 November 1929.
2. Letter from Stefania Wilczyńska to Fejga Lifszyc, 18 November 1929.
3. Letter from Fejga Lifszyc to Stefania Wilczyńska, 14 December 1929.
4. Letter from Stefania Wilczyńska to Fejga Lifszyc, 13 March 1930.
5. *Hayntige Nayes*, 12 February 1936.
6. *Nasz Przegląd*, 29 November 1932.
7. *Nasz Przegląd*, 10 March 1935.
8. J. Korczak, 'Farewell', tr. by Sean Gasper Bye, in *How to Love a Child…*, op. cit., p.127.
9. Quote from: A. Poznanska-Hagari, 'Janusz Korczak i Stefa Wilczyńska w oczach ich wychowanków', *Rocznik Seminarium Kibuców*, 1982, p.15.
10. *Nasz Przegląd*, 30 November 1932.
11. Ibid.
12. *Nasz Przegląd*, 3 January 1930.
13. *Mały Przegląd*, 21 February 1930.

14. Ibid., 10 January 1930.
15. Ibid., 3 January 1930.
16. Ibid., 8 November 1929.
17. Ibid., 20 May 1927.
18. Ibid., 25 March 1927.
19. Ibid., 14 November 1930.
20. Ibid., 26 December 1930.
21. Ibid., 7 December, 1928.
22. Ibid., 18 January 1928.
23. Ibid., 11 November 1927.
24. Ibid., 28 December 1928.
25. Ibid., 29 April 1927.
26. Ibid., 28 November 1928.

11

January 1930. Stefa to Fejga:

Dear Fajgusia,

100 times already I've wanted to toss everything aside and go to see you. Your last letter made my appetite even stronger, but this year I've taken on all kinds of obligations until 1st September, so I will have to hold out. I already have money set aside for the trip. My mother skimped on everything to leave money for her two youngest, enough that I can even afford 2nd class. But for now I have to look after the Orphans' Home and the Hostel, and think about Gocławek, because we're losing half the staff there.

[…] I'm not writing you enjoyable letters, but that's life – I worry about Basia and Rózia, they're like porcelain figurines […]. I devour your letters.

So the children over there are so toughened-up. But maybe only the ones born there? And you haven't written me a word about how the climate is treating you, because not all newcomers can handle it well.

I read snippets of your letters to Perec and Jakub, and others to the Doctor, but I keep choosing different things for our newsletter, because everyone finds it interesting […]. And I recognize the old little Fajgusia from back at the summer camp and in Białystok, and from the Hostel too, but I also see a new one, celebratory, searching, looking around, but very dear to me […]. My worry and fear are no weaker, and I am anxious to see the results of your efforts and struggles.

I have already started learning Hebrew […], but I am finding it very difficult. Whether because it's a tough language or because my old skull's too thick. I want to get the 100 most common colloquial words. […]

I think it's a bit of a shame you're working as a teacher, but maybe that farm was really too exhausting in conditions like those. […]

Here they're opening special two-month courses for prospective emigrants to Palestine, but I doubt they'll help anything. It seems like everything over there is for children – is there nothing for young adults? […]

The Hostel is doing well generally, they're jealous that I'm enjoying your letters so much. And my dear daughter, enough with the formality, you have never been closer to me than now.'[1]

In February, she writes to Fejga again:

My dear Fajgusia,

I don't understand why I have not had an answer to my letter in so long. I know a new job and new people keep the mind busy, but I want so badly to know if you are healthy, at least, because such long silences make me anxious. Or maybe my letter didn't reach you, since I didn't mail it myself?

How pleased I am to be coming to see you. I'm counting the months – October is not far.

It's hard to work here, because everything it's possible to do has already been done. In Gocławek, Ida and Tema are having a grand time building up the preschool and more and more new discoveries. The Doctor is the same as ever, just more serious and deliberate in Bielany district, meanwhile out where you are you can't get enough of experimenting. And on Krochmalna Street it's 'nothing new.' I mean, there's plenty that's new for many people, but for us, economic and social conditions are blocking off further development. The children on-site – as far as I can tell – are doing well, at least for now. And that's good. The mood is sunny, rehabilitations, not many court cases or censorship, a few too many Ds, winter without sleds and skating rinks, which is disappointing for those with skates. Tyla H. (the girl from Sosnowiec) is back from interviewing with various boarding houses around the country. All over the children and young adults are doing badly, are sad, are being harmed! I'm old now, toughened up, but such anxiety comes over me when I hear such stories. And worst of all, I can't see what to do. And people of good will are murdering one another. Conditions for an honest worker are terrible.

I can't write any more today, and I want to mail the letter myself, so at least jot down a couple words on a page saying you are healthy.[2]

(She underlines the last three words.)

March. Stefa to Fejga:

> Our letters crossed. […]
>
> I was so moved, as if by a marvellous fairy tale, to hear you tell about the children's life over there. Is such a thing possible everywhere, or only in these model colonies? […]
>
> You write the least of all about your job. I can only imagine you are absorbed and overworked up to your eyeballs, the way you know best and enjoy. […]
>
> As far as my arrival, coming earlier is impossible. […] I have made commitments for this school year at the OH and the Hostel, and at the *Little Review*, and I can't abandon them midway through the year. […] I'd like to be able to come without ending up compelled to rush back, assuming you're able to find me some organizing work there (without the language), besides, now, in the summer heat, I'd be afraid to risk it. […] Next year the Doctor also plans taking a long leave for six months (not to Palestine) to do some writing, meaning we must coordinate our departures so they don't fall at the same time.
>
> So now you see I must wait patiently. […][3]

May. Stefa to Fejga:

> […] I don't quite understand which school you were saying is meant to be ready for fall, or what job I could have there. Just a new building, not continuation of what's already there, is that right? Although I'm old I don't think anything would scare me away, I'm only afraid of disappointments.
>
> My word, you're writing so cautiously now, as if you wanted to discourage me, I mean, not discourage, but to prepare me for any surprises. Things are bad here, but worse there for not being better.
>
> Did you receive the Dr's latest book, *The Rules of Life*? I sent it to you by registered mail three months ago. […]
>
> I miss you very much and I send a big kiss. I see you're having difficulty finding your way over there.[4]

May. Fejga to Stefa:

> I am a wandering bird, flitting from here to there, never with my feet on the ground, and it's sad. Because everything has changed so much here that I get lost. I can't imagine anywhere else that does

as much for children as we do here. But I still have my doubts and hesitations about whether it's all for the best. Sometimes I think I'm not yet qualified to judge.

May is unusually cool this year. And there are nights when I can't get to sleep.[5]

July. Fejga to Stefa:

I swear, I don't want to write at all anymore. I was patient when I knew it was still a long wait, but now it's only another letter or two before you're already here. The sooner the better. With every passing month I think, oh, this one is the best yet. Unless there are no bad months at all. But now it's really wonderful. Nothing to think about: no pedagogical or child-rearing riddles. It's summer. After the workday, I get a few free hours. I relish nothing more than being alive, to the point of being afraid it won't last. I feel good. I'm a little tan, but not much. I've only had two headaches in nearly a year.

The moonlit nights here are so gorgeous. The quarter moon here is as bright as a full moon in Poland. On nights like those we usually go out to pick and eat grapes.

Now I've been waiting for you to set the date of your arrival, for you to start preparing your passport. In secret I will tell you that I am not at all sanguine about your future work in Palestine and your stay in this kvutzah, but you need not worry now. Now things are good and that's that.

Goodbye, my darling![6]

August. Fejga to Stefa:

I got your page, another disappointment. I have to admit I'm losing faith. I'd set myself up a plan to finish the school year, I'd get time off and then spend a whole month with you wherever you like. But now...today is my first day of leave, because it wasn't worth postponing. I'm not in the mood for it at all. They're encouraging me to go somewhere and relax, but I'm not tired and besides I feel bad for others who are more exhausted and didn't get time off. Once again I feel unhappy about my work to come. I absolutely want to quit the children, but the school does not want to dismiss me and is tormenting me. If they knew me like you do, then they wouldn't start with such a stubborn mule. But I'll convince them in the end. Worst comes to worst, I'll get out of this kvutzah (after all, you know I never see things through; who knows how long that will last, maybe until I die?). I'd like to talk to you so badly, but there's no point writing like this. You're shortening your letters down to single pages and still won't say how long you're postponing your trip for. I've run out of patience.[7]

September. Stefa to Fejga:

What apprehension! How many times have I told Rózia Lipiec, Nacia and Jakób [Kutalczyk]: our Fejga must be sick. She isn't writing. It's suspicious. I've been so nervous. And well! There you have it: a letter came from the hospital. My poor girl, my beloved darling. [...] Tell me, I beg you, immediately, whether you are still even the slightest bit ill. I'm so superstitious that I don't dwell on the health of the people I love best. I have lived through so much sadness, which I don't think is an exaggeration. So write, this very moment. Do you have strength to work? Because I know you and I know that for such natures as ours, work is an essential condition for life. I simply cannot write about anything else now, so I will only arrange our business.

1) Tell me what I should get together for a two-month trip, because I have practically nothing to wear apart from aprons. So if I need to buy something now, I want whatever I will need there.
2) I can attest that Janusz Korczak has not a word of the Yiddish language. He speaks to new arrivals in broken German, and pretends it's jargon. Well then, have you won the bet?

I'm more and more frightened to leave, though I'm happier and happier. And what's also taking away my courage are the people coming here from Palestine on passing visits. Hawa was here again from Jerusalem, and assured me I would be very useful there.

I don't see what use I can be where you are. [...]

And again I know that I won't last two months without work. So I am just counting on you to be smart about setting me up. [...]

The Dr is supposedly resting, but he's actually writing a new novel. I have a hard time without the Dr: I've gotten little new work, but plenty of responsibility. Besides, I'm standing in for the Dr at *The Little Review*.

Does that scorpion's sting not leave any mark?[8]

November. Stefa to Fejga:

> My dear beloved Fajgusia, if you can, keep a tight rein on your nerves for another two months. I am coming, unless I drop dead. If I don't leave Europe in January, you may never believe me again. But you must believe until January (I have already started preparing my passport). [...]
>
> I got your sad letter, my darling child.
>
> I'm reading between the lines, but I'm not worried one bit, because I know this is just for now. The same thing happened to me 15 years ago. I wanted to quit the boarding house. I thought too much and suffered too much. Later...I don't know if it got better. But, yoked to my duty, I had no time for thinking.
>
> I've got no patience for writing either. So I'll keep it brief. Tell me what shoes I ought to bring for January? February? What sort of coat?
>
> Dr G. is coming back to Warsaw at the end of December, 1 January at the latest. I'll stay another 2 weeks to get everything in order and buy the things I need, since I don't have time now.
>
> I'm already looking forward to the journey so much, but I'm afraid I won't last long without work (my nerves won't allow it). That's why I'm thinking about some sort of job.
>
> I've already learned to read Hebrew, but I find speaking difficult, unachievable.
>
> I won't ask you about anything, my dear little daughter, except about your health.
>
> Have a big kiss from me and don't lose patience.[9]

Notes

1. Letter from Stefania Wilczyńska to Fejga Lifszyc, 7 January 1930.
2. Letter from Stefania Wilczyńska to Fejga Lifszyc, 18 February 1930 [?]
3. Letter from Stefania Wilczyńska to Fejga Lifszyc, 13 March 1930.
4. Letter from Stefania Wilczyńska to Fejga Lifszyc, 13 May 1930.
5. Letter from Fejga Lifszyc to Stefania Wilczyńska, 25 May 1930.
6. Letter from Fejga Lifszyc to Stefania Wilczyńska, 8 July 1930.
7. Letter from Fejga Lifszyc to Stefania Wilczyńska, 11 August 1930.
8. Letter from Stefania Wilczyńska to Fejga Lifszyc, 25 September 1930.
9. Letter from Stefania Wilczyńska to Fejga Lifszyc, 28 November 1930.

12

It was then, at the start of the 30s, that Stefa started looking for a new goal. Another way of being needed. Not here in Warsaw, not like this, not in these conditions. But in some community even so.

She reads about Soviet communism. With scepticism. She doesn't believe in it. But nor does she dampen the enthusiasm of her young house children who seek the solutions to their problems in that system. For a moment she even wonders whether to move East.

She looks to Palestine too. She must have read Theodor Herzl's *The Jewish State*. He wrote it when Stefa was only ten years old, but a Polish translation was published in 1917. It's discussed throughout the diaspora, with the religious, the socialists and the assimilators opposing Zionism. The Zionists themselves, who have been holding Congresses since 1897, have a range of visions for the new state. The culturalists have proposed making it into a new spiritual capital for the Jews. Supporters of the Po'ale Tsiyon party want it to be leftist, supporters of Mizrachi organizations – religious, and of the Zionist Organization – liberal. When the so-called Balfour Declaration was issued in 1917, in which the British government stated it 'view[ed] with favour the establishment in Palestine of a national home for the Jewish people', Zionism was gathering strength – including in Poland. In the First Sejm (1922-1927), the majority of the 53 seats won by representatives of Jewish parties were held by Zionists.

Zionism means the rebirth of the Jewish nation through the creation of its own state in Palestine. Collective forms of life, different varieties of colonies, new settlements – which have been founded since the late nineteenth century by Zionist organizations, on land first purchased from the reigning Turks and then from the British. As Arthur Ruppin, one of the fathers of the Zionist settler movement, writes: the land, and the community around it to which one subjugates and subordinates oneself, are to form the basis of life and the first point of reference. The settlers wish to create a system in Palestine without the characteristics of the capitalist principle of economic supremacy. They wish to oppose capitalism with a system based on fairness for the greatest possible number. Cooperatives, self-government, division of labour and obligations, community. All this sounds familiar to Wilczyńska.

Wave after wave of immigrants to Palestine are sailing into port at Jaffa – with every year that goes by, more and more people she knows are making the trip.

In the vast archive of the Ghetto Fighters kibbutz, I look through over a dozen yearbooks. They contain inscriptions, wishes for 'success in Eretz', requests to be remembered, jealousy (like a certain Ryfka in Brześć who can't go with her sister to the 'longed-for Promised Land'), pressed lilacs and lilies-of-the-valley, mailing addresses, blessings for the journey, warm thoughts. A few of the books have a number of then-popular 'Japanese aphorisms.' They begin with the couplet (of warning? or encouragement?) 'there's no art to dying – the art is in living.'

Some return (forever or to collect their families) or write letters. Such as house children. Such as Fejga. Emissaries of Zionist organizations come, including to Warsaw. They encourage and agitate. They advise where to go and how to get there, what to bring along. Wilczyńska sees posters on the streets, information about accounts of the journey to Palestine. She doesn't read Zionist publications in Hebrew or in Yiddish, but the titles alone – *HaTsfira* (Hebrew: Daybreak), *Haynt* (Yiddish: Today), *Der Moment* (Yiddish: The Moment) – are meant to hasten readers along: you've got to go. Now, right away. She definitely reads the regular feature in *Our Review* titled 'Palestinian Matters', as well as correspondence from Palestine, and sees invitations to picture showings, held in places like the Nowości Theatre at 5 Bielańska Street, or to screenings of films with titles like *From Egypt To Palestine.* Maybe she's gone to such an event. Maybe she's read the letters young people send into *The Little Review* from all over Poland as they join the halutz pioneer organizations, or attend camps near Drohobycz, Zamość, Kraków and even in nearby Grochów district. There they learn farm work and Hebrew, and in the evenings, they join hands to dance the hora, a Jewish folk dance.

***

From the 'Phrasebook' section of *A Guidebook to Palestine* by Joseph Ben Adam, some useful expressions while on the ship:

Hineha! Omnam od to tuchal lirot me'eumah – There it is! But you can't see it yet!

Hineh ha'aretz! – There's the country!

(Does she buy the guidebook in the Palestinian Communication Department on Marszałkowska Street, where she arranges the formalities for her departure? Does she need any more than what Fejga and her contacts passed on?)

Tales about colonizing Palestine are already becoming legend. Farming is now 'the cornerstone for rebuilding the ancient Jewish homeland' and

> ...brings the idea of the rebirth and liberation of the Jewish nation through labour; the Jew, oppressed and humiliated in the nations of the Tsar, has long dreamed of his own, free homeland, and when the first pogroms struck at his core and revealed to him the hopelessness of his actions in their entirety, his aimless and substanceless life, he seized his walking-stick. Standing in the first ranks for labour and reconstruction are people of iron will, young men and women inspired by the spirit of noble idealism. The fate of these first settlers, who went with great enthusiasm to be pioneers, was very arduous. They who first joined the ranks of difficult, volunteer labour found in Palestine deserted, uninhabited regions and sandy dunes stretching for miles. Water-inundated places far as the eye can see, muddy fields, millions of mosquitoes buzzing over the swamps, with malaria lurking in these dreary, uninhabited lands."[1]

She knows all this, and that's just how it was with Ein Harod; Fejga wrote to her about it, after all. The settlement was founded in the 1920s by pioneers from Russia and Central Europe at the bottom of the swampy Jezreel Valley, near the source of the Harod Stream. After a few years the colonists moved their tents to the other side of the valley. They live in the shadow of the Gilboa Mountains. There they have quickly created the largest and most efficient communal settlement in Palestine, with its own governance and where private property is unknown.

This is where they've built everything from scratch. This is where Fejga has ended up.

(Is that enough for Stefa to make up her mind to buy a ticket?)

Wilczyńska comes to Palestine for the first time in late January 1931, at the start of the rainy season, in the coldest month in Eretz. She stays with Fejga. She spends a few weeks there.

***

She writes letters back to the children. She picks out what they might find interesting.

My darlings,

Do not be angry that I haven't written in so long. I will explain why presently. I left Warsaw on Monday – I have been travelling for a whole week. You've had lunch 7 times and dinner 7 times, but all the while I was travelling and travelling.

First I took a train through part of Poland, then through Czechoslovakia, Austria, and Italy. In Trieste I boarded a ship and continued on past Italy, around Albania and Greece, to port in Palestine. But the sea was stormy, rough, such huge waves lifted the ship that we couldn't reach Jaffa, the journey took a whole day longer, and we disembarked at a more distant port, in Haifa. The ship can't get to the port itself. So the people go the rest of the way on small boats.

A dark night, pouring rain. Don't think this is rain like you have. Large, mighty, heavy drops – they beat, pound, smash. A heavyset man is soaked from this rain in a minute, and a young boy – in half a minute. So, in this driving rain the boats are approaching, and in them are Arabs. And how they shout! [...] The dark, the downpour, and the savage cries are my welcome to Palestine.

But the next morning: the beautiful sunlight, as warm as May, the blue sea and a strange, strange world. Policeman-Jews, conductor-Jews on the trains, clerks in the post office, bricklayer-Jews building houses and Jews in the fields. Signs in Hebrew everywhere. [...]

Camels – with silly expressions – work seriously and with dignity. But small donkeys are most common: carrying people, sacks, heavy baskets and trunks.

I am very sorry I cannot send you oranges. After the last storm they got cheaper and today I could buy them for a grosz apiece. Just think: for one Warsaw bun you could get 10 oranges today. [...] Warmest greetings to everyone, and anyone who wishes to, please write.[2]

***

The slopes of Kumi Hill descend gently. Wilczyńska often takes walks up to the top – before dusk, when the ground is still steaming with heat, but you need to bring a sweater because as soon as the sun sets, it will suddenly get very cold.

You can see the whole valley from there. *Jezreel* – in Hebrew: God will sow. The specialist-organized commissions told the pioneers: it's impossible to drain these swamps.

The land is empty apart from the kibbutz, the trees are only starting to grow, drainpipes bring water to every palm tree.

'There is a remarkable contrast between these Corbusierian lines and the savage landscape all around,' the journalist Ksawery Pruszyński later noted.[3] Wilczyńska sees the same lines. Long, even rows of white buildings with walls as thin as corrugated cardboard. Cardboard boxes, arranged like children's toy blocks. A new type of architecture for a new type of society.

She must appreciate the tidiness.

Every detail of the settlement has been analysed. Things are to be above all useful and functional. The differences between specific types of agricultural settlements are not great: on a moshav, settlers receive separate plots of land which they can cultivate themselves, unlike on a kibbutz or a kvutzah (a similar, but smaller, type of community)where people work in common fields.

The basic principles are the same: individual labour, equal rights for members – here, women work just as much as men, everyone helps one another, they have self-government and are mutually responsible. The bylaws are applied equally to everyone. There is a general assembly where everyone has one vote. Disputes are settled by a court of conciliation.

And to Wilczyńska, this all seems familiar from somewhere.

Every family has a room for themselves in one of the residential buildings. The rooms are modest ones, at most five by five meters. Beyond the residences stand farm buildings, chicken coops, cowsheds, dairies, processing plants, workshops. And the largest building in Ein Harod, from which all the rows of low, single-storey buildings radiate. It holds the assembly hall, large enough to fit everyone.

(A little – does she think? – like our auditorium.)

When she looks down at the complex from above, to the left and right of the central building she can make out two smaller, but also modern, light-coloured blocks. These are the children's buildings. The kindergartens.

Because in fact, it's when it comes to children that the various types of settlement differ the most. On a moshav, raising children is the parents' concern. On a kibbutz or a kvutzah, it is the whole community's. Those two types of settlement spend the largest share of their budget on their children.

The youngsters sleep in the white building that Wilczyńska sees next to the dining hall – not with their parents. They can visit in the evenings, in free time or after work. In the settlement, the children get the best of everything: cool air when it's hottest in July and August, nutritious meals, the attention not only of their parents but of all the members of the community. The founders of the system believe this will internally shape them into a new kind of Jew, free of influences from the diaspora that will hinder them here. They are meant to be strong, because they're no longer guests, they're home. They are meant to be brave, not fearful. They are meant to think 'we' instead of saying 'I, I, I', and to feel like part of a nation. The kibbutz is the laboratory for this new type of child-rearing.

Wilczyńska observes all this carefully. After all, she herself has doubts whether the way she and Korczak run the orphanage is best for the children. Wouldn't hearth and home be better – leaving them with their parents, in their own house, not a building like a barrack? Or maybe a semi-boarding institution, some middle path?

Or maybe like it is here? There is community everywhere: together, they eat, work and debate the future of their common village. In the evenings, when it's cooler, they even meet again: together, together, together. A collective. Wilczyńska can't yet tell whether people immerse themselves in it or drown.

Many doors remain open.

She compares this with Krochmalna Street. She asks questions, shyly – she's embarrassed by her clumsy Hebrew. She doesn't want to get in the way of their work (because she marvels at how hard they work here!), she waits for the brief breaks, when everyone takes shelter under the still-low palm trees. They reminisce about when their whole community would rest under one meagre tree, for years the only source of shade.

In a photo from the kibbutz, Stefa wears a white shirt, and her skirt is light-coloured as well. Without her black apron with the white collar, she seems younger.

***

The garden at Ein Harod has beehives. Wilczyńska likes to watch the beekeepers working there. She borrows a mask and listens to them talk about the bees. She tells the children about them:

> How smart these little bees are. By scent, by smell alone, they find their way to their hive from as far as three kilometres.
>
> And how they recognize colours! [...] You can't go up to them in a black apron – it makes them awfully mad.
>
> Long ago – Rachel told me – bees lived wild in a hot country, in India. They lived freely in the branches of trees. And when they were brought to Europe, people began raising them in tree hollows and dark hives. But now people think:

'Why did we take the sun away from the bees?'

Now they're building better and better stables, cowsheds and chicken coops – with windows. People are taking greater care with them. That makes the horses work better, the cows give better milk, the chickens lay more eggs.

So they make windows in the beehives too, so the bees have the sunlight they were used to in their homeland. And the bees are healthier, they work better and aren't as angry when they live in well-lit hives.[4]

She signs the letter: 'Dvora from Ein Harod.' Dvora, Deborah. In Hebrew: a bee.

***

The children also write to her. About longing, secrets, worries. Sometimes they complain, or ask about Palestine or sea travel. We still have over a dozen letters.[5]

Dear Pani Stefa,

Are you well in Palestine? How are you doing? How was your journey? Do you miss us? Thank you very much for the figs.

I am not writing much because I have nothing to write.

Please write back to me. Bye bye, long live Pani Stefa!

Fela Fetelbaum

So I'm starting to write my letter. So in school I'm already doing better, I have a bad report card, I have 5 Ds and one B for behaviour and a B for my work here. I'm better now I don't hit kids and I don't get as many cases as when I used to hit everybody. Lewek

Dear Pani Stefa,

I am very, very sorry that I haven't written you a single letter for a whole 6 weeks. I am not keeping up, it's true, but I really didn't have time because I had to prep for my lessons, since our class is going to get visited by a commission of 10 people, that is why we had classes in school on Saturday. Now dear Pani Stefa I can tell you I'm healthy as a donkey in Asia. I got a postcard for the highest weight. Over this year I've gained 8.1 kilos. And how are you feeling right now? Do you look well? And what is the weather like there? Are there many dates in Palestine? Forgive me for asking so many questions, but I'm very curious. I'm jealous that I can't go on a trip like yours.

Farewell! Pani and I send kisses from far away!

Pani Stefa, even though you are not too tough I would like very much if you were nice and wrote me an answer.

Yours respectfully, soon to be former house child Marysia, in Hebrew: Miriam

Dear pani stefa,

The first letter in my life so I am not exactly writing it. I wanted to know how you are doing and how you feel. I miss you. I would like to know about the children there. i am healthy

goodby Pani stefa

Balcia Żelazna

Bye Bye By goodby

To Palestine, to Pani Stefa from S. Elefant

Dear Pani Stefa, our Purim performances are getting close and rehearsals have started. The girls in our school did not get report cards because we didn't pay our dues, but I know what kind of repot card I got. I had two C's: in drawing and German, and an <u>A</u> for conduct. In physics a B, in drawing a B, in Polish a B, in home economics a B, in handicrafts a B. I got a section 200, for leaving my guard shift. Chajcia got a 700 for stealing 1 zł 70 gr from Edzia's bag. I keep ending up in category three, I think it's very wrong that I'm there, because I'm no dirtier than Dorcia (who almost never washes) or Mania, and they're in category two. I wrote a page that was read at newspaper reading. Pani Saba wrote that I'm sloppy and that Mania is in seventh grade, so she can't be in category three, and Dorcia is doing her best. At first the girls thought we'd be freer without you but that's not so at all. Enjoy your vacation, goodbye! S. Elefant

Dear Pani Stefa,

Ever since you left we have been playing with snow. Heniek said: when the girls are on their way to school, let's throw snow at them. So Maniusia Perłowicz was walking by and I was about to hit her then she ran away and I hit the steps and Pani Rózia told me to clean up the steps as punishment. Goodbye, Karolek [annotation in different handwriting: 'Karolek only swept three steps'].

My dearest Pani Stefa,

On behalf of the children thank you very much for your letter, which made a big impression on us. And also thank you for the material for the newsletter. [...] We and the Dr have already had a session of the Judicial Council. There were no tough sentences. The council sessions are going normally. Yesterday the Legislative Committee met and we decided to try out a reform of bedtime. The limit will be pushed back until 8:00, instead of 7:30 like now.

And now I will tell you my secret. I have gone and written an article in response to one the Dr wrote. I wrote it under the influence of outrage, meaning some things I said came out not very delicately. But I wasn't thinking about that at the time. I expected a much harsher response from the Dr and I was prepared for a lot of unpleasantness. But that wasn't the case. Pan Dr wrote me an apology and said he didn't mean to hurt me. When I read that, in an instant I felt happy. My ambition was satisfied.

But then I felt guiltier than even the most unpleasant article could have made me feel. If the Dr didn't mean to hurt me, then I was wrong to be outraged, so I shouldn't have spoken out so harshly. I thought I'd never be able to look the Dr in the eye again. I felt incredibly sorry. Yet the Dr behaved very gently toward me, so on the one hand I was even more furious at myself, but on the other my fear faded away. Now it's all over, but I still feel bad for behaving wrongly toward the Dr.

This has been my main worry while you've been away.

I'd really like to know your impressions from Palestine. But I know you're very busy, so I don't ask for a special response just for me. I'll settle for the general letter to all the children.

I wish you complete happiness with work and relaxation. Respectfully yours, Maria Libman.

Beloved Pani Stefa,

[...] I'm now sitting at table seven and writing to you. I think to myself: Pani Stefa must be so happy right now. Where it's nice and warm, with gardens, the air perfumed with oranges and finally among your own, among Jews, in a Jewish country. I am sure that if not for the duties calling you back here, you would happily stay. I am thinking about what will come later, as we approach the month when children apply to leave the Orphans' Home. I'm thinking about our hostel, and collecting information about the hostel on Dzika Street. Otherwise everything is running like clockwork, school, shifts, Saturdays with family and so on, over and over. Everything's moving at its own pace in the Orphans' Home, someone gets a section 700, because that's what's popular now. But it's a little sad at the table. Everyone is busy with their portion. Sometimes the kids just notice you used to eat the most at our table and they say: Pani Stefa's not here, so we'll get more. But actually it's sad. We mention you a lot. Sometimes people say: here we are eating potatoes with cabbage, and Pani Stefa's eating oranges and figs. Admittedly, there's more to life than food.

Sincerely, Jakób.

So I'll start my letter because I don't want to ask whether you're healthy, since then you'll tell me not to because it's a waste of paper. Meanwhile a few days after you left it was awfully cold, but now it's warmer and we are playing blind man's bluff. Once we even played tipcat, but Panna Rózia took it away, because we aren't allowed to play, but don't be mad at us, we couldn't help ourselves. At school things are the same as ever. Many thanks from the Hard Workers' Club for the 30 zł. you left. Meanwhile goodnight and please let me know if the Arabs have calmed down. Respectfully, Heniek Z.

Letter to Pani Stefa

I was very sad you left to go to a country so far away from us. But I was also kind of glad because once a year you'll get to relax. I really wanted winter to end as soon as possible. Because when you get here it will be warm, and my wishes will come true too, because everything will melt, as if March had come early.[...]Goodbye from far away [illegible signature, Horbeg?]

***

Dear Pani Stefa!!!

I was wondering if the figs that get handed out for morning snack are from Palestine? Thank you for the money you left for the Hard Workers Club. Because we'll be able to benefit more in summer. I miss you. I want you to come back as soon as possible. I'm doing good at school. I'm only doing badly in Hebrew class, Pan Jakób is sending a last case to the Judicial Council. I'm really sorry to admit

> it, but I wanted you to know. I'll wrap up my letter, since I have to go to school!!! All the best from Szlomek Nadel.

***

The file with the original letters in the archive of the Ghetto Fighters kibbutz includes a piece of paper. On it, Wilczyńska wrote down the names of the children who'd sent letters. Some were crossed out (she wrote them back?).

***

April 1931.

On the last day of her several weeks in Palestine, before sunset, she goes for a walk alone around the port city of Haifa, by the German colonists' district and the Bahá'í gardens on Mount Carmel. She soaks up as much as she can of the bright colours, the aromas. She doesn't want her memories of this place to be only of dry ground, of workers' faces, of rocks. Or of unrest: Arabs and Jews are fighting for every scrap of land, disappointed – equally – by British decision-making and the conditions the United Kingdom has set for co-existence in the Mandate.

Fejga to Stefa:

> I remember at home I was afraid I might stay there forever, rooted to the spot. I wanted to see a lot, to gain knowledge. I had no money and no prospects for change. I told myself: you just have to get onto a cart or into a train carriage and go, work it out later. And that's what I did. Of course it goes without saying that this move I'd gotten into my head had no chance of ending well. Now I've come here and I'm back in a quiet corner of the world. You have to shove off from the water's edge in the same way, like it or not, so that you're forced to fight later (because it's fighting for the sake of fighting, without a goal. Rotland says: even if the ideal itself is an illusion, the ascent to it is not). You need a little energy to manage it, meanwhile I care so little about anything. What ultimately attracted me here was the unknown future, but now that I can see its contours more clearly, I don't want it.
>
> All right, enough about me. I can tell from the decisions you've made about your trip here that you'll stay at the Orphans' Home. Maybe you'll be less enthusiastic about working, but there you can always give more to those who have nothing.

> You keep talking about us meeting under different circumstances. I don't believe it. And if I'm going to keep on as I am, and stay this way for years, I'd rather we didn't meet at all. That's cowardice on my part. I dreamed we were both coming here. My dream clearly meant to justify my coming here without you.
>
> I got two letters from you on the road, two postcards, I myself sent a second and a card. I hope our correspondence continues like this. Once you're back and overwhelmed with work again, you'll forget that a girl is stuck here in Ein Harod. As is said about people like me: neither of use to God, nor to men.[6]

Stefa to Fejga, while on her return journey:

> My last southern night, the moon is out on the ship. I still find it hard to focus my mind on the work waiting for me in Warsaw. And I think, when will you stop being so sad, or as you call it, 'bored.' I have no choice but to believe in you. I can't simply give up. Because I think that I'll miss you and I won't want to travel anywhere else ever again. And that is what you've inherited from me, my spiritual daughter.
>
> Remember you promised me you'd take your temperature twice a day for a week. And write me. And say what new sicknesses you've caught, apart from all your old chronic ones. Biiiiig kisses! Our farewell at the harbour was too cold, but you understand that was better for us both.[7]

***

The ship is swaying, Wilczyńska writes unevenly. She mentions there's a painter travelling incognito in third class ('he writes a lot, rather than painting, and gazes artistically at the sea'). The French dealer Ambroise Vollard has ordered a series of engravings from him, illustrations to the Bible. He will work on them for a long time, his labour interrupted by the outbreak of the Second World War, but in 1957, Marc Chagall will finally successfully publish 150 etchings of Biblical scenes.

After returning from Palestine, Chagall writes to his friend: 'Returned from Eretz Israel. Happy. Though not a Zionist and not a "nationalist" but as a Jew.'[8] Later, in an interview, he says:

> I wanted to see it all with my own eyes – how they build a country. [...] A Jew walks there assertively, and works – this small group of

> 170,000 people intends to continue what they started, in spite of the political and economic atmosphere […]. And they are all like that – they all have this enthusiasm: the merchants and citizens in the city as well as those in the kibbutzim, where life is, of course, much harder […]. By the way, I felt especially good in [the Jezreel valley], in the kibbutzim…I even wanted to live among them…[9]

On her journey home, Wilczyńska takes every opportunity to keep speaking Hebrew, to learn new vocabulary words.

***

She knows more and more of them, not only the simplest expressions, which suffice on a tourist trip. She collects expressions that are useful in daily life.

(Is she already thinking about leaving for good?)

She feels more and more resignation, her work wears her out, her routine gets under her skin.

> I arrived in Warsaw after 7 days and nights on the road. I stopped at my brother's, where after a bath I slept for 24 hours. Only after three days did I make it to the OH. I felt embarrassed at the simply generous, moving reception from the children and adults in the OH, Hostel and *The Little Review*. Everywhere I found a new order and I felt so unnecessary that I don't feel as bad thinking of leaving. I don't even care about the tasks they left for me. If they knew I wasn't coming back, then they wouldn't wait and would have figured everything out themselves. I am meant to start work in a week, but I am doing my best to set everything up right away so that in future I won't have to arrange substitutes. Among all these pale people I stand out with my dark face. But before long this lacquer will surely come off, because I am absolutely freezing. Snow, mud, cold. But there you've probably got the khamsin!

And she continues:

> I didn't know it was possible to get so far away for two months from what had been your life's purpose for so many years. And I'm sad, but I'm sure I will adjust, once I get to work.[10]

Korczak writes about the Home with similar resignation and disillusion, about there being no one to hand it over to, about getting old. He is looking for a new challenge. In the mid-1930s he parts ways with Our Home and Maria Falska. There could have been several reasons, no explanation is conclusive. Since the start of the Depression, the Orphans' Home has run into huge financial difficulties, cutbacks have been necessary. Our Home – for ethnic Polish children – has been able to count on greater support from government authorities and isn't dependent on philanthropists to keep it afloat. It's a conflict of ideas: the microcosm of the Orphans' Home, which creates an appearance of domestic life rather than confronting the outside world, while in Our Home, Falska has been implementing a different concept, with the boarding house open, literally as well, to the neighbourhood. Finally, emotions might have been the deciding factor, given Falska's independence and openly expressed opposition to Korczak's views.

Even Korczak is tired too. He's thinking of moving out of Krochmalna Street.

***

Except the place both Wilczyńska and Korczak look to with hope, where things are meant to be easier or certainly at least *different* – Palestine – has its own troubles too.

(So is there any point – she wonders – in going? After all, hasn't she said many times you can't run away from yourself, not even to India?)

Fejga to Stefa:

> There aren't any innovations I can introduce, but I can't stand helplessness. I want something different, I demand someone new, but I can't seem to put the finishing touches on anything. So I'm having a tough time. People have worked out a system and a routine over the years, and I remain in the background. Because the conditions are completely different here, after all. Here it's the children who can teach me, not I them. They have a teacher who knows every blade of grass, every hill, every bird in Palestine. What beautiful, rich language. How beautifully he teaches them. And compared to him I'm like a baby barely starting to take her first steps [...]. The children demand answers, they're interested and I must respond. And I keep on saying 'I don't know'.
>
> How different life is here: quiet, monotonous, every impression sinks in and has a powerful effect. I mean moods, which I so dislike

> and which so often strike me. Naturally first and foremost is my awful, ambitious ego.[11]

Wilczyńska to Fejga:

> I won't put a date because I don't know when I'll send this.
>
> When I now compare in my mind, I can see you're mistaken, it *is* easier to work where you are and it's better than here by any measure. But the heart of the difficulty is that you can't get away from these comparisons. Because to forget, to erase from your memory everything you've done so far and start from scratch means to overcome the ego, even if you don't view what you've done so far to be flawed.
>
> You want me to write about myself. I'm finding it difficult to work in the boarding house, after twenty years! The issues and doubts are different from before, but there are no fewer of them.[12]

For the first time she mentions leaving the country for good.

***

Wilczyńska to Fejga: 'Half of a person's life is longing.'[13]

She increasingly finds she doesn't want to write at all. The closer they get to summer vacation, the less time there is; the hustle and bustle, the Hostel residents' exams, the end of the school year. She'd like solitude and quiet, which she seeks out with greater and greater regularity.

In another letter she writes:

> There's more work, but fewer hands to do it. And I was annoyed at myself for my last weepy letter. One must never write under the influence of emotion, and especially when the letter goes on so long. On the 15th I switch places with the Dr and go to Gocławek for 6 weeks. I think that after taking all that time off I should work more in the summer, and I won't stay for so long in Warsaw, where it's empty, quiet and I enjoy it so much.[14]

She has been going to Gocławek for over a decade, but even so feels nervous. She used to be afraid of the work itself, of the rain that poured ceaselessly for day after day, of the children getting sick – now these don't bother her.

It's herself she's afraid of, her *old age*. She doesn't want to frighten the children with her own being, spoil their joy with her appearance.

She's also awaiting news from Palestine and preparing for her next trip. She's waiting for confirmation that she'll have a job there. She's afraid that her Hebrew – clumsy and crude – won't be suitable for anything. She doesn't want to run an institution, which is what they're proposing. 'Once again I'll have to rule, advise, decide – I don't want to, I don't have the moral fortitude anymore. To prepare myself for nursing? An infant? I'm afraid I'll lack the physical strength.'[15]

She mentions to Fejga: 'Yesterday I was in an old-age home for the intelligentsia. I think it's still too soon for that living graveyard.'[16]

A string of house children and acquaintances are leaving for Palestine They come to Stefa for advice. Wilczyńska writes: 'poor Palestine, if it ends up with more of these people who are going to her because "we have no better option here"'.[17]

Though the children want for nothing on Krochmalna Street, they can also see what is happening outside the walls of the Home.

***

She selects this letter for 'Little Corner': 'Wunia asks why we don't make it so no one is poor. And if we can't do that at all, then at least let the poor dream beautiful dreams.'

***

She feels more and more unnecessary.

She puts off her departure. She vacillates. She thinks she's ready to make a decision: 1932 will be her last year at the OH '(and probably the Dr's too). But I can't muster the courage to make the next decision. If I was sure I could master the language, I wouldn't be asking you for advice. So maybe to Russia. Maybe to some hospital. Anywhere but the orphanage, where I feel so hopeless and without a future. I'm too young for an old-age home. Mentally, with every step I bid farewell to this Home, which has been so dear to me for almost twenty years.'[18]

She dreams of moving out of the Home, but does nothing to bring that any closer.

In spring of 1932 she writes to Fejga:

> How I miss the sun and the warmth.

> I'm not working well. I'm like some 'third person'. Cheerfully and—I can't call it 'indifferently', like you do, but not like 'the old me'. I only do my best not to analyse it. And I devote less time to the children than to the Hostel, the personnel, the alumni.
>
> The young adults are more worth helping, because they are raising themselves and find it very, very difficult and tough. But the children I can't yet help in any way at all. At least I don't see how I could help them?[19]

In summer she goes on a short vacation to the health resort of Jaremcze on the Prut River.

(Why there?)

Stefa to Fejga, in late July:

> I feel your silence is punishment for my last, heartless letter. I don't know if I deserve such harsh punishment. You may believe me or not, but I assure you, the only person with whom I would now like to spend my leave is you.
>
> Perhaps you assume that I had many offers from family and to go with generous people, and I turned them all down. But I went on my own. In fact I nearly didn't go, because I'm not physically tired and have nothing from which I need to rest up. I can still feel the effects of relaxing in Ein Harod. But as for my nerves, after a hard winter (material worries, professional unpleasantness, etc.) I've become a terrible shrew. Even worse than I was. But I don't want to let myself be like that and so I went off somewhere a bit quiet to sort myself out. But it's that same old struggle, I'm not brave enough to quit the boarding house, but I can't get the thought out of my mind.
>
> So I sit here and travel around various backwaters, and am sad you're not with me. It's beautiful and wild on the Prut (a river in the Carpathian Mountains, maybe you've already forgotten). And I swim, and also get tickled by little trout-fish. And I have to carefully avoid the rocks so I don't hurt my feet like I did in Ein Harod. Around here it smells like hay and meadows, and forest. The Hutsul Rusyns dress in colourful shirts like your blouse that's embroidered in bright colours at the neck.
>
> Peace, quiet, and most important of all; no one calls me to the phone or asks about anything. The children are at summer camps, two hundred of them altogether. Everything there runs so smoothly

and tidily it's like winding a gramophone when they go to eat or to the forest, or on errands or to the beach, so even the staff seems unnecessary. So why go back?

I'm sure you're laughing, naughty girl, and crowing that you were right. No, miss smarty-pants, you don't know a thing. No one knows, so let's not philosophize.

Anyway, here I sit by myself, spending pennies, because it's very cheap here, the journey is the only thing that's expensive.

Write to Warsaw, because from here I am going to the Romanian border (to Zaleszczyki in Poland), where the heat is +40 degrees, where peaches grow, and grapes in summer. But by 25 August I must be at work. Whenever there's a full moon, I remember saying goodbye to you in Haifa.[20]

***

In the file with the letters from her to Fejga is an undated postcard. 'There's no art to dying – the art is in living.'

(When did she send it?)

Notes

1. L. Süsswein, *Palestyna buduje się…* (Kraków: 1939), p.5.
2. *Mały Przegląd*, 8 May 1931.
3. K. Pruszynski, *Palestyna po raz trzeci* (Warsaw 1933), p.92.
4. *Mały Przegląd*, 8 May 1931.
5. The archive of the Ghetto Fighters Kibbutz, inventory number 12899.
6. Letter from Fejga Lifszyc to Stefania Wilczyńska, April 1931.
7. Letter from Stefania Wilczyńska to Fejga Lifszyc, April 1931.
8. B. Harshav, *Marc Chagall and His Times: A Documentary Narrative* (Stanford: 2003), p.374.
9. Ibid., 375-376.
10. Letter from Stefania Wilczyńska to Fejga Lifszyc, April 1931.
11. Letter from Fejga Lifszyc to Stefania Wilczyńska, 1931.
12. Letter from Stefania Wilczyńska to Fejga Lifszyc, 1931.
13. Letter from Stefania Wilczyńska to Fejga Lifszyc, April 1931 [?]
14. Letter from Stefania Wilczyńska to Fejga Lifszyc, 3 July 1931.
15. Letter from Stefania Wilczyńska to Fejga Lifszyc, 10 July 1931 or 1932.
16. Letter from Stefania Wilczyńska to Fejga Lifszyc, 10 July 1931 or 1932.
17. Ibid.
18. Letter from Stefania Wilczyńska to Fejga Lifszyc, 1 January 1932.
19. Letter from Stefania Wilczyńska to Fejga Lifszyc, 18 April 1932.
20. Letter from Stefania Wilczyńska to Fejga Lifszyc, 26 July 1932.

13

Since Korczak moved out in 1933 ('3 whole days and nights he lives in Bielany district and is here in an advisory capacity, but 4 days he works for himself')[1] Wilczyńska tends to day-to-day business on Krochmalna Street herself.

The daily schedule looks the same. The Home looks the same.

Children keep coming—like Icio Belfer, whom I'd later meet in Tel Aviv as Itzhak. Wilczyńska does mnemonic exercises not to get their names mixed up. She leaves *The Little Review*. She doesn't write about the reasons for her decision. Igor Newerly becomes the new editor. In the anniversary issue of January 1937, he names her as a co-worker.

(Does she reclaim that tiny amount of time for herself, so that she can more closely follow what's in the papers? Is that enough to keep up-to-date with the world? She is 47 and has a lot of catching up to do.)

The news from Germany is constantly troubling. In the elections in early 1933, the Nazi Party won more than 40 per cent of the vote. Before long, Adolf Hitler will seize absolute power and the first concentration camp will be built in Dachau (the words 'Dachau' and 'concentration camp' will prompt concern for several years, but not the dread that automatically sets off a string of associations: skeletons, hunger, brutality, experiments, mass killings). On 1 April 1933, the central leadership of the boycott campaign in Germany receives a list of Jewish stores, shopping centres, lawyers and doctors. At 10 o'clock on the dot, members of the Nazi Party take to the streets of Berlin, Dresden and many other cities. They set up posts in front of the locations on the list, putting up posters on store windows, doors and the walls of buildings reading: 'Don't Buy from Jews'. In Hamburg, all the stores on the list are marked with the word 'Jew' in red paint. There's also a boycott in Breslau, where the store windows show the epithet 'Jew-Pole'. The city police commissioner orders only the second half of this epithet to be erased.

In Austria, Chancellor Engelbert Dollfuss issues a decree suspending parliament. In the Soviet Union, for over a decade Stalin has been bringing in a new order, and for the past year some of those paying the price have been the millions dying of hunger in Ukraine—though the papers won't report on that for a long time. They will, however, write about the World's Fair, taking place this year in Chicago. Its glistening slogan: *A Century of Progress.*

And in Poland? Things are only slightly calmer. The fifteen years of independence have already seen over a dozen prime ministers, three presidents, and the one and only Marshal – Poland's true ruler, Józef Piłsudski.

(Does Wilczyńska vote? For whom? In the most recent election, did she support the government or the minority parties? Although she declares she doesn't care for politics, is she capable of being indifferent to them when so much is going on?)

In 1933 a recession is still raging in Poland, unemployment reaches forty percent. Those who have jobs often work only a few days a week and do not earn enough to live on.

The Institute of Social Economy publishes essays submitted for a contest titled 'Diary of an Unemployed Man'.

> A saddler and leatherworker's family has five members – including two minor children. It sustains itself only on two soups received from the Committee as well as 150 kg of potatoes. Having 50 kg of coal, every day they cook potatoes all day long, they do not buy bread at all, one child is fed at school […].
>
> An ironmoulder's family, with four members, spends 12 złotys a week on food; their two meals a day consist of: potatoes, cabbage, bread, they buy no meat or milk, at most 10 kg of pork fat […].[2]
>
> The family of a locksmith (he, his wife and two children) from Warsaw: 'finding a job in today's economic crisis is like winning the lottery […] we started selling our things off, my wife had a sheepskin, a jacket, it cost 120 złotys, we sold it for 40, later our gold engagement rings […] then my wife got sick, I couldn't pay for a doctor, we sold an oak table and chairs […]. Our most frequent foods are flour, potatoes and kasha, because bread is a luxury now as well. Plenty of times after spending the whole day criss-crossing the city looking for work, I'd come home and even though my belly was cramping from hunger, I'd lose my appetite as soon as my wife asked, 'well, how did it go?' And my boy would run up and shout: dad, give me some bread. And I haven't got a scrap, you run from workshop to workshop, from

> factory to factory, and get nothing but the same response: we work three days a week, layoffs tomorrow, we're closing on the 15th, we don't pay our people because there's nothing to pay with.'[3]

> A leatherworker's family, with four members, supports itself from the mother's earnings, 1.5 to 2 złotys a day; the father has walked out on the family – he lives separately; the mother, who is employed in peddling, does not return home all day, she lives on soup for 30 groszy a day, eaten wherever in the city; the children's daily sustenance is a half-litre of milk for the 10-month-old boy and tea and bread for the older girl […].
>
> An unskilled worker who takes on a variety of jobs: 'I've got nothing left to pawn; I've got nothing to sell either, because I sold my pillowcases for 1.5 złotys each, my sheets for 2.5 złotys apiece, the bedspread for 11 złotys, the dresses for 6 złotys, for three shirts 3.5 złotys. Today I've got nothing to wear because I haven't bought anything in recently. We currently haven't got clothes or underwear, so we wear them all week and wash them on Saturday – by the way, there is soap.'[4]

***

Three linen-makers, nine office workers, five kindergarten teachers, three hairdressers, fifteen salesladies, three housewives, two teachers, eight nurses, four pedagogues and four printers, three electro-technicians, nine locksmiths, eight peddlers, twenty-seven seamstresses and eleven tailors, four carpenters, a musician, a leatherworker, a butcher, a photographer, a painter, an optician, a dance teacher, a manicurist, two beggars, two prostitutes and three convicted thieves.

Almost forty people of whom nothing is known – twice as many as those who spent only a brief time at Krochmalna Street.

Nineteen dead. Fifty emigrants. These are some of the over 400 house children who've now left the Home.

Wilczyńska writes them letters. She sends money, if she has it. She buys presents. She visits them. She keeps them company, discreetly, when they get a job or go hungry because unemployment is constantly rising. She is not in the habit of complaining, people even call her an optimist when she explains that in these social conditions she can do no different.

(Or maybe – she asks herself – this is just her way of accepting things as they are?)[5]

She sees them becoming mothers and fathers, losing children. She worries. They visit her more and more often at Krochmalna Street, asking for help finding jobs. The Home serves them free soup.

Each new generation of children at the Home is more foreign to her. She feels guilty about that. She doesn't know if she yearns for the kibbutz, for Fejga or just for being anywhere else than Krochmalna Street and Gocławek.

Things are changing everywhere but in her own life. When she can, she studies Hebrew at the Tarbut, a Jewish educational society, or on her own, but her heart isn't in it. It frustrates her that she doesn't have the patience for writing letters either. The form feels restrictive, she'd rather talk face-to-face.

***

Late April 1933, Stefa to Fejga:

> For shame, my darling girl, sending me as empty a piece of paper as that. Such distance, so much time and so much waiting, then for me to have so little, practically nothing to read. Even though I sent you a long and detailed letter a week ago, I'm writing again now because I felt so awful (even painful) after reading your calculations of my arrival. Maybe Rywka Zwykielska will tell you in a month or two how hard things are here, how difficult it is to leave. I keep making plans, it's true, it's so good to live in hope, it costs me nothing. It's just too bad you get a disappointment.
>
> I've told you, haven't I? I've been saving up money since I got back from seeing you. I'm stingy with myself, I keep saying no to things, this year I'll even swear off vacation, I'll be gone for a week at most. But if someone from our family isn't working, we have to help them. After all, in my chosen family, this handful of former house children (not all of them) with whom I live, people are also getting married, having children, dying, getting sick, and I would feel guilty too if I were earning money but unable to spend any of it on anyone or for anyone.
>
> And in summer I'm undecided about those heat waves there, and I don't want to see the sunburned fall in Eretz. As for what's happening now in Germany, and as for the (horrible) Depression, can we even make longer-term plans?
>
> I don't hold it against you, my dearest girl, because I know you gave me smart advice, but you've poured cold water over me and so

> discouraged me from my plan to move there permanently, you should understand how prudent I ought to be in setting off on a visit, the last one of my life. After all I'm getting older, I'll find it harder and harder because of my energy and finances. I must think about my quiet corner here, though it's foolish in times like these to wish for security in old age.[6]

She's doing her best to save money, not only to go abroad. For the first (?) time in years, she permits herself to desire something – she plans to rent a room.

> [...] [M]y own small, quiet digs in town, maybe in a new neighbourhood, in the Workers' Assoc. housing cooperative in Żoliborz district (behind Gdański Station), or maybe in town. So I can spend two nights there, two evenings of quiet for a little writing or reading, then in the morning, arrive at Krochm. well-rested.[...] It's an expense to be sure, but I find it a very necessary one. Because I'm already too drained.[...][7]

She underlines the word 'quiet'.

The Warsaw Housing Cooperative in Żoliborz district, which opened for business in 1927, is home to activists and sympathizers of the Polish Socialist Party, to workers, to leftists, and to the intelligentsia, including the architect Helena Syrkus and her husband Szymon, as well as the author and educator Igor Abrambow-Newerly, his wife Basia (a former house child) and their son Jerzy. Apartments in the Cooperative are meant to be cheap, but aesthetically pleasing and functional, and whole complex – socially-minded. The heart of the development is the Social Home, which houses a pre-school, a hostel for young workers and a medical clinic. For the residents' children, it organizes daytime summer camps, a theatre troupe and extra meals. In response to the needs of female residents – who find it hard to balance professional work with their domestic obligations – it creates a mutual-aid labour exchange ('we cannot make progress alone!').[8] The Social Home hosts meetings of the Warsaw Housing Cooperative Residents' Mutual Aid Association, which goes by the name 'Glass Houses.'

(Why does she choose there and not somewhere else?)

Fejga to Stefa, May:

> You can't get out of the habit of always having to help everyone, giving, granting pleasure, but you treat yourself hard as stone and

> God forbid someone give you a present on your birthday.[...]A cheap ride to Palestine and back I think is 500 złotys, I can't imagine that sum is out of reach. You shouldn't find life here costly. There'll be no presents here or in Poland for some time. And I've been so counting on you coming here. Dozens of trees, bushes and flowers have blossomed. I keep doing the math to see if they'll still be here when you arrive. How I wish I could freeze them in place so they can greet you in their finery. I've been feeling guilty for being such a bad host to you back then. Maybe you're still making up your mind? Because I can see that if you don't come now, it won't be for another year and you'll not only see me changed, but already old. Here, among twenty-year-olds, I at 28 already do look old. I've left the most difficult part for the end. You're right: I've been holding back until we can speak in person, and as for gossip, people are gossiping, I don't even know who, because I keep my private business hidden. There's someone here [Chaim Biber], who longs for me, entirely despite my attitude toward him. He's trying everything to get us together, despite my wishes. He believes I will change my mind. And I'm so passive. I've only managed to drag it out. This business has been going on for a year. I'm making him get out of Palestine. Maybe to Poland, maybe to his brother in Belgium, to study. I'm meant to join him a year later. The boy really is perfect, honest, unusually capable, hardworking, conscientious. Homely, trusting, naïve. I think that gives you a picture of him. I feel I'll never be able to love him. But the way he puts it is, 'Why, it's great to have a loyal dog...' He swears I'll be as free as I want. He's heard my stories about you. Sometimes he's afraid of you, and sometimes he sees you as an ally in his struggle with me. If he comes to Poland, I'm sure he'll visit you right away. He'll spend a year there, and then we're meant to meet in Belgium. These are only plans for now, what will really happen I don't know. But I'm not going to make things any harder for myself, I'm not dwelling on it. I'd much rather fall in love again, like before, but without that anguish. Now, looking at him, I keep my feet on the ground.[9]

Fejga is looking for a new place for herself, another kibbutz. She wants a change.

Stefa to Fejga:

> I am sure you already know everything about me. But I know so little of you. To be frank, your not going didn't worry me much. A bout of

> fever again, a scorpion, who knows what, but in the end the grey workday is the same always and everywhere. You will never leave your humours or moods behind anywhere. You will drag that package with you everywhere you go. Like it or not, it's with you. You can't run away from it, not even to India. [...]
>
> By the way, Tyla, that beautiful girl, came to see me. She's looking for a job in Warsaw. She has a little daughter, she's happy and says how much she enjoys having a baby. Such joy. And Basia says that three-month-old son of hers is pure happiness. Both of them are living and working completely for the baby. I think maybe a baby will give you that joy in life that that you've lost.
>
> There are so many unnecessary children. They wander a world where no one has need of what we might call a 'child of the century'. But so many people do need their own child. Maybe, maybe, you too are one of those.[10]

In 1933 Biber comes to Europe and looks for a job there.

Fejga to Stefa:

> I am so jealous of Biber that he got to sit in your room and talk to you. As if the two of us had switched places. You'd prefer me to him – and he'd prefer me to you. I wanted you to meet him. Reading your letter made me sad. It was like you were already laying me in my grave. The only solution is a baby. No, I don't want a baby if it's meant to be my way out, to be my everything. I'm sure you remember me saying the same even then. Back when I needed one even more. It's not actually external conditions that make a person happy or unhappy. Look: I'm healthy, fit to work, fairly well-liked (I have become so much more outgoing, softer and nicer to people, I'm not homely, I look young, boys like me, one of them loves me, I have close friends who care for me). You'd think I'd be happy. But no, I'm still restless. I'm running away from myself. I'm constantly seeking out thrills, even small ones (India! Why, how amazing that would be!).[...]
>
> Now I've started chasing after Biber. Poland. Belgium. His greatest dream is to share one room with me in Ein Harod or somewhere else, just together. Yet when I think of something permanent, fear seizes me, though I'm well aware that if my Biber vanished on me it would be a horrible disappointment. As I write I'm worried you might misunderstand what I'm saying. I wish so

> badly that we could talk, be together, for a little while. I feel that would bring me peace. Like that time, you remember, after you got here. To advise me in person. Now I know I'm dragging you into not only my own affairs, but those of a stranger as well, but I know you'll forgive me, you won't be angry at me for abusing your patience. After all, it wouldn't be the first time.[11]

Before Fejga joins Biber, she writes to Stefa in the fall of 1933:

> I think I wrote to you about Sara? She's living in Jerusalem now with a young man who loves her very much, and she loves him too, though not as much. She's doing better than when she was alone, but still not well. Are we maladjusted to life? People usually say this Weltschmerz young women feel ends when they get married. Why is it different for us? What are we living for? And how can we live differently? This torments me endlessly, though we hustle and bustle to keep our minds off it. No, I'm not contemplating suicide anymore, firstly because I know I won't go through with it, and secondly because I'm finding pleasure on my search too, although momentary and insubstantial. But this sort of life rules out even the thought of having a baby. I've talked about this a lot with Biber, and if you can, get him to talk to you about it sometime. I'd like you to write about yourself, not about the Orphans' Home and the others. Why should you wait, come to Belgium [to see me], we'll send Biber off and it will just be the two of us again. There's so much I yearn for. That's all that I have left of my emotions: yearning.[12]

When Fejga comes to Poland for a few weeks, they spend every free moment (there are not many) together.

***

In 1933 the Orphans' Aid Society celebrates its twenty-fifth anniversary. *Our Review* publishes Janusz Korczak's article 'Twenty-Five Years'.

> As we look through the annual and anniversary report, we feel a sense of embarrassment. Has the press fulfilled its duty? Has it not written too rarely and quietly about this institution over the years? In the balance of information about social work, the cultural life of the capital and the achievements of research on the child – has

Orphans' Aid had the stature that we owe it, that it deserves?[…]We find our excuse in the fact that the last quarter-century has abounded in such jarring, stormy incidents that we have not had enough time for what is quiet and oriented toward the future. In any event, it is in the nature of the harried work of journalism that one must stubbornly demand, repeatedly and adeptly using supporting circumstances to force one's way through the thicket of paragraphs, information and appeals. Who knows how necessary endurance is, so that people learn and remember?

But unfortunately, amid the flood of today's woes and burdens, some fear that the existence of the Orphans' Aid Society might come to an end once its growth has slowed. For years there are no foundations, the number and size of one-time donations has fallen, the Society's membership has been shrinking, donations, once so large in size, arrive increasingly stingily – grants are shrinking –our balance sheet is contracting. […] It is difficult for the uninitiated to realize what cutbacks, and how painful, the Board intends to introduce, for when feeding the 107 children of the Orphans' Home costs 35,000 złotys, when based on membership fees we now predict a draft budget of only 40,000 złotys – when feeding the 50 children of the Little Rose costs a sum of 20,000 złotys – it eats up our income from events and donations.

What about heating, clothing, lighting, teaching and entertainment? Our budget line for water is 3,500 złotys, as much as we make from selling milk at the farm in Gocławek. In the introduction to the report from 1928 we read:

Why do we find it so difficult? Do we only find it difficult, or also worse and lonelier? […] We no longer have philanthropy, but social care, no longer capricious and insufficient private initiative, not one 'drop' any longer but a whole 'sea'. We solicit funds: the size of subsidies is growing, but the quantity of member fees and donations is shrinking. This process of 'rationalizing' aid and care must take place gradually, without sudden jumps. […] We appeal for donors to our cause. […] Our budget for [1928] was closed with a deficit of about 21,000 złotys.

In the introduction to the report for 1929 we read:

We have exceeded 200 children and young people – this is not the extent of our intentions, but a limit at which we must now stop. Our only interest is to maintain, to retain, not retreat, not reduce. […] We receive encouragement from our monitors: contributions

> are flowing in. Even, or perhaps mainly, those also feeling stretched are contributing. [...] There are few one-time donations – this is a large gap in the budget. The budget for next year: 250,000 złotys – of that sum, 35,000 złotys is subsidy, the rest is to come from member fees, donations, fundraising events, etc. A child costs three złotys a day. We cannot cut back without doing harm, and we must not do harm... The deficit for [1929] amounts to 10,000 złotys.
>
> In 1930 it is worse:
>
> The economic crisis has now affected the Society. Revenue from member fees has shrunk by a total of 4,000 złotys. – Fundraising events brought in 6,700 złotys less. Warsaw city hall has contributed 10,000 złotys less.
>
> We commend this to your attention and remind you that a meeting for members and invited guests will take place on 26 Nov at 12:00 at the Orphans' Home.[13]

***

On that Sunday, the auditorium of the Orphans' Home is full. Chairs are set up in narrow rows, but even so there aren't enough seats for everyone. Guests (mainly men in elegant tailcoats and ties, and here and there a women's hat among them) stand against the wall and in the aisles between the chairs. It's packed. Those in attendance include Minister of Labour and Welfare Dr Stefan Hubicki, Deputy Minister of Welfare Dr Eugeniusz Piestrzyński, Deputy Minister of Internal Affairs Władysław Korsak, Mayor of Warsaw Zygmunt Słomiński, a representative from the governor, the county administrator, the heads of the city's welfare and health departments, the eminent historian Professor Mojżesz Schorr, representatives of scientific institutions, social and economic organizations, and members of the Orphans' Aid Society. Now Maurycy Mayzel, chairman of the Society, takes the floor:

> From 1929 to 1933 we have been fighting a new battle, a battle with the Depression, a battle which nonetheless fills us with mounting dread, since even financial aid from the city has shrunken considerably, significantly hindering our continued activity. Our budget, which a few years ago amounted to 250,000 złotys, has now fallen by over one-third. It is true that food prices have gone down considerably, but even so we are going through difficult times. [...] [W]e own our own building, our own summer camp, an open square

> near our building, an agricultural farm, a boarding house, a winter resort, the Hostel, a tailor's shop, a laundry, our own dentist's office and perpetual funds, which now total over 600,000 złotys after devaluation, meaning they were considerably greater when we were entrusted with them [...]. We have no liquid assets.[14]

From the corner, a photographer speaks up: 'Pardon me, mister chairman – one second.' He takes a picture.

Minister Hubicki recalls his student days when he met Korczak. He assures the Doctor that he is moved, that he supports innovative pedagogy.

Deputy Minister Korsak says: 'we give our best wishes to those who stand at [this institution's] head – wishes for growth, success and further recognition in society.'[15]

Mayor Słomiński: 'I am very glad to be celebrating an Institution that is doing great work on its own initiative without relying on either the national or city government. I can only declare that this Institution helps the city, and to the best of our abilities we will always remember it.'[16]

Chairman Mayzel: 'Ladies and Gentlemen, please allow me once again to thank Minister Hubicki for the candy he generously brought for the children, and which I am sure will taste all the sweeter because it comes from you, Minister.'[17]

Anka Pawe takes the floor. I picture her in my mind: she is ten or eleven years old. Here she is, stepping into the middle of an auditorium full of guests in dark suits: ministers, councilmen, lawyers. She is the delegate of the children's council of the Orphans' Home. Maybe she has stage fright, she stumbles over the first sentence: 'as the delegate of the house children of the Orphans' Home, thank you on behalf of all my colleagues for your aid and the care you have given us. I hope that your work will not be in vain, for when we grow up, the debt will be repaid as much as possible in a different way.'[18]

(Shlomo told me a story: 'Once a concert was organized at the Home, with one of our house children playing the violin. I remember how excited Pani Stefa was when his turn came and he was walking into the middle of the room. She followed him with her gaze, as if she wanted make sure he didn't stumble. She had tears in her eyes, she was flushed and her fists were red, clenched with worry. My Frida looked the same when our Yossi was collecting his diploma at school.')

I zoom in on the only surviving photo of the celebration and I look for Wilczyńska. She might be sitting at the table (the photograph was taken from behind it), off to the side, outside the frame, or be hidden by guests in one of the rows (she could also be standing in the gallery, with the children). I don't see her.

***

Korczak also speaks at the celebration. He reads letters from alumni, which they still send to the Home:

> Beloved Pani Stefa,
>
> I received your letter as well as the announcement of 20 May, many thanks.
>
> I understand perfectly that it's difficult for you to write back, since you're perpetually busy, which is also why I was so incredibly happy to get your letter and the photograph of a few former house children. How lucky I am that you've taken an interest in me and took the time to write a little note. God bless you!!!
>
> You send a few questions, which I am happy to answer. I'll actually see my girl soon, since I've already sent the paperwork and the money. I expect that in three months we'll be all married up. But there's a lot of resistance from her parents. She has fairly rich ones, they own a candy factory. On top of all that they're religious, in other words, Hasidim. They would allow the marriage, but only if I returned to Poland. And can I do that? Never. Anyway, she dreams of going away, even to the ends of the earth, to be with me. How beautiful is that, really, my dear Pani Stefa?
>
> You're right. These still-foreign surroundings make me sad, but it's also true that you forget about the bad things.
>
> You and the Doctor have done everything that was and is in your power for society. I don't know if there's anyone who can repay you both. For hundreds of orphans, you are their substitute mothers and fathers. You are more than a mother and a father.
>
> There's one big favour I want to ask. I'd like a photograph. I want to always have you in my memory. So I can always see my Mother…
>
> All my love, Mama.
>
> Your son, who is grateful to you for everything
>
> Bronisław Gelblat[19]
>
> Beloved Pani Stefa, I would like herewith to offer my sincerest thanks for remembering me. Secondly I would like to beg forgiveness for not writing right away, but please believe me that it was no fault of mine.

Here a person is always so busy he barely has a few minutes for a meal. There's no such thing as Saturday, or Sunday, or a holiday. [...] Why, anyway you know perfectly well that I've never liked writing much. [...] An important story from the Orphans' Home comes to mind and how it warms my heart. I remember now – it was in 1921 – once at lunch there was meat for everyone, only I didn't get any. But a year later, on that same day, no one got meat – except me alone!

Dear and Beloved Pani Stefa, Although I stopped writing two years ago, there has never been a day when I didn't think of you. The reason for such a long silence was that I stopped paying my annual contribution to the Orphans' Home. The fact it was my duty to pay, but I could not and still cannot, makes me feel ashamed and I was waiting until maybe I could pay later. It weighs on my heart that I can't even send five dollars a year. We are going through awful times in America. Reading your letter, Beloved Pani, I was so happy that I wept for joy, though I'm not so happy in my heart. I will share my woes. My husband has not worked in three years. There is terrible unemployment, seven million people without work. Now he has become very anxious, he has lost all desire for anything, but I don't let him sulk around the house. I have no time in my day for worrying. I have two adorable boys. Robert turned five in June and Edward is three. I no longer live at the address where you last wrote to me: I have moved four times in three years. I'm living a nomad's life now because rent is expensive, and here we have a nasty custom: if you don't pay your rent, they put your furniture out on the street. And since there are so many people without work, many families have no roof over their heads and sleep in the park. We count ourselves lucky because we still have a roof over our heads. Of those from our Home, Tobcia R. isn't doing well. Her husband has gone bankrupt and she's going through terrible times as well. She has two children: a boy 11 years old and a girl 8 years old. Fela K. has gotten married. The wedding was quiet. It isn't a very good match and she isn't happy. Zosia H. has three children. Sewek is living with me, because he's not working and his wife took their boy to Lolka's. Regina Sz. comes to visit me. She's still unmarried and complains she has no friends. That's all our alumni. Maybe my material situation is very bad, but my spirits are high. I live in hope that times will improve. My children are my wealth.[20]

***

Hana Biber, Fejga's daughter, lives in a house near the borderline between the old kibbutz, which Wilczyńska knew, and the new one, which I get to know when I come here for the first time in November 2012.

The building's interior is very bright. There are a few posters on the walls – photos by Irving Penn (an American photographer who shot portraits with uniform backgrounds and natural light), not many knick-knacks, and almost no signs of use on the pristine kitchen appliances and dishes. A colourful woven throw is ironed stiff. When Hana serves coffee, she sets the coasters under her cup and mine at even distances from one another and the edge of the table.

People in the kibbutz say she's like her mother. Hardworking, stubborn. Solitary. When she was little, she remembers that Stefa's presence in her house (the same one Wilczyńska stayed in on her visits to Palestine) was stronger than the memories of her real grandmothers. Hana remembers Wilczyńska with more tenderness than her own mother, she talks about her categorically: she was like this, she wasn't like that. 'For sure', 'without a doubt'.

She has kept a present Wilczyńska gave Fejga. The only item of Wilczyńska's that she still has. Maybe there's something else, but Hana doesn't want to show me. She doesn't know when Fejga got it. I don't know what it looks like. I know it exists. When I ask Hana about it, she says: I don't remember, I can't find it. It probably got mislaid somewhere, like many things after mother died.

Please, I'll wait.

A year later I come to Ein Harod and Hana once again invites me to her home, though she promises nothing. Yet again she tells me stories about Wilczyńska, her mother, this time fewer than before. And the present?

'I couldn't find it.'

The next day she calls at dawn.

'I'll show you.'

A metal frame, a piece of thick cardboard on the back, a prop. It's a mirror. Ten by fifteen centimetres, maybe slightly more. When she stands it up on the table, it reflects pictures of her mother and Wilczyńska from the shelf opposite.

'You can hold it, but only for a second.'

***

Hana Biber preserves the memory of her mother's best friend as carefully as that mirror.

Jarosław Abramow-Newerly, son of Barbara Szejnbaum and Igor Newerly, thinks of Wilczyńska to this day as 'grandma'. In his memoir *The Lions of my Courtyard* he wrote: 'Though Stanisław Wilczyński was a giant, grandma Stefa will always have the greater stature in my eyes. Than him, than my mother, let alone me – a silly little freckle-faced boy.'[21]

Shlomo couldn't call her 'mother', but he framed his photo of Wilczyńska just like his photo of 'The-Doctor-Papa-Korczak' (which is what he calls him, sometimes in a different order, sometimes putting all those words together into one). He always has to keep their photos close.

***

1934. Wilczyńska still wants change and doesn't want change. Palestine, as she writes to a former house child, is meant to bean extension of her work at the Home.[22] The kibbutz, too, has similar discipline and aims, but new and probably more successful methods. She wants to see whether her knowledge and skills are useful over there, where the atmosphere and opportunities are different, where they don't feel the weight of the Depression, where the politics aren't terrifying. Where more can be done.

And yet she keeps staying in Warsaw. One day she wants to quit everything and go, the next she loses all desire. She doesn't make any arrangements, doesn't prepare. Alumni, acquaintances and her sister – who is saving up money for her – encourage her to go, but she can't make up her mind. She hates feeling apathetic. She isn't used to it. And it bothers her.[23]

***

The letters from Fejga cheer her up. Stefa still responds cautiously to Fejga's indecisiveness about her relationship with Biber.

> Oh! You dear silly thing! [...] There is no art to loving, but not everyone can love like he does, not in quantity, but in quality.[24]

And again:

> Darling Fajgusia,
>
> I cannot write. That is what it comes down to. With events over there, I can imagine what the mood must be like. We ought to speak. Where, when, I don't know. If only you had all the necessary

> documents already and if only I could now greet you two as an 'orthodox married couple' (don't scowl). I like him more and more and I don't imagine you'll ever regret the decision. He's a funny mix of contrasts: at first glance hard, uncompromising, unapproachable as a boulder, but at heart soft, sensitive, subtle. My dear, my darling, don't think I'm trying to talk you around or want to convince you. I'm sure you're thinking as you read this: if I were in your shoes, I'd say the same.
>
> No, when I think of you two, what comes to mind is one sentence by an author (I don't remember who): 'the best a person can do is to make another person less lonely.' And then I think the two of you are the 'best' in that sense. Anything else is silliness. Why, family life is much easier on the kibbutz and avoids much of the drudgery that you rightly fear. Look what a matchmaker I've become in my old age. Basia and Jerzy have such a sweet, smart baby. Jakób Kutalczuk has married a Hostel girl. Rózia Lipiec and her husband live in the Orphans' Home. Some girls want to have a husband, others – a baby, still others are afraid of loneliness. The Dr asks every couple that visits us: you're not getting divorced yet?[25]

She is beginning (finally) making preparations to leave.

Her letter continues:

> I wrote these crossed-out pages two months ago, right after receiving your long letter. Then Harry arrived, then Gerszon promised me he'd pass on the news you told him – I'm waiting, I know he's busy. Then I waited for the Doctor to visit you all, and now… I'm waiting for my trip anyway… constant excuses, anything not to write.
>
> I don't know if I'll come, but I know that I want to – very, very, very badly.
>
> My darling, I don't want to mislead you. I now have a discount for sea travel, money for a concessionary passport and rail travel, but I don't know if I'll get a visa, even though everyone is doing their best for me. They swore to Gerszon that I can get a visa if I travel first class, though I haven't got the cash for that, or if I go in April, though I haven't got time for that, because by mid-May I have to be in Warsaw.
>
> If I get a visa, meaning if they believe I have no intention of staying in Eretz (as if I wanted to), I'll leave Warsaw on 19 Mar via Constanța, leave Constanța on 21 Mar, be in Jaffa 25 Mar, at what

time I don't know. Find out when the *Polonia* arrives and wait for me.

And if I don't get a visa, we'll just have to say too bad.

And you'll get a sad letter from me. You're a little, tiny bit to blame yourself, but only a little, because I thought you were coming here and I didn't want us to miss one another, I was waiting for a letter with an explanation, I started making preparations (and actually allowed myself to make my preparations) at the last moment.

But I'm so tired that I must rest my nerves, though physically I look almost too well. And I'll take some time off, and spend it here at Basia's, outside the city.

It's not work that torments and bores me, but helplessness, powerlessness, not being able to assist those who are suffering without employment.

As for Biber, I've come to like him a lot and that's that.

So either until I see you, or not. All my love.[26]

***

In March 1934, Wilczyńska finally makes it to Palestine. She spends a few weeks there.

Korczak sends her a gift from Poland: a knife for peeling potatoes.

***

After six weeks she returns to her normal duties. She feels even more superfluous. Again she talks about a machine that can get along without her. She doesn't know if that makes her feel sadder or happier. Does it give her joy, because the thing that she believed in will continue even without her? Or does it give her freedom, since the fact that it will continue means that she can leave? Or fear that the Home won't notice she's gone?

She also starts to fear getting old. Fatigue, more and more grandchildren reminding her of the time that passes unnoticed somewhere between repetition and routine. This not noticing amazes her. Her own impatience and lack of strength bother her. She's afraid of falling ill. She doesn't want to be dependent, she doesn't want to be – as she writes to Fejga – 'a ball and chain for my loved ones'.

***

She also helps Korczak organize his trip when he decides to go to Eretz. He's been putting it off for a long time, he wants to prepare himself for the journey, but that's difficult when there's so much else to do.

Wilczyńska feels sad as, for the first time, she fills out a boarding card for a name other than her own.

She writes to her friend Rywka Zwykielska-Simchoni, a teacher in Ein Harod:

> Please listen carefully and write me straight back. Could Doctor Korczak maybe spend a few weeks in Ein Harod? But he absolutely wants to work with the infants, to do everything there that they need. That's his will now. And he can. What he can't do, he will learn. And he strongly requests that no one anywhere find out he's coming, because he wants to stay peacefully in one place. I'd like it best if he lived with you, but go ahead and decide that for yourselves. [...] I've told him a lot about you all and I want him to get a good look, for him to find what fundamental mistake lies at the heart of how the staff is organized in all the children's homes. Because the more I think about it, the more this phenomenon amazes me. So many people for 200 children, and those people are exhausted! As soon as the Doctor gets back we'll be able to talk these things through. As you know, though I don't write, I think of you all a great deal and all my plans depend on the Doctor's return and his assessment of whether I would be useful for you. For now I don't want to tie myself to being here, though they're offering me a job at that large orphanage for foundlings.[27]

She asks them to wait for him at the harbour.

Korczak leaves in September 1934 and stays in Ein Harod. As he wished, he takes care of children. He observes and makes notes, bringing back dozens of pages' worth. He peels potatoes in the dining hall. He's hugely impressed with Eretz, but never stops being a tourist. He doesn't yet feel he could stay there.

For a few weeks, Wilczyńska once again runs the Home completely on her own. She doesn't complain, but she doesn't like it. She only writes: 'I have less time and more responsibility.'[28]

Notes

1. Letter from Stefania Wilczyńska to Fejga Lifszyc, 12 February 1933.
2. *Pamiętniki bezrobotnych. Nr 1–57* (Warsaw: 1933), p.53.

3. Ibid., pp.82–83.
4. Ibid., p.68.
5. Letter from Stefania Wilczyńska to Fejga Lifszyc, 26 October 1934.
6. Letter from Stefania Wilczyńska to Fejga Lifszyc, 28 April 1933.
7. Letter from Stefania Wilczyńska to Fejga Lifszyc, spring 1933.
8. *Życie W.S.M. Biuletyn Informacyjny*, August 1932.
9. Letter from Fejga Lifszyc to Stefania Wilczyńska, 13 May 1933.
10. Letter from Stefania Wilczyńska to Fejga Lifszyc, 10 September 1933.
11. Letter from Fejga Lifszyc to Stefania Wilczyńska, 24 September 1933.
12. Letter from Fejga Lifszyc to Stefania Wilczyńska, 3 October 1933.
13. *Nasz Przegląd*, 19 November 1933.
14. Anniversary General Meeting of the Orphans' Aid Society. Stenographic record, 26 November 1933, in J. Korczak: *Pisma rozproszone. Listy (1913–1939)* (Warsaw: 2008), pp.154-155.
15. Ibid., p.161.
16. Ibid.
17. Ibid., p.156.
18. Ibid., p.163.
19. Archive of the Ghetto Fighters kibbutz, inventory number 12899.
20. Both letters: J. Korczak, *Pisma rozproszone. Listy* (Warsaw: 2008), pp.168-169.
21. J. Abramow-Newerly, *Lwy mojego podwórka* (Warsaw: 2002), p.62.
22. Letter from Stefania Wilczyńska to Jakub Einfeld, 26 March 1934.
23. Undated letter from Stefania Wilczyńska to Fejga Lifszyc, 1934.
24. Letter from Stefania Wilczyńska to Fejga Lifszyc, 13 July 1934.
25. Letter from Stefania Wilczyńsa to Fejga Lifszyc, 1934.
26. Ibid.
27. Letter from Stefania Wilczyńska to Rywka Zwykielska-Simchoni, 11 August 1934.
28. Letter from Stefania Wilczyńska to Fejga Lifszyc, 26 October 1934.

14

She thinks of Sara and her gentle Yochai, of Rachel and her bees, of the joyful face of Simchoni as she shows off the new small masonry houses on Kumi Hill, of warm-hearted M. – who prefers the company of elders and, like a cat, seeks her own paths. Of wise Moshe, who should give practical lectures for teachers, because he might be wasted on this little handful when there's such a hunger all around for scarce specialists. Of dogmatic and fanatical Gerszon, so young, with strong faith in what's new there.

She thinks of everyone she left behind in Ein Harod. She misses them. 'Even the waste-paper basket, which even seems native in a way, not at all hopeless.'[1]

She sees them clearly, like sleeping Chavka, smiling Shaya, work-worn Shoshana, and silly Grun. And wild-haired Aptekar, who likes to paint and would be over the moon if he'd been the one got to sail with Chagall.

***

Since she got back from Palestine she's been spending a lot of time at the library. That's the best place, it's quiet, empty. She can't find a place for herself in Warsaw. ('I'm fit for scrap.'[2]) She doubts whether she'll find one in Palestine.

She's getting ready for another trip and wants to go as soon as possible.

She puts it off again.

She writes two letters to Rywka. She's afraid, she's hedging her bets, she doesn't believe she'll be needed there.

> I'll respond to the board officially after I talk to Korczak yet again. I've already made a start with studying and examining to work out the what's best to see and what you all might find useful. But I'm very frightened of responsibility and I fear you'll find my work disappointing. I must observe and listen, and draw on your experience, before I can be of help with anything. The more I realize the enormity of what you've achieved in self-rearing and child-

> rearing, the more I doubt my own usefulness and the more hesitations and doubts I have of my own activities. Please believe this is how I feel. If not for Korczak, whom I consider an authority and who would never allow an experiment like this one, and if I weren't fit for it, I wouldn't even dare to try.

And four months later:

> I've made up my mind: this winter. We're going to get to work. My heart swells when I hear what's happening over there, how some of my dreams of improvements are coming true. […] I'd be very grateful for a register of the children – if that's possible. The child's first name, who his parents are and a short character description, in a few words, if of course there are no statistical data.[3]

She asks for – and receives – her first long time off in 25 years.

She writes to Fejga:

> For writing me two pages I owe you a speedy letter. […]
>
> I was on Pańska Street and signed up at the Tarbut for Hebrew, 3×/week. I am reading *Ivrit l'chalutzim* starting at the end. I got leave for six months and of course they wanted to give it to me paid, but I won't accept, because I know how empty our coffers are. I'll do without, especially since the approaching war means there's no point getting a round-trip ticket. I told the Doctor that 'news' in Hebrew is *yediot,* which sounds funny to us, and the Dr said: 'an idiot is the one with the most news!' That's how we talk to one another in Hebrew.
>
> Yesterday I spent almost my whole day off in Gocławek with my 'grandkids'. I enjoyed it so much, because they're so sweet and don't yet have any self-interests or doubts (the oldest is five), and there's no need to give them advice. They don't ask about anything that needs deciding.[4]

She doesn't manage to leave until fall of 1935. It's her third time in Palestine. She spends five months there, which, again, we know little about. Only as much as was preserved in her letters to the children – and articles she writes for the kibbutz newspaper.

***

Either – Or

In all childcare institutions – starting with daycare for just-weaned children, through pre-school, to school, for sixteen long years – children are forced to eat *everything*. They must eat everything, even what they don't like. [...] Over these sixteen years they are not allowed to leave anything on their plate. They are not allowed to be 'picky' with their food. *Not allowed*. Meanwhile in nearly every other area of children's life, the rule is total freedom, sometimes even bordering on recklessness; only within the walls of the dining room – at a meal – do cruel regulations apply: they are to enjoy every bite. How much crying, how many futile tears? How much anger over the first six years? And how many needless arguments and disputes in the years that follow? And that is only the children. And for the child-rearers – how much wasted energy that could be put to better use and effect. Now is not the time to describe how clever children are at defending themselves against adult force and how they resist it. At the same time, in the name of a goal – raising people 'who don't sulk' – we achieve exactly the opposite. And so after sixteen years of fighting 'sulking' a child finally moves into the 'grown-up' dining room. Once there, how easy it is to leave radishes or carrots on the plate... The time for revenge is coming. It's very possible that a ten- or twelve-year-old child is already intently observing how the adults in the dining room behave (and after all, father and mother are authority figures), how they waste money and other people's time. How the kitchen staff toils away, cooking meals for many long hours in the heat of a sweltering room... and look... in a single moment we scrape the food from our own plate into the leftovers bowl. I won't remind you of the journeys our food has taken, of the coal, of the labour of human hands and so on and so forth. Nor will I say any more about the expense – after all I am addressing adults, not children. But: either – or. Either we must raise them differently for those first sixteen years, or behave differently after those sixteen years. Here is a concrete proposal: it would be worthwhile to introduce unportioned dishes for the children too. Yet if finances preclude serving all the food in the dining hall this way, then at a minimum we can place separate clean dishes at each table. So if I don't like lettuce or carrots, then – before I begin to eat – I can use a clean spoon to put the food in on those dishes. It will be useful as seconds for those who are hungrier or less picky.

> I would be very happy to help implement this idea of mine.
> Stefa[5]

***

In December 1935 in Tel Aviv, she definitely meets with former house children who live in Eretz. Apparently someone took a picture to commemorate the moment.

She handed the organizer of this celebration a letter with all the house children's addresses. Beside each name she wrote the number they had in the Home.

***

She writes to the children at Krochmalna Street about rain.

> So real Palestinian rain falls, pours, bashes, beats, and in a few hours or the next day, it suddenly clears up and there's not just one rainbow, but two or three rainbows at once. The weather is beautiful again, it's sunny, warm, there's just that mud I've already told you about. If this were the sand of the banks of our good old Vistula River, it would all be quickly washed away.
>
> The farmers here worry that they haven't had time to sow the grain, because apparently the rainy reason has started too quickly this year. It's a good thing I didn't listen to Pani Rózia and left my umbrella behind. Here that instrument would be comical and not help much. We throw whatever we can over our heads, anything to fight our way through the mud and make it home. [...][6]

About the children.

> I go into the classrooms to see and listen, and I hear them teasing one another, *really* teasing one another! How it warms my heart. Everything is right – I think. I have crossed four seas and it's the same here as at home. I hear tender conversations between Abram and Piekołek. And over there someone is arguing over dried flowers. Don't Reginka and Guta shout that way? But no, it's Aza and Chila. Whether in Polish or in Hebrew, whether they have one sort of name or another.
>
> And there are different 'seasons' and 'fashions'. At home I'm sure chestnut season is over and Izaak finally has room in his lockbox,

meanwhile here there's a fashion for 'bows' –these slingshots with strong rubber bands. But there's lots of space here, plenty of empty space for shooting at targets, so it's allowed. […] You remember – when I left a picture book of the Polish kings and a book about the French revolution on a table at home, the girls came up, glanced through a couple pages, then before you knew it they were gone. But the boys, led by Jankuś and Motek, examined the books, talked them over, kept finding new details, then at the end, they started over from the beginning, because a new set of children had arrived to listen and look. Here, in a younger class, I put out a colourful Japanese book – maybe some of you remember it – and the girls looked at it for three minutes. But the boys spent all of their breaks looking at it, even pushed and shoved a little to get closer, marvelled at how different the Japanese writing was, one explained the pictures to another, what it was about and why – and finally made plans to examine it again after class from the beginning. Naturally I'm not talking about all boys and all girls, but just for the sake of comparison. […][7]

About cows.

There are […] clean ones and sloppy ones who as soon as you wash them get dirty again.

Some cows are greedy. You give them all food in the trough, then one of these fressers[8] will dig into her neighbour's portion first and only eat her own afterward. Some cows are picky: they won't let themselves be milked by just anybody. Someone starts milking her and she can tell these hands are different, and kicks up a fuss for as long as it takes for someone else to come.

In general cows don't fight much, but when a cow has lovely horns, right away she rebels, she senses her power, she will kick with her hoof or prod with her horn. Luckily in our herd of 50 we have only two or three of these shrews. The calves are more quarrelsome: why, just like our human calves – they won't let themselves be tied up, they kick, they push one another around. They only become serious once they've grown up and had their first calf. And when it's time for a cow to give birth, they put a sack over her head so she can't see, and they take her calf away. She cries, searches around, she doesn't know what happened. And when they milk her, she thinks that maybe it's her child nursing, and the licks the hand that's milking her. The farmers do this so they don't lose the milk, but there are

> good mothers who can't be tricked. It does happen, though rarely in fact, that one such good mother will not let herself be milked, not wanting to give away the milk that's meant to be for her baby. And there's no helping it: you have to bring her the calf and let it nurse. They have a sort of book of statistics here, like we have for the children. Admittedly the cows do not go to the office to lick a finger and page through, examining and calculating if they deserve a work postcard, but each cow has her own page and everything about her life and health is recorded. It's recorded who her father and mother were, and even where her grandparents came from. [...][9]

About new immigrants.

> [...] We bid a ceremonial farewell to the German youths. You know why they've left Germany. The first such group came to Ein Harod two years ago. There were 60 of them – girls and boys from 15 to 17 years old. They worked here for two years, or rather learned how to work in a field, in an orchard, in hotboxes, in various workshops. And now after two years they have gone 'their own way' to found a self-sufficient kvutzah. [...]
>
> But now the lights are dimming and on the screen we see a movie about the life of the young people working in Ein Harod. It was the first time I saw anyone watching themselves on film and people kept bursting out in laughter and joy, like when good friends meet.
>
> And then the lights came back on and there was dancing. Naturally, the Palestinian 'hora' – in various versions, with singing, with and without harmonicas, in large and small circles. Strong, healthy, powerful, young legs and old, tired and beat-up ones. Slippers, sandals, clogs, shoes, heavy and high working boots. Maybe they'll find it difficult in the new settlement, where there isn't even any water yet, far from their families and the country of their first childhoods, nor so close to their guides and first teachers of life in Ein Harod. But it's good to test your strengths, it's interesting to find out for sure whether even without experienced advice, without help from alert, adult eyes, you can still achieve something.
>
> Meanwhile they dance, as long as their strength allows. And as long as the floor will hold up, I think to myself.
>
> And then I recall the quiet farewells for our house children, who at 14, 15, 16 years old, go out into life. And saying goodbye to the young men and women graduating from school.

I will wrap up now and my apologies to all the younger children for writing a letter that's they'll find so difficult and boring. [ ][10]

About Arabs.

During the unrest in Tel Aviv, I once wanted to go from upper Haifa down to the old market square, but an old Arab man warned me not to. In Arabic, in Hebrew and with hand gestures, he conveyed to me that I should go back up to the Jewish district, that down below things were unsettled, maybe even dangerous.

[…] [B]ut recently the children and I were in an Arab village, not far from Tel-Hai, where very, very few Jews live. It wasn't actually a village, but a Bedouin settlement. Poor tents covered in mats. Inside, poverty and filth, children and goats, a dog, chickens and people – all together. It reminded me of a Gypsy camp.

But what hospitality they showed us. The tent's owner wasn't there – he was grazing the whole village's sheep a long way away. A young Arab woman, gorgeous, her face painted with 'permanent' dye, did not know where to seat us. She rolled straw mats out on the ground, placed pillows on them, little mattress-type things, and invited the children to take a seat. She used a twig to chase away the flies, of which there were whole swarms, and later invited a few Arab women to dance and sing for us.

The teacher speaks good Arabic and she asked the Arab woman to tell us what they eat, how they work, how they raise their children. […] Later, smiling and bowing, she led us a long way, so the dogs didn't bother us, since a bunch of them had come running from all over the village. […][11]

About the khamsin.

They say if you don't like olives you can't be a Palestinian citizen. And I say: you haven't passed the endurance test of the Palestinian climate unless you've felt first hand what the 'khamsin' is. 'Khamsin' means '50 days' in Arabic. That means that there are meant to be 50 days a year of this east wind, the wind of the desert. […][12]

The khamsin is an easterly, desert wind that does not refresh, but blows a wave of heat; when it comes, the sky grows overcast, clouds of dust hover like fog. It's hard to work, and night brings no reprieve either.

> And so after one day, after two, three, sometimes even more, the 'khamsin' passes, as unexpectedly as it arrived. [...][13]

She never gets used to it.

She also mentions her return.

> But time off is like the summer vacation, it always starts too late and ends too early. So when the children from Ein Harod found out I had to leave and I was sad to go, they made a number of different surprises for my children in Warsaw. [...]
>
> So I packed my bags and boarded the ship.[14]

***

Tuesday, late April 1936. She watches the sailors of the *Polonia*. On their breaks from work they try to catch the young seagulls that rest on the mast. They haven't caught any birds, but they did break a wire and the lights went out.

Wednesday. She's met a young boy. The poor thing has a bad case of seasickness.

Thursday. The ship sails into port in Athens. The passengers go to look at the Acropolis. It's spectacular, but she knows about it. And she doesn't know how to look around with tourists, under the command of guides, who always rush you along. She goes into the city on her own. She happens across a park with a playground. There, Greek children play on swings like all the other children in the world. The little ones in the sandbox are working like everywhere else. More want their own shovel and their own bucket, and sandcastle moulds just for themselves. All around is a beautiful park, like a large forest, shady and sweet-smelling. A nanny manages to cause a fuss – she pulled a child too hard. And then to the fish market. Pink, silver, sky-blue and navy-blue, flat and large, slim as little needles. And next to the fish, some odd-looking octopuses, crabs and snails (she must write about them to the children).

Saturday. They are sailing through the Dardanelles. She thinks back to what she learned in school: the right bank is Asia, the left, Europe. She looks at them and sees difference between Europe and Asia here. And the water... so smooth. Beautiful. A shame it's getting dark.

Sunday. Istanbul. Almost all the passengers have disembarked for the whole day while the ship is stopped. Once again, she stays behind. From the deck, she gazes at the distant mosques and minarets, the dolphins and transparent jellyfish floating along the hull.

Monday. Constanța. She waits for the train to Warsaw. Enough time to watch the Romanian children play in the schoolyard.

She arrives back at Krochmalna Street in April 1936.

Almost immediately she writes to Fejga, whose returning depression worries her. She adds presents to the letters and packages passed on by her friends ('3 blouses, you won't like the colour of one, the cut of the second, and the buttons on the third, but tough luck, you can give them to someone less picky').[15]

> My dear child,
>
> As ever our letters have crossed en route. [...] Now I feel physically perfect and I could offer you some of my health. As proof I send you my latest photograph from the street and if you have the ones we took together, please send them. Again, darling Fajgusia, why such sadness again? What happened, was there some specific cause? Was it something from outside? Did it arrive just like a bad wind blowing? Maybe the heatwaves, the general situation in the country, poor physical health? Maybe Biber, your old vexation, or something new? He hungers for you. Let him at least sate himself with you. Maybe, maybe he will be less hungry. Although who knows. How awful it is to be so far away.
>
> I hope it's enough for now that I love you dearly, like my own child, that I often think of you, and I believe this will pass, as it passed once before.[16]

***

That picture from the street is gone, it hasn't survived.

There are others.

A photograph: a middle-aged woman hugs a little boy dressed in a white top and little hat. She's smiling, both of their hands hold a small, square, white mirror. On the back of the photo it reads: 'If you dream of cash to spare, play the lotto at Centnerszwer's.' The boy is four years old and he and Wilczyńska are counting the freckles reflected in the mirror. He's named Jarosław, he's the son of Barbara and Igor Abramow.

The oldest surviving picture shows a young woman (today she would still be a 'girl') of less than thirty: she's 28, though doesn't look it. Her gaze isn't straight ahead, but turned slightly to the right. One arm is bent, placed behind her back, the second is in the pocket of her dark (black?) apron-dress. Her hair (slightly curly) is brushed to the left, maybe she has pinned it up a little. Light falls on her face. It brightens her large eyes, making her prominent nose less obvious.

In this picture, too, Wilczyńska is smiling.

I crop out of the picture two men standing to her left. Moustachioed Eliasberg with a cigarette (?) in his hand and Korczak, who's thrown on a doctor's (?) apron. The young girl with her hand in her pocket remains.

A slightly later picture: a group of girls dressed for warm weather in light-coloured outfits. One wears a headscarf, the other has a short sleeve riding up her arm. The 1930s, summer, the summer camps in Gocławek. Wilczyńska stands in the third row. The photo is over-exposed, her face is barely visible.

Next: 1937, March, right in front of the Home, a wide shot. A group of children, smiling at the camera, extends from one edge of the frame to the other. If we increase the contrast, we can see that on the left of the photo, in the shadow of the portico over the front entrance, a woman stands, turned half away. We can pull her out of the darkness. The figure is blurry, but I manage to make out two details that let me declare, 'that's her': a black apron and a white collar. And a third detail too, evidently less typical of her, but captured in this picture as well: a smile.

Sometimes, in enlarged versions of this photo, people crop out the figure in the shadow.

Yet another photo, early 1930s: children (packed shoulder-to-shoulder) sitting at little tables, along with her. The photo is over-exposed, we can barely make out her short hair and bangs brushed behind her ear.

Another photo: a woman with short hair (or maybe she's just tied it back?) sitting in profile to the photographer. She has one hand over her face and is looking straight ahead. And this eighty-year-old picture is out of focus.

But three photos from that same series are in focus: large portraits. In one, an adult woman with a short lace collar looks straight ahead with a broad smile, in the second the smile is gone. She has wrinkles and bags under her eyes.

Or this one: she sits (or rather has sat down for a moment, stiffly, as if unused to resting her feet) on the wooden steps of a porch in Gocławek. Leather sandals on her feet, a summer dress (though with a collar), longer hair than usual, because it's pinned up. She looks like she's saying something.

The photos from Ein Harod are blurry too. Wilczyńska dressed in a white summer dress with short sleeves (a watch on her left wrist) carefully pushing a baby carriage holding Neta, Fejga's young son; Wilczyńska with

Neta in her arms, smiling and pointing at something high up and out of frame; Wilczyńska with Fejga, her husband and her son. Wilczyńska and Fejga (with two long braids), the only photo of just the two of them.

There are no photos from the later period of Wilczyńska's life.

A photograph: three young women in long dresses (with at least a few thick layers underneath, probably woollen bloomers) and ankle-length coats, knitted scarves around their necks. Their heads are barely visible under fur hats. In the background we see a wall of snow – a Swiss glacier. It's the start of the twentieth century, and Julia, Stefania and their cousin, the mother of Mary Marley, have just climbed down the ice.

This photo, if it was ever taken, hasn't survived. Mary/Marysia insists that her mother told her about one like it. That's how they must – she hand-underlines the typewritten word – have looked back then.

***

Troubling news comes to Warsaw from Eretz. In 1936, Palestinian Arabs are once again rising up to oppose the British colonial authorities and the mass immigration of Jews, in recent years primarily from Germany. Ein Harod is surrounded by villages, it lies in a strategic location, battles take place nearby, people are killed.

Wilczyńska is worried. For Eretz, which she feels closer to in her heart. And for Fejga – maternally, though less so than before.

> It's silly of me, since I don't know how things are there, yet I have such trust in the feeling of safety in Ein Harod. If it's possible for a Jew to be 100 per cent safe anywhere in the world. Here I am rambling, and being incredibly silly. It's not so prudent to start thinking about a new life at fifty years of age. And yet, I'll add by way of excuse, I think this is nothing new, but an extension of the old. Anyway, there's more than one way to skin a cat.
>
> My dear, beloved child, if I didn't fear so for your health, I'd be leaving without any worries at all for you. Without any worries for the first time. Because six years ago – why, you remember – I left you in a state as if you had an unhealed, fresh wound. And two years ago: so unsure, so undecided.
>
> Now despite all your saying 'I don't care', 'I'll do what he wants', and so on, two facts from recent weeks have reassured me that you're not so 'stony' as you think. I'll tell you, because I feel you thinking: she's pushing me into it. But these facts are broader than your coldly

> worked-out logical sayings, because they were drawn from your deepest subconscious. The realm not of thought, but of feeling.
>
> So listen.
>
> When I recently spent the night at your place and you had such a bad headache that you almost fainted and you were speaking to me in Hebrew, you called out so softly, 'Chaim, it's gone now, I feel better.' And when he left, you complained to me in a pained voice: I don't feel any better, but he's so worried and he needs to go to work.
>
> When during that first moment of panic, in Haifa, we stopped in front of that store with the stockings, you suddenly looked around and shouted: 'where's Biber?!' It was just one moment, and before long, when you saw him, you returned to 'your' balance, and he maybe didn't even hear your little shout among the honking and whistling from the cars. Maybe you don't even remember it yourself. It was a second, but one of honesty, because it was instinctual.
>
> But these brief moments let me forget the many things you've said that are hard, mean and tough for Biber. But the point is these moments allow him, not me, to forget, and keep him away from those thoughts that are darker than the darkest moonless night. So I'm not worried about you, since I know you have Biber with you (and I appreciate him very much for that), even though I know no one, even the most loving person in the world, can prevent someone else from being sad when she's sad. Maybe they can lessen it a little, but not completely.[17]

***

Two days after her fiftieth birthday, she spends an evening at the microscope. 'The gorgeous sight of bacteria zipping around!'[18]

***

One generation after another leaves the Home.

In 1936, Salcia Zalcman is one of those leaving for Palestine. Wilczyńska writes her a dedication: 'You were a child: I taught you the difficult art of how one must work. You grew up: you did very well helping me with work. We are quits, my young comrade. Farewell and perhaps… until we meet again.'[19]

She often ends her letters that way.

(Is she doing her best not to get attached?)

At this same time, in July 1936, Korczak takes his second trip to Palestine. For a few weeks he makes visits, has meetings, observes and soaks up what is best in this new, young country – the energy, the potential. Just as Wilczyńska did before. He doesn't believe he's much use anymore at home in Poland, where the anti-Semitic atmosphere is growing stronger. Around this time, Polish Radio takes Korczak's chats off the air. He wonders about leaving for good. After returning to Poland, he sums up his own achievements with an even greater sense of disappointment ('if not complete bankruptcy, then a slim advantage on the side of accomplishments.') [20]

Just like Stefa before.

***

In fall of 1936 she writes to Fejga:

> My beloved and darling,
>
> I won't even try to excuse myself. When the Dr was there, it was as if a part of me was with you all. When he returned and I asked after you, he said: actually I didn't want to ask about Fejga, because I know you write to one another. All I know is she constantly struggles to stay awake.
>
> I've had a bad summer. First walking flu then an ear infection. Pus under my eardrum. Before they drained it I was really suffering, I kept on working because everyone was on vacation. And after they drained it, I went deaf in that ear for 3 weeks. It bothered me so much I couldn't sleep, I had some kind of noise in my ear. But it was all silliness. All the more so because the children didn't get sick, they had a good summer.
>
> How I wish I had one evening to talk with you.
>
> I won't come until I can speak Hebrew. I am really learning properly now.
>
> The Dr says that I have to go for the summer and for a year, otherwise I don't really know Palestine. Those heat waves really got to him. Though he was also leading a crazy lifestyle, travelling all over the place. Even he's amazed how many visits he made in those 6 weeks. But he's like me, he doesn't know how to keep that up. He came back worn out, and didn't manage to do much as he wanted. And he keeps talking about 'the third time'. And saying 'returning to Ein Harod was like coming home.' Nice to hear, isn't it? That's your contribution.

> I have your photo in front of me. Your smiling face, tousled, so sweet.
>
> The Dr and I talk about you often. We fill each other in, because he doesn't know everything I know and vice-versa.[21]

Korczak suggests they both spend half the year in Palestine and half in Poland, so that one is always at the Home. 'Of course if the journey took two days, then maybe I'd agree. ½ the year here, ½ there. I miss everyone in Ein Harod very, very badly.'[22]

Wilczyńska to Fejga:

> The Dr is so depressed, so dejected, that he doesn't care about anything. Imagine that he wanted suddenly to go to Jerusalem this very month – don't tell anyone, because people who don't know him might get the wrong idea. […] In general he's tormenting himself and others […]. I just think it would be a pity if our beloved Home suddenly found itself without either of its two main administrators.[23]

Korczak lectures less and less, he's withdrawing from the Orphans' Home. Before Wilczyńska does the same, she looks for a substitute, 'someone who would have the enthusiasm of Shoshana, the endurance and skills of Moshe, the hunger for collective work of Rivka, the organizational talents of Fejga, as well as the patience of Rywka Zwykielska etc. etc., if only I could someone who came close to that.'[24]

> Then my going there for a year would be appropriate and perhaps useful. Because we mustn't delude ourselves, after all, just as I do not. 25 years of social work (including during the war, those years count double) mustn't pass without a trace like that.
>
> I could convey a portion of my experience to someone over there, but only as adapted to your conditions. […]
>
> Because I'll go further. If Ein Harod develops a system of children's homes, with a methodical rollout of work on raising children from infancy to adolescence, then we'll be able to share this accomplishment with other centres in Eretz. […]
>
> I'd have to make the right preparations, suggest specialists in Poland and Eretz.
>
> I'm afraid you don't grasp what a difficult and responsible task this is, if you're asking me to agree so quickly: come or don't, take it on or don't.

The main thing is that I have to do it without harming the institutions I've worked for so far, because how else can I?

You all don't know me, but having the trust of people with such great ethical standing as you all only makes my duties all the greater and more difficult.

Fifteen years ago, when my work as matron was tormenting me by keeping me out of frequent, direct contact with children themselves, how I envied the house parents, schoolteachers and kindergarten teachers for being able to connect with the children, 'live' with them, not thinking about winter supplies, holes in the roof or choosing schools. Nor do they have that full responsibility for the whole. Whenever I have wanted to quit as matron, Korczak has told me: a general may not become a soldier.[25]

She finds a substitute, Matylda Temkin. But even so she keeps hesitating. (To stay here, where she doesn't feel needed? Or to leave and start over?) She feels like a deserter.

***

My Information for the passport:

Stefania Wilczyńska

Born 26 May 1886 in Warsaw,

Father's name: Izaak Wilczyński.

Is that enough? I can send more, but I don't know what you need. As far as work, I don't know either. I graduated from secondary school in Russian days, a kindergarten teaching course. I have a half-diploma, i.e. a baccalaureate in natural science from the University of Liège (in Belgium). For 26 years I've been working as matron at the OH. I have helped organize boarding houses for children of school age and Hostels for adolescents. I have cared for and directed pedagogic arrangements for around 30 children and staff at various social institutions in Poland and abroad. I am not an honest person, because for six years I've been opposed to residential institutions of our type, and yet the law of inertia has kept me here for the whole of those six years.

What else do you want?[26]

– she asks Fejga in 1937.

***

She is cautious to a fault. She plans. The most difficult thing is to say definitively 'I am leaving the Home.' That's the first step. The most important. The next: to apply for a certificate from the British (permanent leave to remain in Palestine).

There are four eligibility categories. The first includes people who have 1,000 Palestine pounds in cash, a freelance profession, or 500 pounds and a document confirming there is a need for their work. Others who qualify in this category are accredited artisans with 250 pounds in cash, pensioners and retirees if they can demonstrate a sufficiently high income, and workers who bring capital to Palestine and are able to prove their activities will not create competition for already-existing businesses in the Mandate. The second category is for clergy, students who have been accepted to university studies, and orphans. The third category covers immigrants with professions which are in particular demand in a given year. The fourth: relatives of those who have already received a certificate.

(Which group did she belong to?)

The British are not generous – every year they issue no more than 20,000 certificates, and there is no shortage of applicants. In 1920 over 5,500 people immigrated to Palestine – in 1932, over 9,500. Yet when the Nazis come to power in Germany, this wave increases markedly; a half-million Jews live in Germany in 1933, but every year tens of thousands leave the country. For many of them, Palestine is their destination, both legally and illegally. In 1933 over 30,000 people immigrate to the Mandate, in 1934: 42,000 and in 1935 (still before the enactment of the Nuremberg Laws): over 60,000. This is when the Mandatory authorities set a maximum quota on Jewish immigration in all categories, set at 12,000 people a year for five years, starting in 1936. The reason they give for the quota is Palestine's capacity to economically absorb the newcomers.

In 1937 legal migration is barely one-sixth the level of the previous year; a little over 10,000 migrants are let into Palestine. When the war begins two years later, the Jewish press, and later still the League of Nations, will hear repeated appeals, such as this one from Ludwik Süsswein:

> We wish to believe, however, that the honour of England will not allow her to break the solemn vow given to the Jewish people and that England must understand that in these difficult times the Jewish nation is currently facing, Palestine is nearly the only sanctuary, the last ray of hope in the life of a homeless people with a terrible legacy of the past, whose sole offence and the cause for cruelty to them is only that they were born Jewish.'[27]

But all that is still to come.

For now, the Mandatory authorities are screening applicants ever more strictly. They demand a skills certification in their new chosen country and presentation of the necessary evidence.

People Wilczyńska knows in both countries help her sort out the paperwork – Julia, her sister, makes sure she doesn't deplete her bank account on presents for loved ones, family, and alumni.

Wilczyńska is afraid that if she doesn't get a certificate, she'll only be able to go as a tourist for three months. She's heard that after two years you can legalize your status, but she doesn't want to live in fear, keeping her head down.

In spring of 1937 she writes to Fejga:

> Because I won't stay here as matron any longer than the first of July, I've already said firmly. 27 years is enough. In July and August I want to relax somewhere cheap with former house children. I'm very tired and I want to arrive at work rested for the start of the school year. That's my plan. And if they won't let me into Palestine by any route, I'll move out of the OH anyway and found a cooperative and a job agency for former house children. Because they're the only ones I want to work for now.
>
> You know this decision has cost me a great deal of nerves and thought. You yourselves have encouraged me quite a lot (and again talked me out of things here), so that now only a higher power can change my mind. And the fact that I am over 35, but under 55, why, that is a higher power.[28]

And also:

> It's harder to write. And there would be so much to say in person… But you sometimes write as though it were up to me whether I come or not. Now that I've already made up my mind, which was the hardest part, I fear I might not manage to. Not even the climate scares me so much anymore. And the Dr will be there too, if so, in Jerusalem. And my sister is sad, but seeing how badly I want this, she wants it too, for me. She is an impeccably honest person and lacks any great selfishness.[29]

She reads newspapers: an Arab revolt is taking place in Palestine, Arabs are being killed, so are Jews. It's too cramped on that scrap of territory for both peoples. And it will get even more cramped, because as every month goes by, more and more Jews want to come in. Legally or not, young people with no prospects are leaving, sometimes taking their parents along with them.

Over a decade before, in 1923, the orientalist and professor at the University of Warsaw Rev Dr Władysław Szczepański wrote:

> Does Jewish immigration to Palestine influence changes in the ethnic makeup of Poland, and if so, how much? It is very difficult to answer this question on any scientific basis. Two hypotheses emerge. In one hypothesis (unlikely in any event) of a population of five million in Palestine, and assuming the same percentage as today (33%) departs Poland for Palestine every year, in this hypothesis we could perhaps conclude that in 150 years today's Jewish population density in our country would shrink by around 1.5 million. [...] Compared to the great influx of Jews to our country from Russia, this is a quite insignificant percentage. As I wrote a few years ago, granting Palestine to the Jews would not solve the Jewish problem here. We must now seek its resolution by other means, unrelated to Palestine.[30]

Emigration is becoming more difficult, most countries are closing and tightening their borders. For several years, an initiative has been underway in Poland to aid Jews fleeing Germany – in many cities, aid committees are springing up spontaneously, and *Our Review* has also been holding fundraisers. The November 1938 issues name donors including:

> the philosopher Tadeusz Kotarbiński,
> the historian Maria Czapska,
> the poet Józef Czechowicz,
> the critic Karol Irzykowski,
> the novelists Zofia Nałkowska and Maria Kuncewiczowa,
> a Christian named S.L.,
> the Christian and Jewish workers of the Brennmiller Brothers' factory – jointly contributing 17 złotys,
> Miss Lenusia Lipszyc from Mława, who has cancelled her birthday and is sending five złotys,
> and also Antoś Lewkowicz and the two złotys donated from his savings.
> The children of the Orphans' Home receive donations as well.

***

Ten years ago, Jews went to Palestine brimming with idealism and impatience, now they are more often driven by fear.

In 1939 the sociologist and Zionist Aryeh Tartakower writes: 'Today's wall of restrictions closing off the world from emigrants is not an easy phenomenon to overcome. This wall was built on the sickened soil of conditions after the war, a general restriction of freedom, a growth of nationalist and racist sentiments, and on more than one occasion, panicked fear of what tomorrow will bring.'[31]

Wilczyńska also fears she won't succeed. She reads the newspapers too, listens to the radio and hears the loud shouting on the street about 'Jews taking over' (she has good hearing, after all).

In several letters she repeats the refrain that in this social and political situation, there is no point making any plans. She returns to the idea of emigrating to Russia.

She must be needed.

(Maybe by Fejga? In early summer she gets a letter from her saying: 'I'm pregnant. I didn't want to write so you wouldn't worry.')[32]

So before the certificate – her to be or not to be here or there – she herself takes the first step on the path to something new.

It's 1 July 1937, in three months she'll reach her twenty-fifth anniversary of living on Krochmalna Street. She moves out.

She writes to Fejga:

> What are you thinking by writing: 'maybe we'll never see one another?' Dark thoughts again: why, now you must live for the baby! And if I don't come, too bad, it doesn't matter, you'll have a 'substitute' – you see, he's not born yet and I'm already jealous!!
>
> I've decided to leave Krochmalna for a year, at a minimum. I'll find a job easily. I am a 'whizz', after all, so it won't be hard. But I must earn a living and only in the Orphans' Home am I incapable of working for money. And if I don't get a certificate, there are others waiting longer, who are more deserving, they know the language, are more needed over there. I'm aware of this and I'm not complaining. But I beg you, don't torment Bragiński or Cizyrling, don't say anything, don't mention it. It's really embarrassing, because after all I don't feel at the top of my powers, that is, I don't believe myself capable of offering anything without the language. What's needed is a 'decent person' who must prepare the material and drive the whole machine along. But I don't believe I can be that person. And please, my darling, don't ask them, don't torment them, don't pester, because

> you'll get nothing but disappointment and embarrassment. And you're right: I can't live in uncertainty. I've already cancelled my vacation trip and once I've rested a little, I'll commit to a three-month position at Centos, 'on a trial basis'. And while I'm there we'll see how things go. As far as what's happening now and may happen, unimportant personal matters, the individual is truly unimportant and I'm waiting calmly, without any nerves, for what will come out of the congress in Zürich, the parliamentary debates in Britain, the negotiations in America. You don't read newspapers, but I think they know better here what's happening where you are. We're not the only ones yearning…
>
> I spent a week with Basia and Jarek in the country just now. What a marvel how much that little four-year-old brat has already managed to learn of the world. A good, sweet child. A pity he's too sensitive – he'll suffer too much. I beg you, tell me if your troubles are truly past now. It weighs on me that I can't keep my promise.
>
> Until I see you again, in spite of everything! Or rather 'until you give birth', I think. One day the Doctor claims he's going straight to Palestine, and the next day says he's not going at all. He keeps going back and forth.[33]

In September she starts working at Centos, the Federation of Jewish Associations for the Care of Orphans and Abandoned Children. It was founded in 1924 and by the late 1930s it already includes institutions in over 200 cities and towns across the country.

She will visit them, write reports, advise.

At this time she writes to Fejga:

> Although Biber sent a telegram (my great thanks to him – you're always protesting, my darling, I could have been happy for you two earlier!), though I now have your handwritten letter, but when I read the message in the *Yoman*[34]: 'Mazzal tov!' I didn't want to believe it: *l'Feiga v'Biber nolad ben.*[35] I've got to get used to this idea and this fact, but you think you can get right over it and into your day-to-day routine.
>
> I'm not surprised at all your nerves haven't held up. The books describe it very poetically: 'becoming a mother, the halo of maternity, that sacred emotion' and so on and so forth. But I know so many sensitive women who didn't get through the brutal shock of giving birth to their first child unscathed – especially after six or twelve

years of marriage. For instance Różka Stokman (that house child-turned-housewife of ours), who might seem so stable, gave birth at almost the same time as you. Also two weeks premature, according to the doctor's calculations. Their first baby after nine years living together. And in the first weeks, instead of being happy (they both wanted a daughter and have a daughter – and love one another very much), she kept crying and crying. She was practically ashamed of the state she was in, because she couldn't explain it to herself. There clearly must be something in it, since even the Health Service – which was hardly democratically set up – in all the world gives a woman two weeks off after having a baby. The physical process of recovery doesn't take so long, after all, yet evidently they take mental attitude into account as well, besides wanting a mother to have more time for her baby in the first two, most difficult, months. It's different on the kibbutzim, but you're only human, after all. Perhaps today you're already 'on the road to recovery,' since you wrote on the 12th and it's now 25 Sept, but when you see these words it will be the second or third of October and your son, yours and Biber's, will already be two months old. And every day you'll be looking to see what he got from who, and every day will find new resemblances. And, why, you've both known and seen so many children, but in truth you haven't seen any. Only now will you see what a smart, clever creature he is, this month-old or months-old person.

From watching my grandchildren I have learned to watch and marvel at what progress they make from day to day, how they cope, what they got from their fathers and mothers, what they gain on their own every day, every hour, every minute. And I am sure, my dearest Fajgusia, that with him you'll feel less and less lonely and (you'll say this is selfishness) I'll be less and less needed.

Because who knows when we'll see one another. Reading the papers I can see that hardships are coming and that one person's concerns are truly unimportant compared to what's happening all around.

Big kisses and give my best to Biber, and give Neta a little kiss on the hand from me, and write about him, because after all I want to get to know him.[36]

She underlines the words 'yours and Biber's'.

***

Finally she can be alone when she wants to. Though she considered the Warsaw Housing Cooperative, she ultimately rents a room in Wola district, on Działdowska Street (we don't know which number).

It's modest, small, but sunny. No one knocks or comes uninvited. But most importantly: she doesn't have to give anyone advice or answer questions. She can even sleep when she wants. She knows (she fears? she hopes?) that in six months she'll have had enough of this freedom, but for now it's wonderful.

She calls this joy selfishness.[37]

To get from Działdowska Street to Krochmalna Street takes less than fifteen minutes.

***

At Centos she writes reports in the pedagogical clinic on almost 200 children's homes all over Poland.

From a letter to Fejga:

> My job? I will tell you briefly: I don't believe in it, but it's a living. It's not my old job at the Orphans' Home, absolutely and unreservedly. I had to commit to six months, but I can see that I should have made it a year, to build something and hand it off later. There's not much work here in Warsaw, and it's even interesting, because I get many children from homes and people wanting to do social work passing through my room in the office.[38]

She works three days a week.

***

Over six months she makes 200 visits; she notes precisely 120 conversations in her report. Some people, she notes, came five or six times. Asking for different things: a recommendation of a child-rearer, advice on running a children's home, what toys to select for a pre-school, information about adopting orphans.

She starts her notes with an appeal for less bureaucracy. She herself knows that a bored, exhausted house parent has no time to write. 'He writes when he must.'[39]

She thinks in concretes. She points out what, in her opinion, must be changed.

> The director of such-and-such an institution writes with a request for recommendations of a preschool teacher, a kindergarten teacher, an elementary school teacher etc. No specific information: how many children, their age, what working conditions, etc. Is this a misunderstanding or carelessness? Or candidates submit applications for a job. I agree that the least valuable candidate may write the most beautiful application, and I know the worn-out platitudes about 'love for children' and 'understanding the whole.' But I have demanded a short application and a detailed autobiographical statement: starting in early childhood with all the details, how and what, where they went to school, whether cared for their younger siblings, what routes they sought out and what paths they took to reach the broad, stony, potholed road of a pedagogue's labour. No frills or literary pretensions, only dates and facts. Anyone who knows how to read between the lines can fish out the rare honest candidate, and discredit the deceiver and phrasologist who gets muddled up in a flood of vague information.[40]

She sets aside ten days a month for site visits – in Pińsk, Białystok, Łódź. She visits orphanages where only Yiddish is spoken.

She does not appear anywhere without warning. A few days before visiting she sends a message: 'I am coming not as an inspector and critic, but as an experienced and generous advisor.' She wants to give them time to prepare.

> Or… even to hide whatever they don't wish to reveal, whatever is inconvenient for them or not regulation, what might be looked upon badly. They have the right to 'mistrust.' […] To sleep in the room of a child-rearer, perhaps in a dormitory with children, eat not at the staff table but along with the children. Then there's no fear that – despite a general clean-up before the 'commission's' arrival, despite changes to the menu for this special occasion, putting the children in their 'Sunday best' and so on – they might have the energy or opportunity to change the atmosphere of the day and the character of the night at a given boarding institution.[41]

She wants to see the dormitories in the evening, at night, and in the morning, the night WC's, how – and not only what – they eat, how they spend their free time, whether on Saturdays they visit their families and if alumni come to the facility.

> Seeing how many beds are empty at night because children are sleeping in pairs, because it's warmer, less scary, because it's tradition, because there aren't enough blankets or mattresses. How many snore, cough, play with themselves, scratch (scabies), wet themselves. How the dormitory wakes up – gently, cheerfully and politely, or grimly, sluggishly and abruptly. These observations open one's eyes to everything that even the most shrewdly staged performance might want to conceal. They betray the secrets of those impeccably made beds covered in their white bedspreads. And conversations with the personnel and words spoken in confidence by child-rearers add to the general image, though often one of questionable integrity.[42]

***

She looks at all this very carefully. Every detail is still important. Nothing escapes her attention. Discipline, order, control.

She looks at what she herself has achieved. ('I know neither how to speak beautifully nor write much. I can only work, and do that slowly, carefully.')[43]

In an article to the press, she proposes not separating siblings. She says that before she dies she will write one book: *Down With Orphanages.*

(Three words to judge an entire life?)

***

At the end of 1937, the board of Ein Harod kibbutz receives a letter: 'We have received all the documentation and we declare a licence to make Aliyah has been confirmed for Stefania Wilczyńska. It will be sent to the Jewish Agency as soon as possible.'

Aliyah, 'return to the land of the fathers.' She does not yet know if she is leaving for good. She doesn't want to make up her mind.

Maybe she doesn't have to. She has the certificate in hand. These days they're in such demand, her friends say, that they're the 'Jewish medal of honour'. Hers is one of almost 11,000 issued that year.

For the fourth time, she packs her suitcase.

It's December.

She writes to Fejga:

> The Doctor is very distressed – maybe I'll bring him along, because I find it very hard to leave him in this condition. And the Home on Krochmalna is not standing firm. And that is very sad.[44]

***

'Maybe you can explain this to me,' Itzhak Belfer says when we speak in Israel. 'Because I know everything: the Doctor moved out, Stefa moved out, she even went to work somewhere else. But she kept ringing the gong every morning, I remember it. I'll tell you more, I even remember the last time I saw her. It's 1938, I'm graduating from school. "Icio", she says to me, "I know things at home are tough, that it's hard for you to leave here. Write an application to our court to let you stay another year. Emphasize," she advised me, "that you'll help the children play and teach drawing." Naturally I wrote what she suggested. And they accepted me for another year. And is somebody going to tell me she was in Palestine then, that that couldn't have happened?'

Notes

1. Letter from Stefania Wilczyńska to Rywka Zwykielska, 10 July 1935 [?].
2. Letter from Stefania Wilczyńska to Fejga Lifszyc, 26 March 1935 [?].
3. Letter from Stefania Wilczyńska to Rywka Zwykielska, 25 May 1935.
4. Letter from Stefania Wilczyńska to Fejga Lifszyc, 19-24 September 1935.
5. 'Yoman: Meshek Ein-Harod', 7 January 1936.
6. *Mały Przegląd*, 3 January 1936.
7. Ibid.
8. Yiddish: gluttons.
9. *Mały Przegląd*, 3 January 1936.
10. *Mały Przegląd*, 24 April 1936.
11. *Mały Przeglad*, 26 June 1936.
12. Ibid.
13. Ibid.
14. Ibid.
15. Letter from Stefania Wilczyńska to Fejga Lifszyc, 8 May 1936.
16. Ibid.
17. Letter from Stefania Wilczyńska to Fejga Lifszyc, April [?] 1936.
18. Letter from Stefania Wilczyńska to Fejga Lifszyc, 28 May 1936.
19. Korczakianum – the research centre of the Warsaw Museum, document with inventory number 0571.
20. Letter from Janusz Korczak to Jakub Kutalczuk, 26 December 1936, in: J. Korczak, *Pisma rozproszone. Listy (1913–1939)* (Warsaw: 2008), p.210.
21. Letter from Stefania Wilczyńska to Fejga Lifszyc, 22 September 1936.

22. Letter from Stefania Wilczyńska to Fejga Lifszyc, 3–11 May 1936.
23. Letter from Stefania Wilczyńska to Fejga Lifszyc, 4 April 1937.
24. Letter from Stefania Wilczyńska to Rywka Zwykielska, undated, 1937.
25. Letter from Stefania Wilczyńska to Rywka Zwykielska, undated, 1937.
26. Letter from Stefania Wilczyńska to Fejga Lifszyc, undated, 1937.
27. L. Süsswein, *Palestyna buduje się…* (Kraków 1939), p.291.
29. Letter from Stefania Wilczyńska to Fejga Lifszyc, 8 May 1937.
29. Letter from Stefania Wilczyńska to Fejga Lifszyc, undated, 1937 [?].
30. Rev Dr W. Szczepański SJ, *Palestyna po wojnie światowej. Światła i cienie* (Kraków: 1923), p.300.
31. A. Tartakower, *Emigracja żydowska z Polski* (Warsaw: 1939), p.59.
32. Letter from Fejga Lifszyc to Stefania Wilczyńska, 8 June 1937.
33. Letter from Stefania Wilczyńska to Fejga Lifszyc, 14 July 1937.
34. A weekly published in Ein Harod kibbutz.
35. Hebr.: A son has been born to Fejga and Biber.
36. Letter from Stefania Wilczyńska to Fejga Lifszyc, 25 September 1937.
37. Letter from Stefania Wilczyńska to Fejga Lifszyc, 15 October 1937.
38. Letter from Stefania Wilczyńska to Fejga Lifszyc, 25 September 1937.
39. S. Wilczyńska, 'Sprawozdanie z półrocznej działalności Poradni Pedagogicznej przy Związku »Centos«' in: *Słowo do dzieci i wychowawców*, B. Puszkin and M. Ciesielska (eds) (Warsaw: 2004).
40. Ibid., pp.80–81.
41. Ibid., p.82.
42. Ibid., pp.82–83.
43. Letter from Stefania Wilczyńska to Rywka Zwykielska, 1937.
44. Letter from Stefania Wilczyńska to Fejga Lifszyc, 23 December 1937.

15

She writes to Fejga in January 1938: 'I can't leave as if I'm running away.'[1]

She fears whether she'll be able to tolerate the climate in Palestine. The desert wind, the dust that gets under your eyelids, into your lungs pins you to the damp ground, because in summer that's the only source of coolness. Her body resists. This made her anxious last time too.

And the language – she still thinks she understands too little, that she speaks Hebrew too badly.

Although she informs Fejga that this will be her last trip after all (she underlines the word 'last'), she wants to bring along only absolute essentials.[2]

(What's absolutely essential to her?)

Before leaving she writes to Fejga:

> And before I get to work I'll need to have a good night's sleep (when do I ever get a good night's sleep in life – that's our chronic illness now) [...]. Leaving here is unpleasant and difficult, because my sister is so sad and I'm not leaving the Orphans' Home in order.
>
> It's all foolishness.
>
> The Doctor is furious I'm leaving and keeps saying I should come back. The alumni too. Well, we shall see.'[3]

She leaves in March 1938. She plans to be there a year and a half, initially. She is breaking up 'for good' into pieces.

By then Ein Harod is a model kibbutz and Eretz, one giant testing ground. A new state, a new way of bringing up a new man. A new type of upbringing. It's fascinating.

In the 1930s, the kibbutz is visited by the famous authors Hanna Mortkowicz-Olczakowa (the daughter of Jakub Mortkowicz, Korczak's publisher), Maria Kuncewiczowa and Ksawery Pruszyński. After his visit in 1933, Pruszyński writes:

> [Ein Harod] was a swamp, now it's a pure-bred, full-blooded kibbutz. In it, the first farming collective I have encountered on my path in life, a new type of agricultural settlement reports for duty.[4]

He is enchanted by the children born on the kibbutz. He compares them to the Jewish children of the shtetls and Warsaw's Nalewki Street.

> These children were already born in Palestine, not in exile. To them the pogrom in Proskurov and German attacks will now be history. [...] [H]ere they call them *sabras*, from the name of a wild bush that is common in this country. [...] If we can compare two of these – sons of one and the same nation – simply place them side by side and show them to people, this would perhaps be the best manifestation of the enormous distance that lies between the world of Exile and the World of Rediscovering the Homeland.[5]

Maria Kuncewiczowa also notices the children. 'Tan, gorgeous, unwilling to be touched, independent.'[6]

Pruszyński spoke with immigrants on his way to Palestine. Mojżesz Schamrot told him why he's going: the end of the diaspora, the return home, the Depression. 'The Palestinian communes and Russia are the only spots where the world is really looking for new forms of life, where it's now freed itself from the domination of the unproductive classes… Our Palestine will show the world the way.'[7] Klara Zalatkowska, a young halutz from Romania also mentions the need for freedom and change. 'We are moving in opposition to the way things are, and we're trying, maybe in communism we'll find a good fit for us. We're also searching in Zionism. And sometimes we switch to one and sometimes the other.'[8]

Others say: we don't want to wait. We want to create the life we want. We're seizing the nearest opportunity to it. If not everyone likes it – it will change. If I don't like it – I'll leave. To them, Palestine is a country with no past tense, only future. The kibbutzim are places with no singular, only plural.

The ship's cabins are small and stuffy, the trip is long. Wilczyńska often goes out on deck, speaks with the halutzim (at this time there are nearly 100,000 of them in Europe, preparing for the journey.)

(When asked why she is going, does she answer: 'to fight against superfluousness'?)

***

In Ein Harod she works in the school with the youngest children.

She lives in a wooden house high on the mountainside. The house is divided into four equally-sized rooms for four families. The entrance room leads to a narrow, extended interior. To the left is a corner kitchen, a connecting room no one knows what to do with because it's too small and oddly shaped, and a bedroom. It's seven large strides from the entrance to the window.

The space is cramped. The walls are thin and you can hear what the neighbours are up to. There's mildew. The house stands on a platform to keep it off the ground, but the ground gets up to it anyway: worms crawl up through the gaps. The worms, like everything else here, are celebrated. They're ours, say the inhabitants with pride, our grasses, our grain, and our worms too, our life in our land.

The living room is lined in plywood like a cigar box. On the other side of a narrow wall is where Fejga and Biber sleep, along with their baby son on days off.

At night, if you peer through a little window with a mosquito net, you might sometimes see the stars. Or during the day, the faint outline of Mount Gilboa.

The door creaks when the wind is picking up.

Wilczyńska gets a section of floor and a sleeping pallet to herself.

Not much room.

Room enough.

***

She's not a guest anymore. As if her earlier trips had been for reconnaissance. She's no longer enchanted by everything like she was back in 1931 when she came for the first time – by the cultivated fields, the little train station with no schedule board where she disembarked seven years ago, when there was still nothing around. By the bizarrely shaped cactuses (only one of the ones she brought home survived at Krochmalna Street). By the vegetables in the cafeteria. Back then she didn't yet know the name of that vegetable you could apparently prepare 80 ways, just like potatoes – the big, long, purple one. Or those bitter little cutlets, made not of meat – which is good because she's vegetarian (with a slight exception for herring) – but of nuts, like the children on Krochmalna Street sometimes got.

Such surprises are behind her.

Now she works, from early in the morning. A few times a week she also has a night shift at the children's home.

When she has a day off, she still goes on walks. Short ones, on which she sees the farmers coming home from work, the shed for 25 cows, the dairy. And the labourers lifting the bright concrete blocks of the museum. The people here aren't even firmly established, she thinks with an admiring smile, and they're already putting up a building for art.

Her longer hikes take her up to the Mount Gilboa range, the feet of which the pioneers left ten years before. They worked, often with their bare hands, doing their best to tear a patch of cultivated land out of the mountain. They told one another stories recorded in Scripture. This is where David defeated Goliath. This is where King Saul and his sons perished.

***

A narrow path leads up to the peak of Gilboa. It passes an overgrown, now-wild vineyard, and tall cypresses mark out the path on either side. They built a cemetery on the mountain, far from the tents.

She often visits it. She stands on the Gilboa mountainside and looks at the slopes of Kumi, descending gently into the valley. The white dots are the children's blocks in the kibbutz.

And here she can also see the bright but dusty city of stone blocks – 140 of them.

Not all the pioneers gave in to the mountains and swamps and moved where everyone else is to build a new settlement. Some stayed behind.

They had their first burial only three months after founding the kibbutz. Back there, in the mires. His name was Nachman. He was 24.

Then after him there was Izaak, who'd come from Russia, and little Leah, as quiet as a mouse. She said she'd come here to give her life meaning. And then Rivka and Chaim. David, who emigrated from Germany in 1933 as one of the many still managing to escape. They wrote on his gravestone: 'He died by his own hand.' The list is long.

They usually noted down each of the deaths in the books of the kibbutz archive. Where they came from, how they remember them. Many have empty spaces by their names.

How to write: frustrated hopes, unpreparedness, conditions that were too difficult and didn't reward their efforts? Or disappointment?

This would look out of place alongside statements such as 'he came to build Eretz', 'he drained the fields', 'he built the first house', 'she had the collective's first baby'. Nor do they look right alongside 'he died poisoned by impure water' or 'after being stung by a scorpion'.

Because, after all, pioneers don't turn back.

The cemetery was active for less than ten years.

They left it behind when they moved across the valley. They founded a new one over there. Near the fields, the houses, the dairy.

***

I am fifty-two years old.

Have I lived?

(What does she think of as she stands on the hill and looks down at the kibbutz?)

***

She writes again to the children of Krochmalna Street:

> I'm sure you're already getting ready to leave. And I'm enjoying the countryside too. The wind carries from a long way off the smell of blossoming orange trees, through my window the pomegranate trees are blooming with red, fleshy flowers. And the roses will barely have time to emerge from their buds before they wilt. Yet there are so many of them that one is always flowering. That's how it is in the gardens, but in the fallow fields and on the roads, the sharp, prickly, thorny thistles have already gone yellow and dried out. They are tall as a grown man and so unapproachable, unwelcoming and unpleasant that it would be more comfortable to take the long way around in the most scorching heat than go cross-country through a thicket of prickly, dry thistles. This is why you can't work barefoot here, nor even walk in the greatest heat because the land is so hard. It demands great sacrifices, effort and labour, though it was said it was 'land flowing with milk and honey.'
>
> [...] Do you know, since I've been here is the only time I've felt the New Year is truly new. [...] I've received many cards with best wishes from children, different from you in the city. Because they don't have money, and anyway there are no stores here at all. So the girls draw on the cards, paint them or paste on pictures and dried flowers, and hand them out around the rooms. [...] And we drank wine from local grapes, good wine – wishing well to all people around the world. Because we don't know whose

fault it is that things are bad – one little girl said. And another added:

'People always say "Arab bands". But when the Arabs look down from the mountains at our village, maybe they think we're a "band" too?'[9]

[...] You ask what I am up to. Apart from my specialty of squeezing lemon and grape juice for 200 schoolchildren, I've gotten one more duty. It's pleasant work, namely sewing on buttons and marking underwear. [...]

Perhaps this will encourage you and will teach you that everything is useful, especially on the kibbutz, where the painter bakes bread at night so during the day he may paint, the doctor scrubs the floor of his room because there are no servants here, and so on. A former teacher cooks, and does it well, in the children's kitchen, while her husband, also a teacher, works in the cowshed, and a former assistant to a good tailor is pleased she can transform an old, tattered coat into a 'nearly new' children's jacket. Because here oftentimes you must turn something 'double inside-out'.[10]

[...] On Friday at school we held a beautiful celebration for the female workers. The children and teacher Moshe did a fantastic job organizing it. It was like Mother's Day, but celebrating working women at the same time. This is an international holiday commemorating the liberation and equal labour and rights of women, on par with men. [...]

The choir sang songs about labour and hoping for a better tomorrow, four older girls recited poems about working women, two read testimonies of Palestinian working women about the early days of their toil, and notes from night guardswomen in the current self-defence militia. Teacher Moshe showed pictures through an epidiascope. That's a kind of machine: you just put in an ordinary postcard, and you'll see a huge picture. In the countryside it takes the place of a movie theatre. So we saw pictures by famous artists who painted women – mothers of various ages and nationalities, up to present-day photographs of women from the war in Spain.[11]

***

Whenever she tries to introduce a technique from Krochmalna Street, the kibbutz resists.

In her articles, Wilczyńska calls for changes:

> Wherever he is, the child has a strong inclination to separate himself […], in this way he creates movable worlds, places where a child can live according to his own imagination, far from the intrusive supervision of adults. Perhaps this is his escape from the strict prohibitions of a home that is not 'his' home. Let us not be naïve but rather openly admit that under the guise of caring for our little ones we very often demand something that's for the benefit of adults. 'Enough of that, stop making noise.' Yet traditionally we talk a great deal about the child's right to movement, freedom, 'self-fulfilment.'[12]

> […] Maybe someone has seen the German film *The Superfluous Man* about the tragedy of a man who, despite being respected, remains unneeded. A similar feeling comes over me (of course not such a tragic one) when it comes to my work at the school. Here I feel unneeded and useless, and some people don't even feel very comfortable around me. There's already a certain group of comrades who avoid meeting me in the dining hall. Because I ask, demand even, time not only for adults but for children too. I demand punctuality for things that are important to them and in general constant thought about the children.
>
> Does this sound funny? Might we find anyone in Ein Harod who wouldn't think about a child? And yet there are many who don't notice the children. Or on the contrary, they notice them, but only when the children are making noise in the dining hall, getting underfoot, playing pipes and disrupting the hours of rest. […] These people do not see that children spend eight months a year no less busy with obligations than grownups are. And that in public places […] they are strongly chastened, yet they don't yet have any rules protecting their rights, as adults do. […] Perhaps my mental condition, recently so full of tension, and my difficult material situation, my fatigue from the climate, have combined to mean the child has 'slipped away' on me and given me the feeling that child-rearing issues have been pushed off into the indefinite future. […] Children, as such, are very rarely noticed. There is simply no time for them. But no solutions have yet been found for these issues in community education. We are only groping blindly for an answer. […] There are some who categorically declare that a child needs *x*

> hours of sleep. How do they know? Have they measured and weighed this in the same way one measures and weighs food? [...] [H]ow do they know with such certainty what's harmful? How do they know it's essential to drink three cups of milk? How do they know that talking during meals is harmful? [...] Or maybe there's something I don't know? Does the relationship between the school and the family not cause a certain number of children to flee from school and from home, to create their own world with no 'allowed' or 'not allowed', those symbols of their grown-up masters? [...] It's hard for me to work in circumstances like these. While it's true everyone listens to my grievances, appreciates them, but when it comes to action, it's an all-too-familiar, politely stated 'no'. I trust that I will be useful, but I'm unable to work without faith. That's the reason why I left my work in Europe and my place of work...[13]

***

A response is published in the kibbutz newspaper:

> Stefa stands haughty and straight-backed in the door of our reception. A favourite teacher and pedagogue who has positively influenced our habits and truly taught – such is the image I always have before my eyes. But here's a disappointment. [...] S. asks for advice. She has been overcome by a feeling of depression. She's spotted obstacles and suddenly her haughtiness is abandoning her. [...] I'd like to remind Stefa of her own words: 'When a worker thinks only: it's not worth it, it's not possible, that's the first step to defeat, it's a failure in child-rearing work. [...] [H]aste is the child-rearer's enemy.'[14]

Another edition carries an ironic statement: 'A miracle! An issue without a piece by Stefa.'

In a letter many years later, Stella Eliasberg will write: 'I don't know what kind of disappointments Stefa and the Doctor had. Why they went back. [...] [A]fter returning from Palestine he often came to see me, showed me the pebbles he'd collected as mementoes. He was very depressed and unhappy with himself. Stefa was the same.'[15]

***

Wilczyńska doesn't understand them and they don't understand her. It's not the language, maybe they just think the way people ought to think here, maybe it can't be taught.

Fejga's place is crowded – her, Biber, little Neta and one tiny little room.

It's hot, it's difficult to work, especially without faith that your work has any purpose.

She starts her shifts at the pre-school at eight in the evening. She hears the children's conversations, about the military, about airplanes. About how not all Arabs are to blame, after all. Sometimes they can hear jackals howling out the window, and sometimes gunshots. The Arab Revolt is underway, there's no prospect of an accord and the Mandatory authorities, the British, are preoccupied with what's going on in Europe.

Once the children are asleep she'll darn something or tidy up.

She wakes up before four with the rest of the kibbutz. At five she returns through the backyards, still quiet at this hour. She's free until evening. 'But I waste a big chunk of the day, because I sleep until 12 like a grand dame after a ball.'[16] She avoids the auditorium. She interjects less and less. She performs her tasks and finds herself jobs to fill every free moment. She squeezes juice out of citrus fruits and although the kibbutz has a machine to do it, she prefers doing it by hand (and finally can feel 'what it means to be 'squeezed like a lemon').[17] Another evening it's cleaning the children's shoes. Two hours later, 50 pairs are ready to go.

***

Many of Wilczyńska's ideas, such as a room for quiet time, praising the children, a self-government, their rights to move and to respect, are introduced in the kibbutz after she leaves.

***

It could have been 1929, or earlier, or later, hard to be sure. Definitely in the evening, but though late at night would be best. Lights out, no one in the hallways and quiet in the Home on Krochmalna Street.

'Look, here's little Helcia's ping-pong ball.' Wilczyńska is walking among the beds in the girls' dorm. Carefully, quietly. 'She put it on the windowsill and forgot it. She was crying. But I told her it would turn up,' she whispers (the Hostel girl following her doesn't know whether to her or to herself).

She sets aside what's lost, covers what's uncovered. She stops on her way past a bed if she hears heavy breathing (her hand – delicately – on the forehead, to check: a fever?), she slows down for a moment if someone is raving in their sleep. She stops to put someone on the chamber pot when they've just gotten out of bed and are groping their way along. Or when someone awakened by a nightmare needs reassuring: there, there, it's all right now.

Her night rounds, every night, most often solitary – it's her favourite daily ritual.

Ten years later, in Ein Harod, she titles her notes from her two-hour shift in the children's dorm, the place where everyone spends the night in accordance with the rules of the kibbutz: 'Chronicles of a Night Watchwoman in the Children's Home'.[18] Every night she writes down whom she puts to bed and when, and who wet the bed and when.

26 October: 'N. asked: am I allowed to sing quietly, really quietly, so only G. can hear?' She allows the children to whisper in the evening.

> 27 October:
>
> L. and M. cover themselves up at night with a blanket – over their heads. L. was crying, she was afraid, a bad dream. And her parents don't want to cover her up at night, they say it's hot out. L. explains she's less afraid when she's under the covers. In the dorm, a child awakened for a moment hears his neighbours snoring or talking in their sleep, water dripping from the faucet, he sees an unfamiliar darkness or creeping shadows. For him, the blanket covers up black night.
>
> 1 November:
>
> Non-independence of four-and five-year-olds when undressing themselves. Their parents mainly undress them, lay out clothes, carry their children – even big ones – to bed. But after all, many children would like to do these things 'themselves'. Untie their shoes themselves, unbutton themselves, make the bed themselves. But it must take longer, and father is in a hurry because he doesn't have time or is tired. Or mother must go take care of younger brother.
>
> 2 November:
>
> C. was shouting in the night that his stomach hurt. He didn't cry, he

> lay quietly, clenched his lips. I asked him: should I leave a nightlight by your bed?
>
> 'Oh yes!'
>
> I lit it – he fell asleep. And when S. had an awful dream, I sat with her with a light until she fell asleep. And when later G. couldn't get to sleep, and everyone around was asleep, I also lit a light in the hallway for him. So he felt more at ease and not so lonely. We know what the torture of insomnia is for an adult person. But when C. was awake for five minutes, the next day he said: I didn't sleep all night.

She invents the initial letters of the children's names, so they won't be embarrassed if they recognize their fears in the stories she describes.

***

The buildings scattered over the Kumi mountainside still look like cardboard models cut out of Bristol board. I look at them from the old cemetery on the other side of the valley. I know I won't find any traces of Wilczyńska here, that she couldn't have seen the same thing: the rail line is gone (though the little brick building of Ein Harod station has remained), a paved road cuts through the bottom of the valley, large water tanks have been built on the slope of Mount Gilboa.

But as I look down from the peak of Kumi, the view is nearly the same. Fewer than twenty houses, with red-shingled roofs, and in the middle a larger cube – the dining hall with the auditorium, smaller ones to the right and left, but then also the tallest: the store, where the kibbutzniks buy without having to pay, and the former pre-school. The houses in even rows are no longer uniformly white, which makes them look like someone's coloured them in.

When I go further down, nearby I see two rows of palm trees. Tall, maybe as high as the fifth or sixth floor of a skyscraper, they go down as far as the boundary that once marked the kibbutz. To Wilczyńska they were shoulder-height.

The air is full of the smell of mandarins; their low, small trees grow everywhere here. Amid the houses, bushes blossom pink, white and orange. Narrow dirt paths meander up toward the peak, taking dozens of turns. The grass is still irrigated, but by dusk the ground – baked all day long in the sun – burns anyway. Then the blades crunch under your feet like straw.

Despite that, this section of the mountainside looks like an oasis. Where the kibbutz ends, the green begins – clumps of lavender, and trees whose branches sag with heavy, juicy grapefruits.

Here, right here, it's still beautiful. Empty.

In the evening, the sounds of everyday activity don't escape the houses: music is played softly enough to stay within four walls. Quarrels, if they happen, take place in quiet. The many dogs visible during the day don't bark as you walk past a house after dark.

The nights are hushed.

The old kibbutz is shrinking. The dairy has been privatized, the shares divided. All that occasionally breaks the evening silence is the buzzing of old golf carts, driven by the last people who listened to the stories of the pioneers.

***

One of them is Yael, petite and frail, who cries and apologizes. She is, she says quietly, over ninety years old and really shouldn't get so carried away, but she can't help it.

'We were so bad to her it was practically shameful. It was our fault. But we were silly little brats back then. This older lady showed up (to us anyone over thirty was already old) and she kept wanting to praise us for doing such a wonderful job. And besides that, she spoke so strangely, this woman who'd come from *Polin*, with an accent. And she was constantly wanting to do something, make some improvements of her own, but we were fine with how things were. Or she wanted to help, but we did everything on our own here. I remember she taught us songs.'

Like the Polish national anthem. Yael still remembers the words and the rhythm: *Jeszcze Polska nie zginęła, póki my żyjemy…*

'Maybe if we'd been better, she'd have stayed? Would she have encouraged Korczak, maybe they'd have brought the children, what do you think?'

And tears again.

'We had parents, we weren't orphans,' says Ruth, the youngest of three former students of Wilczyńska's. 'We didn't need as much as she wanted to give us. She was breaking down an open door.'

Ruth was late meeting me for tea – as she used to be for the lunch that fell during Stefa's shift – because 'I was staring at the war on television.' It's mid-November 2012, Israel has launched yet another military operation in Gaza. Before long they turn on the TV in the café too, so we can hear about it.

Ruth:

'She used to praise us to the heavens. She wanted to write about the children's accomplishments in our newsletter. And we used to look at her like she was crazy.'

On a kibbutz, doing work is like breathing. Praise for breathing? Ridiculous.

'She was sort of...' Yusuf speaks up for the first time and maybe that's why he takes his time looking for the right word. One after the other he rejects 'sad', 'serious' and 'intimidating'.

And he explains: the village was their whole world.

'Even when the Arab Revolt was going on and people were being killed all around us, we were in paradise. We knew nothing of money. What mattered was work and resting after work. We walked around with our heads held high. We were spoiled, the centre of the world, the first children born in Eretz. We felt pride. We actually spent the day together and the night in the children's home, but still we were kings of the kibbutz.'

(Yusuf can't decide: was she more *galmuda* or *bodedet*. Lonely or solitary?)

As I leave, Yael Tabenkin, Ruth Ofer and Yusuf Richtenshtein are fifteen again, stealing chickens and reminiscing about the pioneer days of Ein Harod.

***

'There is no greater solitude than on the kibbutz,' says Amela Einat, who's spent twenty years as a therapist on Israeli kibbutzim. 'From morning to evening you blend into the mass, after dusk you shut down to escape from it. But there's no escape, because the kibbutz sees, watches, knows. Even though you cling to the illusion that somewhere here you've got something that belongs only to you, something of "your own", and you stick close by your loved ones.'

***

'Yusuf asked me to tell you,' says Ilana Bernstein from the kibbutz archive, 'that she wasn't *galmuda* after all. He finally decided she was *nifredet*, though he doesn't know exactly if such a word exists.'

Nifredet, which Yusuf thinks is closest to the truth, means 'apart'.

***

From the kibbutz meeting minutes, spring and summer of 1938:

> The word 'no' is common in schools, and likewise pedagogues and parents also say 'no.' Because it's much easier to say 'no' than 'yes', but is this a solution to the matter?
>
> I remember people accusing me because I didn't want to force the children to drink milk with their afternoon snack. And if I served more than one portion, I was told that's not allowed. Why are there children who don't like sugar and some who like herring? [...] [E]ven a cow knows herself what she needs to eat. In this world, doctors' recommendations are often made because of the needs of the market, the needs of sellers.

> Although you have all given the children a different life than the one you remember yourselves, you govern them as you were governed, as it was in your parents' houses. And what feelings did you have toward your parents [...]? We idealize the past. Were we really so well-behaved, devoted and caring to our parents? To excuse ourselves, we sometimes say: 'true, our parents didn't understand us so well, didn't give us as much and weren't as devoted to us as we are to our children.' This is untrue. [...] [P]erhaps I'm wrong, I don't know relationships between parents and children so well, but I must ask: is it always necessary, fair and responsible for parents to give their children everything they have, everything they can give, and make sure not to touch them or offend them even once they're grown up? And yet at the same time parents demand that children understand and participate in their own serious troubles [...], I believe, moreover, that children suffer all of your woes very profoundly, yet *differently* from adults.
>
> Children can see and hear not only what's happening in their parents' rooms, but also what's happening in other rooms. I believe they know more than adults think. They watch, observe, listen and talk among themselves about all these issues. I hear snippets from time to time: 'This or that teacher's acting differently, and they tell us that's not allowed.' How true, we demand more of them than of ourselves, yet we know, after all, that when raising children the example is more important than the words.

> I must tread carefully, because anyone could say to me: You don't have children, so it's easy for you to talk.[19]

***

In January 1939 she speaks for the last time at a meeting about the rulebook (she reads the one Korczak developed for the Home). Discouraged, she explains to the kibbutz members why she won't be introducing any changes: "I think there are more appropriate people than I. Younger and with time to wait. I can't wait any longer. I haven't had any luck with certain issues. I have initiated a few changes and they haven't gotten anywhere positive. [...] I can only assist."[20]

***

In Ein Harod, in the evening, people gather after work to listen to the radio. Newspapers arrive too, and letters from relatives.

In spring of 1939, the evenings are more and more often spent talking about war. People nervously discuss how to get their families out of Europe. They gather documents and apply for certificates.

***

The workbook of Rózka Sternkac, a Hostel resident, is full of dense notes. In 1934 what was giving here the most trouble were the oldest house children, the 14-year-olds, about to leave Krochmalna Street.

She told Wilczyńska: 'Szlomek wrote an obituary: "Adolf Hitler, a housepainter by trade, has kicked the bucket. RIP." He gets very emotional when people talk about Germany in school. When they do, he shouts: get lost! Get lost! When someone talks about their chemical industry, he shouts: yeah, that's right! They're making gases for the war!'

***

Shlomo:

'So, was I wrong? We talked about practically nothing else. 1937, 1938, 1939, war was at our borders. The Anschluss, Munich, the Danzig ultimatum, Minister Beck's speech, to this day I remember, we followed it. There was a joke going around Kercelak market: "Hitler is very reasonable.

He wants the living room, but he'll settle for the corridor." I don't remember if I was afraid of war.'

***

Fejga:

'You promised to stay.'
Stefa:
'My children are there.'
(1939, Ein Harod)

***

From the kibbutz newspaper, 2 May 1939: 'Today Stefa left for Poland.'

Notes

1. Letter from Stefania Wilczyńska to Fejga Lifszyc, 15 January 1938.
2. Letter from Stefania Wilczyńska to Fejga Lifszyc, 19 January 1938.
3. Letter from Stefania Wilczyńska to Fejga Lifszyc, 8 February 1938.
4. K. Pruszyński, *Palestyna po raz trzeci* (Warsaw: 1933), p.92.
5. Ibid., pp.94–95.
6. M. Kuncewiczowa, *Miasto Heroda. Notatki palestyńskie* (Warsaw: 1939), p.92.
7. K. Pruszyński, *Palestyna*..., op. cit., p.13.
8. Ibid., p.15.
9. *Mały Przegląd*, 25 November 1938.
10. *Mały Przegląd*, 20 January 1938.
11. *Mały Przegląd*, 13 May 1938.
12. S. Wilczyńska, 'Liczby czy wrażenia' in *Słowo do dzieci i wychowawców*, B. Puszkin and M. Ciesielska (eds) (Warsaw: 2004), p.102.
13. 'Proszę o radę' in S. Wilczyńska, *Słowo do dzieci*..., op. cit., p.95.
14. 'Milczeliśmy! (w związku z wypowiedzią Stefy)' in S. Wilczyńska, *Słowo do dzieci*..., op. cit., p.207.
15. Letter from Stella Eliasberg to Ada Poznańska-Hagari, 24 January 1953, Korczakianum – Research centre of the Museum of Warsaw.
16. *Mały Przegląd*, 15 November 1938.
17. *Mały Przegląd*, 21 January 1938.
18. 'Zapiski wartowniczki nocnej w domu dziecięcym,' in: S. Wilczyńska, *Słowo do dzieci*..., op. cit., pp.106-111.
19. 'Protokoły zebrań kibucowych (fragment – wypowiedzi Stefy)' in S. Wilczyńska, *Słowo*..., op. cit., p.194-201.
20. Ibid., p.202.

16

The girls, in dresses and dark smocks, sit barefoot. They are focused on their task, not looking at the lens. Peelings (taken from the white aprons laid on their laps) go into a wicker basket, the potatoes, into a shared pot. The war is already here. The ghetto is not, yet. The garden where they sit is blooming, it's warm out.

Just like on that early morning when the first German planes flew over Krochmalna Street. The children playing in the courtyard think it's the Polish air force. They cheer. In the first days of September 1939, the Home doesn't escape the bombings, but isn't badly damaged either.

They organize a shelter in the basement, and Wilczyńska also runs a nursing station there. Life tries to continue on its old rhythm, to make its way through ruins, air raid sirens and bombs (when the bombardment is heavy, the children move from the dormitory to a bathroom on a lower floor).

(Do they still make job lists, now expanded with new positions? The plumbing's out – need to draw water; the wounded are arriving – help with bandaging.)

When the general mobilization was declared, Korczak once again tried to enlist and even sewed himself a uniform. They refused him due to his age. He doesn't take off his uniform. He wears it until Polish Radio is forced off the air.

Despite the fighting and the civilian population's support, at the end of September the city surrenders. The occupation begins, and soon Warsaw finds itself in the military occupation zone known as the General Government. The whole city does its best to carry on as before. By October, stores and shops are already opening in significantly damaged Wola district. Polish Radio goes underground and its broadcasts of classical music are interspersed with speeches. Even Korczak presents an appeal to children (including about how to behave during an air raid). The city is adapting, though most people believe this isn't for long and the war will be over by spring at the latest.

The Home's residents are also doing everything they can. Wake-up with the strike of a gong, breakfast at a fixed time (though with each day prices are rising at a frenzied pace), keeping the children busy since they aren't going out to school. The court also ought to be in session since, after all, regardless of the war if someone violates an article, they need to be held responsible. There are fewer court cases, though – the house children have acquitted themselves bravely during the siege of the city. Korczak even rewarded them with a present – a banner like the one the main character dreams of in Korczak's *King Matt the First*, and apparently also coloured green. They march with it down Okopowa and Gęsia Streets – which will soon form part of a closed district – in a procession from the Jewish cemetery following the funeral of Józef Sztokman, an employee of the Home. They march in their Sunday best to Krochmalna Street, proud and sombre, waving their new flag.

Wilczyńska must be worried. Winter is coming, they have no reserves and they don't know how long their supplies will last.

(How often does she think back to the last war? Famine, typhus, fear as she made sure the roll matched up every day?)

The roll, if they are checking it at Krochmalna, is only getting longer for now. Children are arriving who were orphaned in the first months of the war, or got lost in the mass of refugees from other cities. Although Centos continues to operate and is offering support to the orphanages, boarding houses and children's centres of Warsaw and the surrounding region, money is short. Korczak sets out to appeal to pockets and consciences.

What about Stefa? She's probably prepared.

The year was 1925 (or maybe 1928?). She pinned a piece of paper to the inside of the door of the wardrobe in her room: 'After my death please give my body to the anatomy laboratory. And the children's studies should not be interrupted.'

In 1929 *Our Review* wrote (once again): 'Every year, students of Jewish faith in the medical department encounter difficulties due to a lack of Jewish cadavers.' Everything should serve a purpose – this message stayed with house children long after they left.

Usefulness, prudence: qualities in particular demand in the event of war.

(Is that enough? The only thing that's enough is to prepare for everything.)

***

After the fall of Warsaw, an American delegation of the Red Cross comes to visit orphanages. When Korczak finds out German officers will also be in attendance, he categorically refuses to come out. Wilczyńska argues with him for a long time – and convinces him. He emerges dressed in his Polish uniform (under his coat).

The occupation has also brought with it the persecution of Jews. Their bank and savings accounts are blocked, they are forbidden from possessing more than 2,000 złotys in cash, they are banned from trading in textiles and leather goods, pawn brokers are forbidden from returning Jews their items on deposit, Jewish companies are forbidden from registering, apartment buildings are taken over, Jewish bookstores and libraries are closed. Before long, schools for Jewish children are shut down as well. Soon Jews will be banned from travelling by train, entering certain parks, medically treating Aryans and registering to practise law.

The atmosphere is ever more stifling. But this is barely the beginning.

On 1 December 1939, Governor Hans Frank issues an order requiring Jews throughout the General Government to wear a visible distinguishing mark. Wilczyńska puts an armband, at least nine centimetres wide with a Star of David in the middle, on the right sleeve of her coat. Korczak refuses to wear one.

Children under ten are exempt from this order – and also from forced labour, which is obligatory for men between the ages of 14 and 60. Some will flee to avoid it.

***

Shlomo Nadel expects a certain level of engagement. It's not enough to sit and listen. He waits for the moment when interest usually gives way first to impatience and then a stubborn reminder: 'Keep going! Come on, tell me, what happened next?'

His pauses grow longer and he waits. He sinks into his soft armchair, rests – and waits. It's not his first time telling this story and he knows when to stop talking. He has to repeat the part about the SS officer saving his backpack more loudly, and carefully enunciate his escape across the Bug River. And deliver the build-up to that moment in a hushed voice.

And wait.

He has already been here with his story hundreds of times. Now, if you want to reach the moral, then you're going to get a little worn out, impatient. Listen intently, pretend you understand, find an appropriate facial expression.

He waits for that expression. Without it, he won't start.

'Was it warm then or cold? Was it drizzling that day? What colour was it, exactly, Shlomo, what was she wearing?'

'You're not listening carefully,' he says, already getting irritated. 'Come on, I'm telling you that doesn't matter, listen better.'

He's ticked off, you've got to wait it out. Sit tight, because he'll get back to his story momentarily. After all, this the only reason that he's still here, and that you are too.

But you've got to interfere. Knock him off his rhythm, drill into the cracks in his smoothed-out story, into the places where he says 'I don't remember, I think that's how it was'. Force him, yet again, to go back and tell you how he met her, what stuck in his mind. How he said goodbye to her. This isn't what he agreed to meet for.

Yet here he is, getting back on track, falling into the rut of retelling the same story, he nestles down into it. He's calm, he's at home.

***

'What can a young man do when he's 19 and war breaks out, how can he not run away? I went to ask what to do next. To say goodbye to Korczak and Stefa. He told me: "Shlomo, don't go believing that over there with the Soviets you'll lie on the sofa all day and get nothing but free lunches. People there work hard for a crust of stale bread. Don't believe that communism of theirs is so beautiful. We were counting on you boys, that when you grew up, you'd work, that you'd help us in the war. But may luck help you to survive, run away."'

Shlomo breaks off, cries.

'And I spent four years hungry, four years on the run, four years away from them and the next seventy, even more without them. What was it like, how was I going to escape? I asked my mother to give me my little brother, he was four years younger than me, we called him Samek although his name was Simcha, that's "joy" in Hebrew. She told me: "He's little. Why, they won't do anything to him." Here's a photo of him, the only thing I have left of my brother. Mama said: "Let one of you at least stay with me." There was nothing I could do, I had to obey her. I set off. I brought along a photo I'd taken in the Home, my guardian Felek Grzyb had first shown me how. And out there, on the run in the East, me and another boy got robbed. There were two of them, Polish men. I didn't know they were robbers. I was making my way from Warsaw to the border on foot, we did forty kilometres on the first day. I wouldn't have made it that far on the second day, but we had another hundred kilometres to go. So when a cart drove up, we were thrilled. These two guys go: "Don't walk, it isn't safe, if you got ten złotys we'll give you a ride." We gave them the money and climbed on. And we hadn't gotten far before they started whipping us, shouting: "git off, git, ya little kikes." They beat us on the head, in the face, in the eyes. They threw us off the cart and took everything. Those photos of mine as well. I wouldn't have done this now, but in those days I still had Korczak inside me. And he used to tell us: "if you know what you've done, if you're in the right and you know it for sure, then even a king will hear you out and acknowledge it. If you're sure of yourself, stick to your guns." And, foolish hero that I am, I stand in the road and when I see a little vehicle coming, I wave my arm, I flag it down. We're standing there, my friend and me, holding our hands up in the middle of the road, and this vehicle stops a metre from us. The door opens… the fact I didn't shit my pants right then makes me a *gibor*, a hero. It was a German officer! I could hear the driver tell him "don't bother with them." And he says back: "this'll just take a few minutes." What were we worth? Two little garlic peels, that's all. *Ping, ping* and two little Jews are gone. But he shouts to the Poles over there, "halt, come here." He shoots once in the air, they turn around. The one that beat us up starts shouting: "they're Jews, they're communists, they're running away to the Reds." The German officer said: "I didn't ask you what they are, I asked who you are. Who gave you permission to rob them?" As this was happening I thought I was in some movie, something was all out of whack. "Give them back what you stole." And he tells me: "on the way there's a German commander's office, you're supposed to register there." They chased the Poles away and left us on the road.'

'What happened then?'

'I went, what else could I do, I'd given my word.'

'You went to register?!'

'I mean, lying wasn't allowed. You know what Stefa would've done if she found out I'd lied? One of my friends from Krochmalna says Korczak raised nothing but fools, but would you believe when we got there they let us go? And to this day I'm sorry I didn't ask who he was. The fellow who saved me. I don't know his name, nothing. I had no way of helping him, but what if he needed it? He knew Polish, maybe he was from somewhere near Poznań, maybe from Gdańsk? What if he was a good person and I needed to help him?'

***

Through the wall I can hear shouting.

'Give it back.'

'I'm not giving it back.'

'Give it back!'

'I need to have it!'

Shlomo is arguing with his Moldovan care-giver.

She soothes him:

'Come on, it's just going to sit right here, it won't get lost.'

'I won't let you have it!'

And so on every night.

Now too, he keeps placing his hand over his hip, checking through the fabric that the contents of his pocket haven't changed, haven't fallen out, haven't crumpled.

He wraps his talisman, four centimetres square, in a ragged handkerchief (which he changes every few years, though they're always equally grey) with a pale-blue edge, five times. Then he lays it flat in one palm and covers it with the other. And slides it into the very bottom of his pocket. He pats it: it's close.

'You want to see?'

Taking it out takes longer. The narrow pocket resists, his hands tremble, his clumsiness frustrates him. At any moment he might drop the thing he's so carefully guarded, so the whole action demands precision and patience. Unwrapping (the five turns around its axis are five chances for it to break, so he does it slowly), it looks like a child playing at passing a ball from hand to hand. When the finally freed amulet appears in his open hand, the sight is disappointing. The object isn't even solid plastic, but a cocoon of Scotch tape. At the very centre is a bulge – one or maybe two (the tape on it is broken, protruding, 70 years' worth of dust is stuck to it), smaller than a grain of coffee. It's a walnut shell.

'I once went to Germany and at customs they asked me: "what's that?" I answered: "Das ist mein Talisman." The customs guard looked at me and said: "Schließlich ist es nichts." So in the end it's nothing.'

***

More and more goodbyes. Wilczyńska is anxious for the house children fleeing Warsaw.

They are also anxious for her. In spring of 1940 she receives a letter. It's from Fejga Lifszyc by way of the Red Cross, asking for a return message.

On a postcard dated 2 April 1940 she replies: 'My Darling, we are healthy. I am working in the Orphans' Home a little, and Korczak a lot. I haven't come because I don't want to go without the children. Your Stefa.'[1]

Six days later, maybe in fear that the first postcard won't reach Fejga, Stefa sends another: 'We are working in the Orphans' Home. Without the children I don't want to come and therefore you must have patience. Give my love to everyone, Stefa.'[2]

***

With every order, life in the General Government grows more difficult, especially for Jews. They are now banned from, among other things, borrowing books, and are refused spaces in hospitals. On 2 October 1940, Warsaw District Governor Ludwig Fischer signs one more document addressed to the Jews: on the creation of a closed district.

The Home at 92 Krochmalna Street doesn't fall within the designated borders of the Jewish district. It must move to 33 Chłodna Street, the building of the Roeslers' renowned business school.

In November, Wilczyńska oversees the relocation of: 100 (120? 150?) plates, bowls, mugs (metal ones?), sets of cutlery, dish towels, brushes, pillows, quilts, bed sheets, chamber pots (how many could there be, twenty?), and beds (how much furniture are they allowed to bring?). So maybe better to bring mattresses, they're transported in piles a storey high. How many sets of underwear? Books (which?), dolls, arithmetic slates, balls, the microscope (does she take it?), rags (they might prove useful if the kids put on a show)?

She leaves the bunch of keys to Pan Zalewski, the janitor, who wants to go to the ghetto with them (they don't let him; he'll stay to look after the Home and wait for their return. The Germans will shoot him in the courtyard in August 1944). The potatoes brought from Krochmalna Street to Chłodna Street are halted and confiscated. Korczak, in his Polish uniform with no armband, goes to the Germans to protest. He ends up in Pawiak Prison. Wilczyńska remains (unbegrudgingly) alone at the head of the Home.

They share the building on Chłodna Street with others. When she finds out that one of their new neighbours knows Hebrew, she speaks with him whenever she can. She doesn't want to get out of practice.

(Does she believe the war will end soon and she'll leave for Palestine? When does she stop believing that? Is it when in spring of 1940 she hears about the surrender of Belgium, the Netherlands and then France? Or when in mid-November the ghetto is closed and she becomes one of 40,000 imprisoned inside it? Or maybe slightly later in November, when the Home has 150 children and a staff to feed, but the yellow ration card – ethnic Poles receive pink ones with higher values – for a single person corresponds to 369 calories?)

Though social welfare is overseen by the Judenrat – the Jewish self-government formed on Frank's orders at the start of the war – and the Department of Welfare and Jewish Social Mutual Aid (made up of organizations like Centos), aid is also delivered by the American Jewish Joint Distribution Committee, known as 'the Joint'. Yet neither their funds nor their capabilities are sufficient. Rachela (Rokhl) Auerbach, who runs a soup kitchen for the poorest writes: 'all our charitable institutions' activities should be called breaking death up into instalments'.[3]

The Home receives bread only ten times a month, in portions of 250 grams per person (later even this ration is reduced to two kilograms per month), and180–200 grams of sugar per person each month.

She doesn't know that she's still lucky. The roll still matches up, and their wards will not be among the 96,000 ghetto children first swollen with hunger (in hiding, in apartments, in basements) and then dead from starvation (on sidewalks, in courtyards, on steps).

She must see them when she walks through the closed district (where she, like everyone, gets seven by seven metres for herself, squares without green space, and cramped streets): bald children-skeletons, the still living and the no longer living, are propped up against walls or not propped up at all, blocking way in the middle of the sidewalk, abandoned. In fall of 1941 they will wrap them in posters for a Centos campaign. (September 15 to October 15, 1941 was 'Month of the Child'. The slogan: 'Children must live'.) In two years there won't even be paper left.

(How often has she managed to avoid going outside?)

***

From Korczak's notes: in January 1941, the 140 children at the Home on Chłodna Street lost 17 kilograms,

in April: 12,

in May: 55,

in June: 18.

The total weight lost in the first half of the year amounts to 3.1 kilograms per child.

And the ghetto is getting denser. New people keep arriving. At the Home, too.

***

On 30 April, Rózia Dratwa dictates:

> By the time they deported my mama and my sister to who-knows-where, my papa was dead. One young Christian lady I knew placed me in a convent. I spent a whole year there. And I was all right. They fed us four times a day, both soup and bread, and we were never hungry. We played with dolls. They told me to pray. Even though they knew I was Jewish, no one teased me. Sometimes we'd go for walks in the park, but it's better here, because I've got my aunt here and I go to lessons. I wouldn't want to go back there, but I don't know why.

Michaś Krzeczanowski tells a story:

> As soon as the war started, by that Saturday German and Polish planes were already fighting, and on Monday three bombers flew over us. On the morning of 8 September there was still a Polish patrol, but by the afternoon a German one had arrived. At first they gave out candy and laughed as the kids grabbed it. I didn't want to take any. A few weeks later the Germans announced that all the Jews had to gather on a large square […]. And they taught us how to take off our caps: how if a German was coming, we had to step off the sidewalk and take it off. Afterward they rounded everybody up. They showed us their loaded rifles and said: you're the ones we'll be shooting at. Later they said we had to wear triangles on front and on back. Then they ordered us again to close all the stores. They said: if you want us to resettle you like humans, we had to give them silver and gold, because if not they'd resettle us like animals. They said: you've got ten days to make sure there's not one Jew left in the county.

Jerzyk Rott:

> We were making our way to Warsaw on foot. In the distance we'd see a plane coming and before long we'd hear rattling. People would start jumping off their carts and hiding in ditches, I'd hide under a bush, so

> you couldn't see me at all. Then back to the carts. You were constantly terrified. Here you'd see someone torn in half, there one arm, a leg. Then there was the ghetto. Mama got sick right at the start. That was two weeks ago. Every day another person died. Papa did his best to get a job as a courier – they overworked him and he got sick. He lay down in bed and the next day I woke up and saw papa lying on the floor, he'd been thrashing around in convulsions. A heart attack. Mama, papa… in such agony. A week ago my brother got taken away to a camp.

On 13 May, Marceli Zabinowski told his story:

> Papa told my sister, my mama and me to hide in the bedroom, because the shutters in there were closed and he thought that if the Germans saw there was no one there, they'd leave. But they got really worked up and started pounding on the door with rifle butts and shouting. As they were looking for the caretaker, papa opened the door with a skeleton key and told us to run away. I managed to take my sister. When I went to the Poles' next door, they were afraid to keep us because it was a huge responsibility. We had to leave, so we joined our neighbours who'd been arrested. I didn't want to go without our parents, but the soldiers were pushing us. My sister was wailing, she was cold, and they just laughed. I gave my sister my cap, because I could do all right without it.

A note: 'He dictates confidently, constantly looking and checking to see if I've written it down correctly. He's playing the hero a little.'

On 13 May, Marysia Sznajberg (eleven years old) says:

> Papa was working in a factory, he was a weaver, not earning much. Mama worked at home and I helped her. We were doing well. When summer came, papa, mama, my sister and I went on a trip to the forest, we sang songs, it was really fun. Then we heard war was coming and we had to cover our windows with black paper. Then, when the bombing was over, the Germans came and chased out almost all the Jews. And us too. While they were chasing us, since we still had money, we decided to go to Russia. We rode, and then we walked, across the no-man's-land between Germany and Russia. We lay down on the ground there. And then Russia didn't let us enter, in the harshest cold. Many people starved to death. There were no houses there at all. So we lay there on the ground for a long time,

> until a German train came and took us away. We rode for two days, to some town where all the Jews had been shot. They took us into this big room where the wall had ice on it. They took us there to shoot us. And once we were standing there in pairs, an order came to send us to Warsaw instead. But there was nowhere for us to live there, so they told us to stay in a synagogue, in Praga district. It was really cold there, even colder than outside. And then we were in quarantine, two days a week we got a piece of bread and we couldn't leave, women and children were in one room, men in another. After two weeks they let us out, and then did it again. And it made my mother sick, because she was anaemic, she went to the hospital and died. And then papa did his best to get me into the Orphans' Home. Now papa is selling everything we have and still living in the synagogue, and my sister is with him. She's also going hungry, she's not going to school, she's forgotten everything.

Note: 'The girl is very reasonable, she tells her story calmly. She's accepted her fate.'

Felunia Frydman, eleven years old, arrived from an orphanage on Wolska Street. She says:

> There were lice there, there was scabies, a hundred and fifty children had it. And horrible hunger. We didn't change our underwear because there wasn't any, just one pair of stockings for the whole winter. Rats in the dorms, there was no bathroom, just a bucket, everyone argued over who had to empty it, no one wanted to, so it just sat there. It stank so badly that if you went in there, ma'am, you'd have to come right out again. Then we moved to Dzielna Street, there was nowhere to play there, we were surrounded by Pawiak Prison. And there was no light and no teaching. We sat in the dark, we couldn't go up to the window because of the shooting. There were five hundred of us there and kids died every day. One night fifty-eight died. Anyone new who arrived was gone before long.

Note: 'She tells her story exceptionally eagerly, she draws conclusions herself, she thinks carefully.'

Cyrka Klejner (nine years old):

> At the start of the war planes flew over and dropped leaflets saying to surrender. But Poland didn't want to. Then the Germans broke

> something to do with the water and lighting. And then Poland gave up. The Germans came in. First they pretended to be good, and then they kept getting worse. Mama was working in the basement of the Home. She got me in here. I like it here.

A woman records the children's accounts: where they came from, what they experienced before they were accepted into the Home. Is this Wilczyńska? We might think so, but we can't be sure. The notes have a familiar tone, they show how much she knows about the child she's describing in a few sentences. But what about the questions she didn't write down? The follow-ups? Whoever was making the notes knew what and how to ask the person responding. In the Israeli archive of the Ghetto Fighters kibbutz, the inventory attributes the notes' authorship to Wilczyńska without any doubt.

The children bring with them: nightmares, screams in their sleep and bedwetting, orphanhood, hunger, fear, typhus, typhoid fever, dysentery, trachoma, bare feet, sweaters with holes in them, lice.

In April 1941, Thursdays fell on the third, the tenth, the seventeenth and the twenty-fourth. In May there were five of them: the first, the eighth, the fifteenth, the twenty-second and the twenty-ninth. June, luckily, again had one fewer: the fifth, the twelfth, the nineteenth and the twenty-sixth.

Thursdays were when Wilczyńska processed applications to enrol in the Home.

(Did she hate Thursdays?)

***

Prices keep getting higher in the ghetto, the smuggling can't keep up, there's a shortage of everything except anxiety. In fact, there's even more anxiety than usual in June 1941 – when Germany attacks the Soviet Union – and in August – when typhus is raging. They can't clear the corpses fast enough.

By now nearly two years have passed since Korczak's appeal 'To Christian Citizens' in 1939 (he attached these appeals to the letters he sent). In it, he evoked section three of the declaration of the General Council of the International Save the Children Union of 1923: A child should receive aid ahead of others in a time of distress. Korczak: 'The task of the Orphans' Home today, is to care for children whose families have left to seek a new berth. It is our aim to return them after a few weeks or months, as orphaned children – not louse-ridden – not scabrous – or ravaged and disfigured by destitution. This would not befit Poland's Honor, but discredit the care and defense owed to the Jewish child in the face of undue injustice.'[4]

There are few places where they can ask for help, but they never flag in their efforts. They also ask for geranium seedlings – to keep the children busy. They get them.

In September they send a postcard (signed: 'Henryk Goldszmit/ Korczak and Stefa') to Canada, to former house child Leon Gluzman: 'Inform others who still remember their childhood years.' They ask for food packages. The ration cards are not enough.

It's getting harder to find fat for lunch, sometimes horse meat is the option. They cook sweet milk soup, cholent from rutabagas with powdered egg substitute, and they drink coffee made of beets and barley.

But she still strikes her gong for mealtimes.

Despite the fact that smuggled grain is being ground in dozens of illegal mills in the ghetto, in attics and basements, there is still a shortage of bread. Any that you can get has walnut shells and sawdust in it. It's damp and sour.

Korczak in his diary: 'After my rude letter to the dignitary, we received a not half bad boost of sausage, even ham, even a hundred pastries. [...] And then a surprise in the form of two hundred kilos of potatoes. [...] A tormented "Did I do the right or wrong thing?" is the gloomy accompaniment to the children's carefree breakfast.'[5]

At Centos they prefer to talk to Wilczyńska than to Korczak. She listens calmly, sometimes even smiles slightly, she doesn't raise her voice or slam doors. Helena Merenholc, an employee there: 'She understood we couldn't always fulfil their unrealistic demands.'[6]

Korczak to Zofia Rozenblum, head doctor of Centos (in spring): 'To your question about the children's health I have the right to answer as one usually responds to bothersome and thoughtless questions: What's new? Nothing much. [...] Giving to the Orphans' Home is not some favour, it is their wretched duty. They may hate me, scorn me, swear, whatever they want and as much as they want; but they do not have the right, for the sake of this scorn and hatred for me personally, to steal the children's fish oil, or sugar, or eggs, or anything that belongs to them.'[7]

Centos, in response: 'The fact that the Orphans' Home has fish oil was communicated to us not by detectives, but by Pani Wilczyńska. The commission [of which she was a member] accepted the principle that institutions that have already received fish oil will be excluded from the distribution.'

What's going on in the home? Well this, for instance: 150 children sit behind long tables with white tablecloths. A choir sings Palestinian songs, one of the boys reads the Haggadah – the Passover story of the Israelites' departure from Egypt. 'This year we are slaves. Next year we will be free people.'

They're doing the best they can.

***

A phone call from Shlomo. He says excitedly:

'There's so many important things I forgot to tell you! About the acacia tree, the avocado tree and the lemon tree. The acacia tree grew in front of our Home and cast shade on Wilczyńska's windows. She brought the avocado tree from Palestine. It wouldn't grow because how could it grow there, in the wrong soil, the sun was wrong. But she watered it and waited for it to sprout, she kept it in the sun beside her cactuses. The lemon tree, because she liked them. Not for herself, for us. We'd make a face, but we'd take a bite. And she told us how it had vitamins, it would make us healthy. I heard that even during the war, in the ghetto, she'd go to get the lemons, but I don't know if that can be true.'

***

The president of the Warsaw Judenrat Census Department of the Board of the Jewish District informs Dr Janusz Korczak of population changes in the closed district (internal correspondence):

October 1941. Deaths: 1,221. Note: this line indicates only the number of registered dead. The number of deaths according to cemetery data was 4,716.

November 1941. Deaths: 5. Number of funerals according to the cemetery: 4,801.

December 1941. Deaths: 3.Note: According to the cemetery the number of funerals was 4,366. The number 3 refers only to registered deaths.

***

'A postcard came from you. I can still recognize Marszałkowska Street and Łazienki Park, but the rest is a totally different city now.' Shlomo always calls early in the morning. 'You know how sorry I am that Frida can't see it! I told her about what's on the postcard, about the city I don't recognize there, the one you know. But she… She's not long for this world and there's nothing I can do about it. She doesn't even recognize me anymore and but I still say 'good morning' to her every day. I greet her that way every morning. You know, when I was coming out of the Holocaust, I didn't think to get married, I didn't think at all of being with someone, because what for? But I met her and she made me brave enough to try again. We've got two sons. One handles our groceries, the other drives us to the doctor, buys our meds. Frida's the one who raised them, those sons of mine, so good. 'Dad, you were always busy. When we needed you, you were out taking pictures, you weren't there,' that's what they told me. 'Cause that's how I was my whole life, snap, snap, photos. I started taking them in the orphanage and then for the rest of my life. Snap, snap. To leave something behind.'

A year earlier, in Israel, he showed me other postcards he's kept:

> Date: 16 Apr 41
>
> Dear Szlomek, mother's worried why we haven't heard from you in so long. Maybe you didn't get my postcard. Lots has changed here, mother's still working in the same place, but with no money. I'm in the Hostel of the Orphans' Home, Dr Korczak's hostel, currently at 33 Chłodna Street. I run the wood shop, from 9 to four, after that I read, write or go for a bit of a walk. Here it's full spring, we had the Easter vacation with bread. I'm earning a few złotys. Once again I'd like to please request, if you are able, to send me a package, and please know that I'm in need. I'll make it up to you for sure. Don't forget about your brother who's in need. I beg you. How are things with you? Are you healthy? Tell us all about everything. Be sure to write back, because mother is worried. Stay healthy, all my love from afar, and once again, please send a package. Write back right away, your brother Samek Nadel
>
> I'm very sorry we're writing back so late, but it isn't our fault, because we had some difficulties, we can't take pictures because we can't send them. I'm still in the Hostel of the Orphans' Home and am in charge of the wood shop, sometimes my stomach gets demanding, so I pick up a book and read. Much has changed in the Orphans' Home and at home. Every week I buy more black bread for 6 zł a kilo. Mother is working in the same place and is only getting ten złotys a month. We're luckily healthy. How are things with you? Tell us about everything precisely. I have one big request. If you can, please send a package for me to mother's address. Is there any chance you can try for us? Regards from the family and for our friends, once again please send a package, because I'm in need. I'll make it up to you for

> certain. Warmest regards and please write back quickly. Your brother Samek Nadel and mother Gela Nadel. All our love.

'See what a fortune I have here. Four postcards from my mother and brother, faded, that's all I have left. Snap, snap, I take pictures of them so I have more, practically even a whole handful of these postcards, enough for a box, not just a slim envelope.'

While Shlomo – who gets conscripted into the Red Army's labour battalions – is working in a mine in the Urals, in Warsaw in October 1941 the ghetto once again tightens up its borders.

Maria Falska offers Korczak help getting out to the Aryan side.

(Does anyone offer to get Wilczyńska out of the ghetto too? Maybe her brother, who lives in Żoliborz district?)

Meanwhile Stefania organizes for the Home to move once again, this time to 9 Śliska Street/16 Sienna Street – the building spans a narrow block. Before the war it was the headquarters of a traders' and industrialists' society, it has large, tall window, a ballroom with a gallery, and a second large gymnasium. The Orphans' Home doesn't take up the whole of it. There's a café on the ground floor where a famous pianist plays, on the fourth floor they serve soup for the hungry (in the entire ghetto over 100,000 soups are served a day).

They have less space than they need. A large room is divided by wardrobes and beds, which act as the walls – during the day they move them aside. They eat in shifts, there aren't enough plates or chairs.

Wilczyńska doesn't have her own little room here, she has a bed squeezed into a recess in the main room. It's stuffy, the courtyard has been shrunk to a dead end.

The opposite side of Sienna Street falls outside the ghetto and first a barbed-wire fence and then a wall run down the middle of the roadway. From the windows on the third floor they can see the gap left by a demolished building and the rest of Warsaw.

(Does she look?)

***

From an article by Wilczyńska about architecture being unsuitable for children's needs, written during her stay in Ein Harod:

> Windowsills in classrooms are also found at a height of 120–130–140 cm; on balconies, even higher. I have asked specialist doctors:

> does this 'blocking out' the sun have a purpose, must windows necessarily be so high? The school principal responded with a question: 'Have you ever been a teacher? If not – then you don't know that this nosy and undisciplined "crowd" can't keep themselves under control even for the most interesting lesson and will stare at the street through the window.' And I remembered one section of the drama *Eros and Psyche*, which tells the story of a certain nun who is punished by imprisonment in a locked tower and is supposed to only ring the bells for prayers. And when the prioress of the convent asks: 'Is the sinful soul now sufficiently protected from temptations from the outside?' one of the nuns gives voice to her doubts: 'Why, her eyes can see the sky and the clouds driven by the wind, and who knows, maybe some lost bird will fly there as well...' Even that meter-and-a-half height for a window in a classroom is too little, because they might see the sun or an airplane in the sky – is any lesson more interesting than an airplane, especially a military one?[8]

The windows that looked out on the street have been covered up.

On Saturdays, the children still leave to see their families.

***

Israel Gutman, though he is not yet even 20 years old, is active in the resistance, meaning he has little time to regularly visit Sienna Street. Yet one morning he manages to finally make it there. He finds his sister Gina in the main room. She's playing with some children. The rooms are clean, the Home as noisy as before. The Home – he notes – has brought stability along with it. Inside, it feels like there's no ghetto. Gina spots him and takes him to see Wilczyńska.

'In recent days many parents and care-givers have been coming to take their children; others believe the little ones are safest here with us. I won't stop you. Gina can leave if you think that's what's safest for her and it will be better that way. But we ourselves aren't encouraging people to take them.'

The Judenrat assures them: there is no reason to fear.

(Does she believe that assurance?)

In the Home they've made a rule: children who have been taken away will not be allowed back.

Wilczyńska tells Israel that she might make an exception for Gina.

He goes back to his sister and sits down with her on a bench on the patch of courtyard. They talk – he tells her that he promised their mother he'd look after his sister, that people are getting deported who-knows-where, that the two of them should stick together. She says she's already thought this through: yesterday in the corner of the room where she sleeps, two children got picked up by their families, including her best friend. She thought about what to do when someone comes for her. She doesn't want to leave the Home. She likes it here – she's terrified of the street, the crowds, the unfamiliar. What if he doesn't come back one day? These days people don't come back. So better to stay here, where it's warm and there are the children, the Doctor and Pani Stefa.

He doesn't know how to tell her that nowhere is safe anymore. He looks his sister in the eyes. 'She knows even without me telling her. All the little ones know it.'

He kisses Gina and leaves quickly.

Within a year, he'll be fighting in the Ghetto Uprising. He'll go through Majdanek, Auschwitz, Mauthausen. For the whole rest of his life, as a historian, he'll document and research the Holocaust, and even run Yad Vashem. For the whole rest of his life, as a brother, he'll think of how that day, he didn't look back.

***

The ghetto doesn't hear the news about the decision made in Wannsee in January 1942. Yet soon it does hear from Szlamek Ber Winer, who escaped the camp in Chełmno. He tells of exhaust fumes being used to kill people there. The ghetto doesn't know that Wannsee and Chełmno are directly linked by cause and effect, nor that this is only the beginning and that they are already approaching their final reckoning.

At this time the closed district contains 50,000 children between the ages of 7 and 14. The underground *Information Bulletin* reports on 30 April 1942 on the conditions they are living in:

> The Warsaw Ghetto. Poverty, hunger and cold, and catastrophic hygienic conditions have created horrible circumstances here […].
>
> There is a row of so-called special houses, where the greatest paupers live, where death takes its greatest toll. For instance, in the house at 46 Miła Street, currently with 500 residents, so far 233 have died. […] In the house at 63 Pawia Street, with 794 residents – 450 have died, including 200 in the last two months. The record in this tragic statistic was broken by the house at 21 Krochmalna Street,

> with 400 residents, and the same number of deaths, i.e. 400 people. [...]

At almost the same time, Mojżesz Chonowski from Centos reports from an inspection of the storeroom in the boarding-house on Sienna Street: 'it was impossible to conduct an inspection on 29 March, since because due to an overload of work before the Easter break, the staff did not have the necessary available time to weigh their food products. It was agreed with the matron to postpone the inspection.'[9]

The reason they didn't have the necessary time available was that they are still doing their utmost to ensure that the ghetto, despite ever more virulent efforts, still does not alter the order of the Home. For instance, the seminars Korczak and Wilczyńska hold on Monday evenings with the Hostel residents. Some selected topics of discussion:

what is duty,
evil and anger,
symbiosis,
loneliness.

Wilczyńska often runs into Zivia Lubetkin, an underground activist, as they both wait in line for the same ghetto aid organizations. They become friends. Zivia invites Stefa (they're on first-name terms) to 34 Dzielna Street, where she lives with Yitzhak 'Antek' Zuckerman and others in a halutz-style commune. Wilczyńska brings Korczak, who delivers lectures for them; for a year, both he and she have been taking part in underground seminars for people coming from all over Poland, and give independent speeches at Dzielna Street in January 1942. Wilczyńska, seeing the conditions they're living in, tries to support them. When the halutzim recover a farm in Grochów that was abandoned after the air raids – their own kibbutz – against Korczak's wishes, she sends them tools rescued all the way from the Home's farm in Gocławek. She mothers them. 'A general with a toothache cannot lead an army.'[10] She tries to convince them to take better care of themselves. 'If leaders of a movement are hungry, their discretion is impaired.'[11] It will be another year before their discretion faces its strongest test. In April 1943, Antek and Zivia, along with other members of the Jewish Combat Organization (ŻOB), launch the Ghetto Uprising.

(Would she also have told them, as she used to tell rebellious house children, 'get your revolution over with?' Would she have tried to talk them out of it?)

The staff are also busy with lockboxes. At Krochmalna Street every child had their own, and used it to hold items that belonged only to them. Their treasures (what is a treasure in the ghetto? Vegetable peelings can still be boiled, there are no seeds because there's no fruit, so probably pebbles, pieces of debris, there are still plenty of those). On Sienna Street, the children also have something to keep their belongings in. The staff have prepared them 200–250 cans, boxes, pieces of cardboard.

(Did she prepare them?)

Then there's also Passover. In April 1942, organized killing operations begin in the closed district. Fear of deportation is growing, on the streets there is talk of nothing else.

At the same time on Sienna Street they're organizing a Seder, as tradition dictates. Estera Winogron and the children are rehearsing *The Post Office* by Rabindranath Tagore. The plot: Amal, a sick, young Indian boy chained to his bed on his doctor's orders, can only observe the world through the window. He hears it, feels, has it at arm's length. The boy wants to escape his tiny, cramped room, but the guard reassures him: the time will come when someone will take him by the hand and lead him out, the boy only needs to get a letter from the king, which will bring freedom. The messenger is right around the corner. Before he arrives, Amal falls quietly asleep.

***

Right around the corner. That's really very close.

But life in the Home doesn't slow its pace. Sienna Street only gets festive for the holidays, from day to day they must simply exist. Keep the children busy.

They're bored.

They're afraid.

The younger ones write diaries. Marceli notes: 'I found a penknife. I will give fifteen groszy to the poor. I vowed it to myself.'[12]

In May, Zygmuś, Semi, Abrasza, Hanka and Aronek write to Father Marceli Godlewski, the parish priest of All Saints Church on Grzybowski Square, now on the edge of the ghetto: 'We respectfully request [...] permission for visits to the church garden on Saturdays [...]. We will not damage the seedlings.'[13]

Korczak notes at this time in his diary: 'this quiet might yet be disturbed by a visit from [Pani] Stefa with some good news, or something requiring tiring deliberation, a desperate decision.'[14] He mentions her barely a few times in the diary, in these stories she's a side note.

In June, they march through the city with their banner a second time, on the anniversary of Dr Eliasberg's death. They swear at his grave that they 'will live in love for people, justice and truth.' It's a beautiful, sunny day and they are beautiful as they march through the ghetto.

On the afternoon of Saturday 18 July, they invite guests to Sienna Street for a second performance of *The Post Office*. When Amal falls asleep, Korczak hunches in a darkened corner. He is more and more depressed, trapped by the ghetto. Wilczyńska also sits in the audience in the ballroom, in the last row.

'Right around the corner' means barely four days. On 22 July, the great deportation operation begins. From then on, every day at the Umschlagplatz – the loading point in the north of the ghetto –people will be gathered and then loaded onto trains heading 'to the East'.

From Korczak's diary, late July/early August:

> All our efforts to get Esterka [Winogron] back have come to nothing. […]
>
> 'Where was she caught?' someone asks.
>
> Maybe it's not she, but we who are caught (by staying behind).
>
> I've written to the police to send away Adzio: he is mentally backward and maliciously insubordinate. We can't jeopardize the home for some stunt of his. (Collective responsibility.) […]
>
> I don't know how and what the soldier of a victorious army feels…[15]

Shortly before this, Korczak stopped weighing and measuring the children. He's no longer interested in the results. He's in very bad condition, he tires quickly, every few hours he has to rest. We don't know if he knew (did they know? did they believe?) that those being deported 'to the East' were not going for labour.

***

The end of July, maybe it's already August. Wilczyńska makes two visits.

At Centos, she says to Helena Merenholc: 'The children don't know anything, we're doing all we can to keep them from panicking. They trust us. Whatever happens, we'll all be together to the end.'

Her voice is calm.

She also comes to see Stella Eliasberg. With a request for cyanide. She says: 'I want to have it on me. I'll take it at the last moment, when there's no hope left.' Eliasberg says years later: 'I gave it to her.'[16]

(Did she want it for herself? For Korczak? For the children – which ones, how to choose? And – did she take it in time?)

She's in a hurry, she has to get back to Sienna Street as soon as possible. 'So they don't take them without me.'

All we know for sure is that on 5 (probably) or 6 (less likely) August, the Orphans' Home was targeted for the deportation operation. A procession of children and their care-givers crossed the ghetto to the *Umschlagplatz*, where they were placed in at least two of the more than 20 cars of a train, which set off for Treblinka. There are more stories about how the children, the Home staff and Korczak looked as they walked than there are people who could have witnessed it. Apparently Wilczyńska led a second group (others say she walked at the end); she'd made the children sandwiches for the journey and prepared them clean clothes.

***

At first, Shlomo shrugs.

'What kind of question is that, what was it like? Does anyone think that makes any difference?'

'The point is to establish the scenario that's closest to the truth.'

'But what happened there wasn't close to the truth.'

Now I'm the one who gets mad.

'I know you go see kabbalists, Shlomo, but even you should know that's not what I'm asking about. I just want the facts.'

'But I wasn't there, how am I supposed to know? I heard that Korczak could have saved himself, chosen to get out to the Aryan side, hide, run away. Maybe she could have too. But seems to me: if he, and Stefa too, lived the whole life they did – with us –then what else could they have done? There was no choice to make! None, you understand? There was only a theoretical possibility.'

Notes

1. Archive of the Ghetto Fighters kibbutz, inventory number 13395.
2. Ibid.
3. *Getto warszawskie. Przewodnik po nieistniejącym mieście*, B. Engelking, J. Leonciak (eds) (Warsaw: 2013), p. 332.
4. J. Korczak, *How to Love a Child…*, op. cit., vol. 2, p.223.
5. Ibid., p.283.
6. *Janusz Korczak. Życie i dzieło. Materiały z Międzynarodowej Sesji Naukowej* (Warsaw: 1982), p.126.

7. *Janusz Korczak w getcie. Nowe źródła*, A. Lewin (ed.) (Warsaw: 1992), p.85.
8. *Mibifnim*, 19 April 1940.
9. Archive of the Jewish Historical Institute, catalogue number 200/3.
10. Yitzhak Zuckerman, *A Surplus of Memory: Chronicle of the Warsaw Ghetto Uprising*; tr. and ed. by Barbara Harshav (Berkeley: 1993), p.117.
11. Ibid.
12. J. Korczak, *How to Love a Child…*, op. cit., vol. 2, p.308.
13. Ibid., p.289.
14. Ibid., p.281.
15. Ibid., pp.324–325.
16. Recollections of Stella Eliasberg, *Pani Stefa*, manuscript, Korczakianum – research centre of the Museum of Warsaw.

17

In accordance with schedule no. 548 of 3 August 1942 – set by the German General Directorship of the Eastern Railroad for daily journeys of the special train for deportees running between Gdański Station in Warsaw and Treblinka, from 6 August onward – an empty train leaves the rail siding at Treblinka station, having completely emptied its cargo.

Treblinka II – the largest of the camps designed under Operation Reinhardt for the sole purpose of killing – went into operation several weeks before final preparations were complete. Its fake station waiting room with the painted-on clock (whose hands did not move) was not yet built. Its performance was considered unsatisfactory – the gas chambers were over capacity, meaning some of the human cargo transported through the gates the camp was killed by shots to the back of the head shortly after disembarking. Daily processing capacity fluctuated between 8,000 and 10,000. Order had to be brought to the killing. We do not know if the transport of 5/6 August arrived at the camp before this optimization or after.

***

> *'Did you ever talk to any of the people who arrived?'*
>
> '[...] [T]hey were standing there just after they'd arrived, and one Jew came up to me and said he wanted to make a complaint. So I said yes, certainly, what was it. He said that one of the Lithuanian guards [...] had promised to give him water if he gave him his watch. But he had taken the watch and not given him any water. Well that wasn't right, was it? Anyway, I don't permit pilfering. I asked the Lithuanians then and there who it was who had taken the watch, but nobody came forward. Franz – you know, Kurt Franz – whispered to me that the man involved could be one of the Lithuanian officers – they had so-called officers – and that I couldn't embarrass an officer in front of his men. Well, I said, 'I am not interested what sort of uniform a man wears. I am only interested in what is inside a man.'

> But don't think *that* didn't get back to Warsaw in a hurry. But what's right is right, isn't it? I made them all line up and turn out their pockets.'
>
> '*In front of the prisoners?*'
>
> 'Yes, what else? Once a complaint is made it has to be investigated. Of course we didn't find the watch – whoever it was had got rid of it.'
>
> '*What happened to the complainant?*'
>
> 'Who?'[1]

Franz Stangl, the commandant of Treblinka II after its reorganization, was captured after the war in South America and sentenced to life imprisonment in 1970 for his role in the killing of over 900,000 people. He agreed to give an interview to the British journalist Gitta Sereny.

In his cell in a Düsseldorf prison, he read a great deal. One children's book fascinated him. Yet he wouldn't have bought it for his grandson, who lived in Brazil. He said: 'I've studied it, […] I know why [Germans] don't want to buy it. […] "When a soldier gets an order, he must obey it. He must not ask questions, he must not hesitate, and must not think: he must obey." […] Of course parents here don't want their children to read this. […] That is exactly the sort of thing they must not read, ever again.'[2]

Stangl meant Korczak's novel *King Matt the First.* The section he was questioning reads: 'Now Matt understood that the colonel of the engineers had been right to be angry yesterday, and that in war every order must be carried out quickly and without any unnecessary gab. Yes, a civilian could do what he wanted, hesitate, and waste time talking, but a soldier knows only one thing: an order must be carried out without delay, every command fulfilled to the letter.'[3]

Until the end, Stangl maintained that before he arrived at Treblinka he didn't know what his duties would be. When asked whether, once he'd learned his true role in the camp, he wanted to change anything about how it operated, he replied: 'This was the system. […] It worked. And because it worked, it was irreversible.'[4]

***

Once the methods were optimized, the time needed to completely unload a train's cargo was estimated at no more than 180 minutes from when it entered the camp. The respective stages were timed out by specialists from the newly-founded logistics branch: specialists in managing subhuman resources converted into cargo (15–20 minutes from opening the train cars to lining deportees up on the road to the gas chambers), specialists in efficient deprivation of life with the aid of combustion gas (10–25 minutes) and specialists in large-scale cremation (2,000 corpses – one-third of a transport – laid out on steel grates in no more than 25 minutes).

4:20 p.m.: planned arrival of the transport.

4:20–4:40 p.m.: opening the first 20 train cars, collecting baggage, directing a share of the deportees (the sick, the old, the youngest) to the 'field hospital', killing them by a shot to the back of the head and/or pushing them into a burning pit; separating the remaining men and women, undressing, cutting off the women's hair, confiscating personal possessions with no monetary value or utility (and which were therefore, for the Reich's purposes, worthless) as well as documents, and burning them.

4:40, maybe 4:45 p.m.: lining up on the road to the gas chambers, the truth becomes clear, opening up the next 20 train cars.

5:00 p.m.: gassing begins. There follows, in stages: pressure in the head; reddening of the skin; convulsions; vomiting; involuntary excretion; loss of vision, hearing, smell, orientation; significant drop in arterial pressure; cerebral oedema, heart arrhythmia.

At around the twelfth minute the screams subside.

5:25 p.m.: gassing ends.

5:45 p.m.: emptying the gas chambers, transferring corpses from the gas chambers to pits, burning.

6:00 p.m.: opening up the last train cars.

6:20 p.m.: lining up the remaining share of the cargo on the road to the gas chambers.

6:40 p.m.: gassing.

After about twelve minutes the screams subside.

7:00 p.m.: gassing ends, transferring corpses from the gas chambers to pits, burning.

7:00 p.m.: planned departure of the empty train toward Gdański station in Warsaw.

***

'We had this custom in the Home that on Passover, during the Seder, the Doctor would sneak a walnut shell into a meatball. Whoever got that one had good luck. And I got it once. I wrapped up the shell and carried it with me. And when I went to Krochmalna Street that time to say goodbye before running away to the East, I told him: "This will bring me luck".

Shlomo had the shell with him when he escaped first the ghetto and then occupied Poland. During his wanderings in the East. When the war ended. When he returned to Poland and shortly later, when he learned there was no one waiting for him. In the short-lived Jewish settlement in Dzierżoniów, in the transitional kibbutz where he waited to leave for Palestine. When he met Frida and when a week before our last meeting they celebrated their sixty-fifth wedding anniversary (they got an enormous bouquet of roses from both their sons, and a gang of grandchildren and great-grandchildren – because as he said, there are Nadels again – also standing in the shade on the terrace).

He had it when he came to Eretz in 1950 and when, unemployed, he wandered aimlessly through the streets of Tel Aviv in the first years of emigration, and long after, when he finally found a job in a photography studio. At all the wedding shoots he was commissioned for. During the long hours he worked, which made his sons later accuse him of never being there. At all the speeches he gets invited to schools for, to tell children about the utopia on Krochmalna Street. When he was granted the Order of the Smile (number 952). Every time Israel fought one of its wars. The first time he got paid a pension. When Frida got sick, and then stopped getting out of bed and no longer asked him, as she had through all those years of their marriage: 'Shlomo, now tell me something you've never told me before.'

He brought it with him to the kabbalists that he asked: why me and not my little brother? And when they told him: because it was your destiny. *For you to stay alive.* Tell the story of what you went through and ask no more questions. But don't make a long face, you've had nothing but luck, you have nothing more to be absolved from. Leave it be, don't ask.

He also has the shell at every one of our meetings, including the one when he tells me: I'm a realist, but in the end even realists have to believe in something, so I believed in it and stopped asking questions. And then you came here and once again I have no peace.

'What about Wilczyńska, did you say goodbye to her?'

'She gave me something too. You want to see? I've never shown this to anybody…'

(He takes my hands in his.)

'…she didn't say anything, she just looked in my eyes, sadly, like this, and squeezed tight…' (he squeezes mine into a fist) '…and gave me this…' (he squeezes my hands tighter, and waits) '…don't you feel it? She gave me this…'

He opens my closed hand, it's empty, he points at the centre of my palm.

'Don't you see yet?' He waits again, getting impatient. '…she gave me something that meant I was never alone again.'

He puts some fruit in a shopping bag.

'So you don't get hungry on the road.'

Notes

1. G. Sereny, *Into That Darkness: from Mercy Killing to Mass Murder, a study of Franz Stangl, the Commandant of Treblinka* (New York: 1983), p.170.
2. Ibid., p.260.
3. J. Korczak, *King Matt the First*, trans. Richard Lourie (New York: 2004), p.61.
4. G. Sereny, op. cit., p.202.

Timeline

1933: Anniversary of the Orphans' Aid Society. The lawyer Leon Lichtenbaum, a member of the Society, gives a speech. He asks it to be minuted, because '*verba volant* – words fly away – but *scripta manent* – what is written remains', so he also makes a formal motion and asks 'that the minutes record that Dr Henryk Goldszmit and Pani Stefania have served our Society well.'[1]

January 1942: Janusz Korczak writes a polemic letter in response to an article by Guta Ejzencwajg in the *Jewish Gazette*:

> The Orphans' Home was not, is not, and will not be Korczak's Orphans' Home. I am too small, too weak, too poor, and too foolish to select very nearly two hundred small children, dress them, gather them, feed them, heat them, care for them and introduce them into life. This great work has been performed as a group effort. [...] They include many wonderful names, there are also many unnamed. [...] Wilczyńska, Poz, Korczak (if names are required) – they are clerks and administrators of a considerable fortune. [...] We are wrong to identify scope, technique, competence and outcomes of work with the individual administrator who was given the task of carrying it out.'[2]

1942/43: Emanuel Ringelblum in his diary/chronicle of the ghetto:

> The whole time, before the war and during the war, Korczak worked alongside Pani Stefania Wilczyńska. They worked together their entire lives. Not even death separated them. They went together to die. Everything to do with Korczak individually – the boarding-house, propagating love for children – everything is their joint achievement. It is difficult to define where Korczak begins and where Wilczyńska ends.[3]

The Liquidation of the Warsaw Ghetto – A Report, published in November 1942 by the Home Army Office of Information and Propaganda. Antoni Szymanowski notes under the (incorrect) date of August 3:

> Yesterday saw the deportation of the entire children's boarding-house run for many years by the renowned child-rearer and author Janusz Korczak. The Germans gave him permission to remain – but he did not accept the offer. He went the children on their final path. Such behaviour is growing more frequent here. Korczak's assistants also went with him. I want to shout: hail his heroic decision, this death that crowned a beautiful, beneficial life.

10 December 1942: London, Foreign Minister of the Polish Government-in-Exile Edward Raczyński sends a note to the Allied governments: 'All of the children from the Jewish schools, orphanages and children's homes were deported, not excluding children from the orphanage remaining under the care of the famous pedagogue Dr Janusz Korczak, who refused to leave his charges, though he was given the opportunity to remain behind.'[4]

3 January 1943: *Polish News*, London, an item on page five: 'The Heroic Stand of Janusz Korczak'.

4 April 1943: *Polish Weekly*, New York, Gustaw Bychowski writes his 'Recollections of J. Korczak'. 'Although the lives of saints belong to the distant past, I have always known that we have one true saint living among us, for I have always considered Janusz Korczak, that is Doctor Henryk Goldszmit, a saint.'[5] Four columns speak of Korczak's life, and the last one, of his death:

> The Gestapo assassins appeared arrived at Orphans' Home and hauled the children out to annihilation. The executioners generously allowed him, Korczak, who had never in his life raised a hand to any child, to stay. But that is not how our holy friend was to end his life, for to him, life without the children would be meaningless. He therefore did not feel heroic in the slightest when he went willingly with the children to destruction. If somewhere above our bloody and disgraced earth there is a heaven, then there in a great meadow, surrounded by all the martyred children of the whole of Poland, their holy care-giver Janusz Korczak is fulfilling his divine mandate.

24 August 1943: *Free Poland*, Moscow, Stanisław Skrzeszewski writes an article about Korczak (title: 'To the Martyrs of the National Cause'). He closes it with the words: 'the captain of the orphans' ship remained onboard until the final moment'.

1 October 1943: *On the Road*, Jerusalem, the journalist Paulina Appenszlak writes an in-depth 'Recollection of Janusz Korczak'. She also remembers Wilczyńska: she was the one who introduced Appenszlak to Korczak at the orphanage on Franciszkańska Street; she had a little room near the girls' dorm.

1946: Stefania Beylin publishes an article in *Today's Woman*: 'Janusz Korczak and His Children'. She mentions Wilczyńska in the section about the move into the ghetto ('his loyal assistant'). The piece ends with this paragraph: 'Like that legendary youth who played the pipes to lead crowds of children out of the city, so did he lead his children far away, across the vastness of torment and suffering, to a land where no pain could reach.'[6]

June 1947: The President of the Polish People's Republic, Bolesław Bierut, accepts a proposal from the Minister of Education to posthumously grant Janusz Korczak the Commander's Cross of the Order of the Rebirth of Poland for his outstanding achievements in the field of childcare. The document also names other honourees – the Officer's Cross is granted, also posthumously, to Maria Falska. One of the recipients of the Golden Cross of Merit is Janina Bierut, the First Lady, who before the war was a pre-school teacher. Wilczyńska receives a Silver Cross Second Degree. The cross (on a short, red ribbon) still has its identification tag, number 1496.

However the justification for the proposal to honour her has been lost, nor do we know who suggested it (the medal, according to law, is granted to those who 'performed actions beyond the range of their ordinary duties').

September 1958: The Janusz Korczak Children's Home No. 2 opens at the site of the former Orphans' Home.

February 1964: At a meeting of the Korczak Committee, a proposal is made to open a Janusz Korczak and Stefania Wilczyńska museum. The idea is not returned to.

1977

> And one day I selected out Pola Lifszyc. The next day she went to her house and she saw that her mother wasn't there – her mother was already in a column marching toward the Umschlagplatz. Pola ran after this column alone, she ran after this column from Leszno Street to Stawki – her fiancé gave her a lift in his riksa so that she

could catch up – and she made it. At the last minute she managed to merge into the crowd so as to be able to get on the train with her mother.

Everybody knows about Korczak, right? Korczak was a hero because he went to death with his children of his own free will.

But Pola Lifszyc, who went with her mother – who knows about Pola Lifszyc?[7]

(Marek Edelman, one of the leaders of the Ghetto Uprising, asks the journalist Hanna Krall.)

1978: UNESCO declares it the Year of Janusz Korczak.

May 1978: Treblinka. On the grounds of the former Nazi death camp, the ceremonial unveiling takes place of a memorial stone in honour of Janusz Korczak and the children. The monument at Treblinka is made up of 17,000 of these stones – this is the only one with an inscribed name. To this day, teddy bears and cards (with children's and adults' handwriting) are regularly left at its base.

Summer 1979: Shlomo Nadel comes to Poland, to Treblinka. He finds the silence there terrifying. He calls out: little brother, mama, Doctor, Pani Stefa, it's me. He cries. The next day, in Kraków, he collapses in the street. People think he's drunk, he can't get to his feet. He loses consciousness.

1990: The première of the film *Korczak* (directed by Andrzej Wajda, screenplay co-written by Agnieszka Holland). In the final sequence, lasting less than thirty seconds, the car with the Home children disconnects from the train, the doors open from the outside and the children run out into a meadow.

Wajda explains: the easiest thing would have been to show the children dying in the gas chamber, there wouldn't be a dry eye in the house. He wanted to get away from literalism.

The French *Le Monde* runs a review: the author accuses Wajda of revisionism. Claude Lanzmann, director of the documentary *Shoah*, is also critical of the film. One of the defenders of the movie, including its ending, is Marek Edelman.

Wajda's Wilczyńska is played by Ewa Dałkowska. In one scene (time and place: the ghetto), she is talking to Korczak. Her voice breaks, she's close to tears. She keeps saying: 'what will become of us?'

There's no one who could say whether that tone, that near hysteria, was appropriate for Wilczyńska (at that time? at all?).

1999: Shlomo Nadel fills out a 'Page of Testimony' for Wilczyńska – a Yad Vashem document, a sort of symbolic 'tombstone'.

2009: Krzysztof Warlikowski, a theatre director, first stages *(A)pollonia.* This play is about a casualty of human fate, about sacrifice and its futility, opens with a recollection of the performance of *The Post Office* by Tagore in 1942 in the ghetto, at the Home. Warlikowski refers to the contents of an invitation sent from Sienna Street to the guests: 'We are not quick to promise as we have no certainty. We are certain, however that this hour spent with a beautiful tale by a philosopher and poet will stir emotion of the highest level of feeling.'[8]

Warlikowski closes out this thread with the words: 'A fortnight later, Amal and the rest of the orphans from the Home would march off to the boxcars. Korczak would help the children climb to that "highest level of feeling," up the boxcar steps.'[9]

September 2011: The Polish parliament passes a resolution naming 2012 the Year of Janusz Korczak.

2012: The Office of the Children's Ombudsman in Poland publishes *How to Love a Child* and *A Child's Right to Respect* by Janusz Korczak. The print run is small, it only reaches libraries. It was the first time Korczak had been published in ten years. The print runs sold out and even today his books are hard to buy; they appear sometimes in used bookstores and sporadically on internet auction sites.

The Children's Ombudsman places PDFs of Korczak's most important texts on their website.

8 March 2012: The Mojżesz Schorr Foundation declares Women's Day in 2012 Stefania Wilczyńska Day. Short articles appear in the press revisiting Wilczyńska's memory. A Facebook page dedicated to 'Beloved Pani Stefa' receives 486 likes.

9 May 2012: Warsaw. Paintings are hung on the fence of General Gustaw Orlicz-Deszer Park – an exhibition titled *In Memory of a Remarkable Pedagogue*, dedicated to Wilczyńska. A score of people view:

A piece by eleven-year-old Zuzanna Bethencourt – Korczak, a row of smiling children, Wilczyńska (a blue knee-length dress, a bun, blue high-heeled shoes) and the Orphans' Home in the background. Zuzia says: 'everyone is in my painting, it's too bad they're no longer with us'.

An outline of Wilczyńska's face (by Piotr Habierski, in black-and-green embroidery on a white sheet – a technique available and possibly used in 1942 in the Warsaw Ghetto),

A portrait by Jakub Żeligowski (black, acrylic on canvas), under a figure of Wilczyńska, a caption reads: 'The way she lived means she's still here'.

Early February 2013: The press reports that the Lublin-West Regional Court has suspended proceedings to establish a date of death for Janusz Korczak. This means the 30 November 1954 ruling of the County Court in Lublin stands. That ruling did not determine a date of death but considered him dead as of 9 May 1946 (nine months after the end of the Second World War – at that time the courts accepted this de-facto date if a precise one could not be established). The controversy over 5 or 6 August 1942 also affects the dates of death of over 200 children, girls and boys, including: Abasza, Srulek and little Gina Gutman, Róża Azrylewicz-Sztokman, Romcia Sztokman (no one remembers anything about her, not even what things she liked), Henryk Azrylewicz, Henryk Asterblum, Róża Lipiec-Jakubowska, Sabina Lejzerowicz (supply manager), Dora Sokolnicka (seamstress), Nacia Poz (with the warm smile). And Stefania Wilczyńska.

December 2013: The Polish website Eretz Israel puts out an appeal: Warsaw should honour Wilczyńska. The city could give her name to a street or a square. The campaign's leader Dana Rotschild tells *Gazeta Wyborcza*: 'The annihilation of the ghetto is about more than just the rebels' heroic attacks or the actions of the Righteous, it's also – and maybe above all – about the memory of those who were murdered, and whom Wilczyńska symbolizes.'

2014: For Women's Day, the author and social activist Sylwia Chutnik tells an interviewer which women, in her opinion, ought to be commemorated in the capital. 'A monument to Wilczyńska maybe shouldn't be physical at all. Maybe it should consist of the idea that no child in Warsaw should live in a children's home.'

In March, the railroads shorten the Janusz Korczak train line (named after him as part of the Korczak Year). This means it will still terminate at Kraków–Płaszów station (located very near the grounds of the former Płaszów concentration camp), but will start in Warsaw rather than Białystok, meaning it will no longer stop at Małkinia (today the nearest station to Treblinka).

The Warsaw City Council's Commission on Naming makes a statement on commemorating Wilczyńska: 'The Commission on Naming notes that the figure of Stefania Wilczyńska should not be singled out without simultaneously commemorating the figure of Janusz Korczak.' The Commission also assessed a specific proposal. Its representative Andrzej Sołtan told *Gazeta Wyborcza* newspaper: 'There are applications to honour other people at this location too. We get a lot of proposals in. Maybe the solution would be a memorial plaque?'

2015: Winter, Shlomo and I are talking on the phone.

'Do you think they heard me that one time at Treblinka?'

Notes

1. J. Korczak, *Pisma rozproszone. Listy (1913-1939)*, p.165.
2. *Gazeta Żydowska*, 7 January 1942.
3. E. Ringelblum, *Kronika getta warszawskiego* (Warsaw: 1983), p. 605.
4. *Dziennik Polski*, 11 December 1942.
5. G. Bychowski, 'Wspomnienie o J. Korczaku', *Tygodnik Polski*, 4 April 1943.
6. S. Beylin, 'Janusz Korczak i »jego dzieci«', *Kobieta dzisiejsza*, August 1946.
7. H. Krall, *Shielding the Flame: An Intimate Conversation with Dr Marek Edelman, the Last Surviving Leader of the Warsaw Ghetto Uprising*, trans. by Joanna Stasińska and Lawrence Weschler (New York: 1986), p.45.
8. J. Klass, K. Duniec, J. Krakowska (eds), *(A)pollonia: Twenty-First Century Polish Drama and Texts for the Stage* (Kolkata: 2014), p.3.
9. Ibid., p.5.

Selected Bibliography

Sources:

The letters of Stefania Wilczyńska from 1925–1940, above all to private addressees from Palestine and Poland.

The official writings of Wilczyńska composed about the Orphans' Home

Wilczyńska's entries in a few dozen surviving notebooks of trainees from the Orphans' Home in the 1930s.

Documents written about the Orphans' Home signed by Wilczyńska (certificates, announcements and others)

Articles by Wilczyńska published in Poland and Palestine concerning pedagogy, in the mass media, in kibbutz periodicals (in Polish and Hebrew)

Wilczyńska's statements in the minutes of kibbutz meetings

Subject Literature:

Abramow-Newerly, Jarosław, *Lwy mojego podwórka* [The Lions of My Courtyard] (Warsaw: 2000)

Battenberg, Friedrich, *Żydzi w Europie* [Jews in Europe], trans. Anna Soróbka (Wrocław: 2009)

Bednarz-Grzybek, Renata, *Emancypantka i patriotka. Wizerunek kobiety przełomu XIX i XX wieku w czasopismach Królestwa Polskiego* [An Emancipated Woman and a Patriot: The Image of women at the turn of the nineteenth and twentieth centuries in the journals of the Kingdom of Poland] (Lublin: 2010)

Blady-Szwajger, Adina, *I więcej nic nie pamiętam* [And I Don't Remember Anything More] (Warsaw: 2010)

Bogucka, Maria, *Gorsza płeć. Kobieta w dziejach Europy od antyku po wiek XXI* [The Lesser Sex: Women in the history of Europe from antiquity to the twenty-first century] (Warsaw: 2005)

Chutnik, Sylwia, *Warszawa kobiet* [Women's Warsaw] (Warsaw: 2011)

Cytryn-Miodowska, Bella, 'Matka żydowskich sierot' [A Mother of Jewish Children], *Nowiny Kurier* (Tel Aviv), Dec 18 1952, pp.264-265

Czerniaków, Adam, *The Warsaw Diary of Adam Czerniakow*, ed. by Joseph Kermish, Raul Hilberg, Stanislaw Staron, trans. by Stanislaw Staron (Chicago: 1999)

Dębnicki, Kazimierz, *Korczak z bliska* [Korczak Up Close] (Warsaw: 1985)

Edelman, Marek, *I była miłość w getcie* [And There Was Love in the Ghetto] (Warsaw: 2009)

Eisenbach, Artur, *Emancypacja Żydów na ziemiach polskich 1785–1870 na tle europejskim* [The Emancipation of Jews in the Polish Lands 1785–1870 in the European Context] (Warsaw: 1988)

Engelking, Barbara and Jacek Leociak, *Getto warszawskie* [The Warsaw Ghetto] (Warsaw: 2001)

Falkowska, Maria, *Kalendarz życia, działalności i twórczości Janusza Korczaka* [A Timeline of the Life, Activity and Writings of Janusz Korczak] (Warsaw: 1989)

Falska, Maria, *Nasz Dom. Zrozumieć, porozumieć się, poznać* [Our Home: To understand, to communicate, to know] (Warsaw: 2007)

Fuks, Marian, *Żydzi w Warszawie* [Jews in Warsaw] (Poznań: 2011)

Gilead, Zerubavel, *Gideon's Spring: A Man and His Kibbutz* (New York: 1985)

Grupińska, Anka, Jan Jagielski and Paweł Szapiro, *Getto warszawskie* [The Warsaw Ghetto] (Warsaw: 2008)

Hannam, June, *Feminism* (London: 2007)

Herzl, Theodor, *Der Judenstaat* (Vienna: 1896)

Jagodzińska, Agnieszka, *Pomiędzy. Akulturacja Żydów Warszawy w drugiej połowie XIX wieku* [In Between: The Acculturation of the Jews of Warsaw in the late nineteenth century] (Wrocław: 2009)

Janusz Korczak in der Erinnerung von Zeitzeugen [Janusz Korczak in the Memory of Contemporary Witnesses] (Gütersloh: 1999)

Janusz Korczak. Źródła i studia: Wspomnienia o Januszu Korczaku {Janusz Korczak: Sources and studies: Recollections of Janusz Korczak], ed. Aleksander Lewin (Warsaw: 1981)

Jaworski, Wojciech, *Syjoniści wobec rządu polskiego w okresie międzywojennym* [Zionists and the Polish Government in the Interwar Period] (Sosnowiec: 2002)

Johnson, Paul, *A History of the Jews* (New York: 1988)

Kirchner, Hanna, *Nałkowska albo życie pisane* [Nałkowska, or A Written Life] (Warsaw: 2012)

Koper, Sławomir, *Wpływowe kobiety Drugiej Rzeczypospolitej* [Influential Women of the Second Republic] (Warsaw: 2011)

Kopówka, Edward, Piotr Tołwiński, *Treblinka. Kamienie milczą – ja pamiętam* [Treblinka: The Stones are silent – I remember] (Siedlce: 2007)

Korczak Janusz, *Dzieci ulicy. Dziecko salonu* [Children of the Street: Children of the Salon, (Warsaw: 1992)

– *How to Love a Child and Other Selected Works* (vols. 1 and 2), sel. By Olga Medvedeva-Nathoo, ed. by Anna Maria Czernow, various translators (London: 2018)

– *Jak kochać dziecko. Momenty wychowawcze. Prawo dziecka do szacunku* [How To Love a Child, The Events of Child-rearing, A Child's Right to Respect] (Warsaw: 1993)

– *Mośki, Joski i Srule. Józki, Jaśki i Franki* [Mosieks, Joskas and Sruls, Józeks, Jasieks and Franeks] (Warsaw: 1997)

– *Na mównicy. Publicystyka społeczna 1898–1912* [At the Lectern: Articles on Social Subjects 1898–1912] (Warsaw: 1994)

– *Pamiętnik i inne pisma z getta* [Diary and Other Writings from the Ghetto] (Warsaw: 2012)

– *Prawidła życia. Publicystyka dla dzieci* [The Rules of Life: Articles for Children] (Warsaw: 2003)

Krajewska, Joanna, *„Jazgot niewieści" i „męskie kasztele". Z dziejów sporu o literaturę kobiecą w Dwudziestoleciu międzywojennym* (Poznań: 2010)

Krall, Hanna, *Shielding the Flame: An Intimate Conversation with Dr Marek Edelman, the Last Surviving Leader of the Warsaw Ghetto Uprising*, trans. Joanna Stasinska, Lawrence Weschler (Ann Arbor: 1986)

Krzywicka Irena, *Teraz się nie umiera* [Now Is Not When to Die] (Warsaw: 2011)

– *Wielcy i niewielcy* [The Great and the Little] (Warsaw: 2009)

Landau-Czajk, Anna, *Syn będzie Lech… Asymilacja Żydów w Polsce międzywojennej* [Our Son Will Be Called Lech…: Jewish Assimilation in Interwar Poland] (Warsaw: 2006)

Leociak, Jacek, *Spojrzenia na warszawskie getto* [Views of the Warsaw Ghetto] (Warsaw: 2011)

Lifton, Betty, *The King of Children: The Life and Death of Janusz Korczak* (New York: 1997)

Margines społeczny Drugiej Rzeczypospolitej [The Social Margins of the Second Republic], ed. Mateusz Rodak (Warsaw: 2013)

Merżan, Ida, *Aby nie uległo zapomnieniu* [So It Is Not Forgotten] (Warsaw: 1987)

– *Pan Doktór i pani Stefa* [The Doctor and Pani Stefa] (Warsaw: 1979)

Miłosz Czesław, *Wyprawa w dwudziestolecie* [An Expedition into the Interwar Period] (Kraków: 1999)

Mortkowicz-Olczakowa, Hanna, *Janusz Korczak* (Warsaw: 1957)

– *Panna Stefania* (Warsaw: 1961)

Newerly, Igor, *Rozmowa w sadzie piątego sierpnia* [A Conversation in the Orchard on 5 August] (Warsaw: 1987)

– *Żywe wiązanie* [Connected Lives] (Warsaw: 2002)

Niepiękne dzielnice. Reportaże o międzywojennej Warszawie [Ugly Neighbourhoods: Journalism on Interwar Warsaw], sel. and ed. by Jan Dąbrowski and Józef Koskowski (Warsaw: 1964)

Niewęgłowska Aneta, 'Drogi do wolności, czyli historia równouprawnienia kobiet' [The Road to Freedom, or the History of Equal Women's Rights], *Wiadomości Historyczne* 2006, no. 4

Olczak-Ronikier, Joanna, *Korczak. Próba biografii* [Korczak: An Attempted Biography] (Warsaw: 2011)

Opoczynski Peretz and Josef Zelkowicz, *Those Nightmarish Days: The Ghetto Reportage of Peretz Opoczynski and Josef Zelkowicz*, ed. by Samuel Kassow, trans. and ed. by David Suchoff (New Haven: 2015)

Ostałowska, Lidia, *Watercolours: A Story of Auschwitz*, trans. by Sean Gasper Bye (New Delhi: 2017)

Ostatnie pokolenie. Autobiografie polskiej młodzieży żydowskiej okresu międzywojennego... [Autobiographies of Polish Jewish Youth in the Interwar Period], ed. Alina Cała (Warsaw: 2004)

Patek, Artur, *Żydzi w Drodze do Palestyny 1934–1944* [Jews on the Road to Palestine 1934-1944] (Kraków: 2009)

Pogorzelska, Olga, 'Zieleń w getcie warszawskim' [Green Space in the Warsaw Ghetto], *Kultura Miasta*, 2009, no. 5

Poznańska-Hagari, Ada, 'Janusz Korczak i Stefa Wilczyńska w oczach ich wychowanków' [Janusz Korczak and Stefa Wilczyńska in the Eyes of their House Children] *Rocznik Seminarium Kibuców*, Israel, 1982

Pruszyński, Ksawery, *Palestyna po raz trzeci* [Palestine for the Third Time] (Warsaw: 1933)

Rajchman, Chil, *The Last Jew of Treblinka: A Survivor's Memory 1942–1943*, trans. By Solon Beinfeld (New York: 2011)

Ringelbaum, Emanuel, *Kronika getta* [The Ghetto Chronicle], trans. Adam Rutkowski (Warsaw: 1983)
Rozensztajn, Szmul, *Notatnik*, trans. and ed. Monika Polit (Warsaw: 2008)
Rudnicki, Marek, 'Ostatnia droga Janusza Korczaka' [Janusz Korczak's Last Path], *Tygodnik Powszechny*, 1988, no. 45
Sakowska, Ruta, *Ludzie dzielnicy zamkniętej* [The People of the Closed District] (Warsaw: 1975)
Sikorski, Dariusz Konrad, *Spór o międzywojenną kulturę polsko-żydowską* [Controversy Over Interwar Polish-Jewish Culture] (Warsaw: 2011)
Smith, Lyn, *Forgotten Voices of the Holocaust* (London: 2006)
Stöcker-Sobelman, Joanna, *Kobiety Holokaustu* [Women of the Holocaust] (Warsaw: 2011)
Szpilman, Władysław, *The Pianist*, trans. by Anthea Bell (New York: 1999)
Tuszyńska Agata, *Krzywicka. Długie życie gorszycielki* [Krzywicka: The Long Life of a Scandalist] (Kraków: 2009)
– *Vera Gran: The Accused*, trans. by Charles Ruas from the French of Isabelle Jannès-Kalinowski (New York: 2013)
Umińska, Bożena, *Postać z cieniem. Portrety Żydówek w literaturze polskiej* [A Figure with a Shadow: Portraits of Jewish Women in Polish Literature] (Warsaw: 2001)
Wańkowicz, Melchior, *De profundis. Ziemia za wiele obiecana. Wojna i pióro* [De Profundis: A Land Promised to Many, War and Pen] (Warsaw: 2011)
Warszawa naszej młodości [The Warsaw of Our Youth] (Warsaw: 1954)
Wilczyńska, Stefania, *Słowo do dzieci i wychowawców* [A Word to Children and Child-Rearers], ed. B. Puszkin, M. Ciesielska (Warsaw: 2004)
Wiszniewicz, Joanna, *A jednak czasem miewam sny. Historia pewnej samotności* [And Ye Sometimes We Have Dreams: The Story of a Certain Solitude] (Wołowiec: 2009)
A World Before a Catastrophe: Krakow's Jews Between the Wars, trans. Jessica Taylor-Kucia (Kraków: 2007)
Wspomnienia o Januszu Korczaku [Recollections of Janusz Korczak], selected and ed. Ludwika Barszczewska and Bolesław Milewicz (Warsaw: 1981)
Zuckerman, Yitzhak, *A Surplus of Memory: Chronicle of the Warsaw Ghetto Uprising*, trans. and ed. by Barbara Harshav (Berkeley: 1993)
Zyngman, Izrael, *Janusz Korczak wśród sierot* [Janusz Korczak Among the Orphans] (Tel Aviv: 1976)

Additionally:

Mały Przegląd [The Little Review] 1924–1939
Daily press 1918–1942 (searches with the keywords: Korczak, Wilczyńska, Dom Sierot [Orphans' Home], Towarzystwo „Pomoc dla Sierot" [Orphans' Aid Society]), especially *Przegląd społeczny* [The Social Review], *Gazeta Warszawska* [The Warsaw Gazette], *Głos żydowski* [The Jewish Voice], *Robotnik* [The Worker], *Ewa* (1928–1933)
Documents of the Orphans' Aid Society, documents in the museum of the Ein Harod kibbutz
Films: *Shoah* by Claude Lanzmann, *Korczak* by Andrzej Wajda